PATENT
TRADEMARK
AND COPYRIGHT
LAWS

1984 Edition

Edited by
Jeffrey M. Samuels
Managing Editor
Patent, Trademark & Copyright Journal

The Bureau of National Affairs, Inc. Washington, D.C.

Printed in the United States of America
International Standard Book Number: 0-87179-445-4
International Standard Serial Number: 0741-1219

Contents

Introduction   v
The Constitutional Provisions   vi
U.S. Code, Title 35, Patents   1
U.S. Code, Title 15, Chapter 22, Trademarks   75
U.S. Code, Title 17, Copyrights.   112
Notes of Other Statutes   199
Finding List for Notes of Other Statutes.   273
Index   275

Introduction

The Bureau of National Affairs, Inc., publisher of *BNA's Patent, Trademark & Copyright Journal* and *The United States Patents Quarterly,* is pleased to present this compilation entitled *Patent, Trademark, and Copyright Laws.* This edition includes Title 35 (Patents), Title 17 (Copyrights), and Chapter 22 of Title 15 (Trademarks) of the United States Code. It also includes miscellaneous sections of the United States Code relating to the practice of intellectual property. All statutory changes enacted through January 1984 are incorporated.

J. M. S.

Washington, D.C.
January 1984

THE CONSTITUTIONAL PROVISIONS

ART 1, SEC. 8, CL. 3. The Congress shall have power . . . To regulate commerce with foreign nations, and among the several states, and with the Indian tribes.

ART. 1, SEC. 8., CL. 8. The Congress shall have power . . . To promote the progress of science and useful arts, by securing for limited times to authors and inventors the exclusive right to their respective writings and discoveries.

UNITED STATES CODE

TITLE 35—PATENTS

PART I—PATENT AND TRADEMARK OFFICE

Chapter 1—Establishment, Officers, Functions

Sec.
1. Establishment.
2. Seal.
3. Officers and employees.
4. Restrictions on officers and employees as to interest in patents.
5. [Repealed.]
6. Duties of Commissioner.
7. Board of Appeals.
8. Library.
9. Classification of patents.
10. Certified copies of records.
11. Publications.
12. Exchange of copies of patents with foreign countries.
13. Copies of patents for public libraries.
14. Annual report to Congress.

Chapter 2—Proceedings In The Patent and Trademark

Sec.
21. Filing date and day for taking action.
22. Printing of papers filed.
23. Testimony in Patent and Trademark Office cases.
24. Subpoenas, witnesses.
25. Declaration in lieu of oath.
26. Effect of defective execution.

Chapter 3—Practice Before Patent And Trademark Office

Sec.
31. Regulations for agents and attorneys.
32. Suspension or exclusion from practice.
33. Unauthorized representation as practitioner.

Chapter 4—Patent Fees

Sec.
41. Patent fees.
42. Payment of patent fees; return of excess amounts.

1

PART II—PATENTABILITY OF INVENTIONS AND GRANT OF PATENTS

CHAPTER 10—PATENTABILITY OF INVENTIONS

SEC.
100. Definitions.
101. Inventions patentable.
102. Conditions for patentability; novelty and loss of right to patent.
103. Conditions for patentability; non-obvious subject matter.
104. Invention made abroad.

CHAPTER 11—APPLICATION FOR PATENT

SEC.
111. Application for patent.
112. Specification.
113. Drawings.
114. Models, specimens.
115. Oath of applicant.
116. Inventors.
117. Death or incapacity of inventor.
118. Filing by other than inventor.
119. Benefit of earlier filing date in foreign country; right of priority.
120. Benefit of earlier filing date in the United States.
121. Divisional applications.
122. Confidential status of applications.

CHAPTER 12—EXAMINATION OF APPLICATION

SEC.
131. Examination of application.
132. Notice of rejection; reexamination.
133. Time for prosecuting application.
134. Appeal to the Board of Appeals.
135. Interferences.

CHAPTER 13—REVIEW OF PATENT AND TRADEMARK OFFICE DECISION

SEC.
141. Appeal to Court of Appeals for the Federal Circuit.
142. Notice of appeal.
143. Proceedings on appeal.
144. Decision on appeal.
145. Civil action to obtain patent.
146. Civil action in case of interference.

Chapter 14—Issue Of Patent

Sec.

151. Issue of patent.
152. Issue of patent to assignee.
153. How issued.
154. Contents and term of patent.
155. Patent term extension.
155A. Patent term restoration.

Chapter 15—Plant Patents

Sec.

161. Patents for plants.
162. Description, claim.
163. Grant.
164. Assistance of Department of Agriculture.

Chapter 16—Designs

Sec.

171. Patents for designs.
172. Right of priority.
173. Term of design patent.

Chapter 17—Secrecy Of Certain Inventions And Filing Applications In Foreign Country

Sec.

181. Secrecy of certain inventions and withholding of patent.
182. Abandonment of invention for unauthorized disclosure.
183. Right of compensation.
184. Filing of application in foreign country.
185. Patent barred for filing without license.
186. Penalty.
187. Nonapplicability to certain persons.
188. Rules and regulations, delegation of power.

Chapter [18] 38—Patent Rights In Inventions Made With Federal Assistance

Sec.

200. Policy and objective.
201. Definitions.
202. Disposition of rights.
203. March-in rights.
204. Preference for United States industry.
205. Confidentiality.
206. Uniform clauses and regulations.
207. Domestic and foreign protection of federally owned inventions.
208. Regulations governing Federal licensing.

209. Restrictions on licensing of federally owned inventions.
210. Precedence of chapters.
211. Relationship to antitrust laws.

PART III—PATENTS AND PROTECTION OF PATENT RIGHTS

CHAPTER 25—AMENDMENT AND CORRECTION OF PATENTS

SEC.
251. Reissue of defective patents.
252. Effect of reissue.
253. Disclaimer.
254. Certificate of correction of Patent and Trademark Office mistake.
255. Certificate of correction of applicant's mistake.
256. Correction of named inventor.

CHAPTER 26—OWNERSHIP AND ASSIGNMENT

SEC.
261. Ownership; assignment.
262. Joint owners.

CHAPTER 27—GOVERNMENT INTERESTS IN PATENTS

SEC.
266. [Repealed.]
267. Time for taking action in Government applications.

CHAPTER 28—INFRINGEMENT OF PATENTS

SEC.
271. Infringement of patent.
272. Temporary presence in the United States.

CHAPTER 29—REMEDIES FOR INFRINGEMENT OF PATENT,
AND OTHER ACTIONS

SEC.
281. Remedy for infringement of patent.
282. Presumption of validity; defenses.
283. Injunction.
284. Damages.
285. Attorney fees.
286. Time limitation on damages.
287. Limitation on damages; marking and notice.
288. Action for infringement of a patent containing an invalid claim.
289. Additional remedy for infringement of design patent.

290. Notice of patent suits.
291. Interfering patents.
292. False marking.
293. Nonresident patentee, service and notice.
294. Voluntary arbitration.

CHAPTER 30—PRIOR ART CITATIONS TO OFFICE AND REEXAMINATION OF PATENTS

Sec.

301. Citation of prior art.
302. Request for reexamination.
303. Determination of issue by Commissioner.
304. Reexamination order by Commissioner.
305. Conduct of reexamination procedures.
306. Appeal.
307. Certificate of patentability, unpatentability, and claim cancellation.

PART IV—PATENT COOPERATION TREATY

CHAPTER 35—DEFINITIONS

Sec.

351. Definitions.

CHAPTER 36—INTERNATIONAL STAGE

Sec.

361. Receiving Office.
362. International Searching Authority.
363. International application designating the United States: Effect.
364. International stage: Procedure.
365. Right of priority; benefit of the filing date of a prior application.
366. Withdrawn international application.
367. Actions of other authorities: Review.
368. Secrecy of certain inventions; filing international applications in foreign countries.

CHAPTER 37—NATIONAL STAGE

Sec.

371. National stage: Commencement.
372. National stage: Requirements and procedure.
373. Improper applicant.
374. Publication of international application: Effect.
375. Patent issued on international application: Effect.
376. Fees.

PART I—PATENT AND TRADEMARK OFFICE

CHAPTER   SEC.

1. Establishment, Officers, Functions 1
2. Proceedings in the Patent and Trademark Office 21
3. Practice Before the Patent and Trademark Office 31
4. Patent Fees 41

CHAPTER 1—ESTABLISHMENT, OFFICERS, FUNCTIONS

SEC.
1. Establishment.
2. Seal.
3. Officers and employees.
4. Restrictions on officers and employees as to interest in patents.
5. [Repealed.]
6. Duties of Commissioner.
7. Board of Appeals.
8. Library.
9. Classification of patents.
10. Certified copies of records.
11. Publications.
12. Exchange of copies of patents with foreign countries.
13. Copies of patents for public libraries.
14. Annual report to Congress.

§ 1.   Establishment

The Patent and Trademark Office shall continue as an office in the Department of Commerce, where records, books, drawings, specifications, and other papers and things pertaining to patents and to trade-mark registrations shall be kept and preserved, except as otherwise provided by law. (Amended January 2, 1975, Public Law 93–596, sec. 1, 88 Stat. 1949.)

§ 2.   Seal

The Patent and Trademark Office shall have a seal with which letters patent, certificates of trade-mark registrations, and papers issued from the Office shall be authenticated. (Amended January 2, 1975, Public Law 93–596, sec. 1, 88 Stat. 1949.)

§ 3.   Officers and employees

(a) There shall be in the Patent and Trademark Office a Commissioner of Patents and Trademarks, a Deputy Commissioner, two Assistant Commissioners, and examiners-in-chief appointed under section 7 of this title. The Deputy Commissioner, or, in the event of a vacancy in that office, the Assistant Commissioner senior in date of appointment, shall fill the office of Commissioner during a vacancy in that office until the Commissioner is appointed and takes office. The Commissioner of Patents and Trademarks, the Deputy Commissioner, and the Assistant Commissioners shall be appointed by the President, by and with the advice and consent of the Senate. The Secretary of Commerce, upon the nomination of the Commissioner in accordance with law, shall appoint all other officers and employees.

(b) The Secretary of Commerce may vest in himself the functions of the Patent and Trademark Office and its officers and employees specified in this title and may from time to time authorize their performance by any other officer or employee.

(c) The Secretary of Commerce is authorized to fix the per annum rate of basic compensation of each examiner-in-chief in the Patent and Trademark Office at not in excess of the maximum scheduled rate provided for positions in grade 17 of the General Schedule of the Classification Act of 1949, as amended. (Amended September 6, 1958, Public Law 85–933, sec. 1, 72 Stat. 1793; September 23, 1959, Public Law 86–370, sec. 1(a), 73 Stat. 650; August 14, 1964, Public Law 88–426, sec. 305(26), 78 Stat. 425; January 2, 1975, Public Law 93–596, sec. 1, 88 Stat. 1949; January 2, 1975, Public Law 93–601, sec. 1, 88 Stat. 1956; and August 27, 1982, Public Law 97–247, sec. 4, 96 Stat. 319.)

(d) The Commissioner of Patents and Trademarks shall be an Assistant Secretary of Commerce and shall receive compensation at the rate prescribed by law for Assistant Secretaries of Commerce. (Added October 25, 1982, Public Law 97–366, 96 Stat. 1760.)

§ 4.   Restrictions on officers and employees as to interest in patents

Officers and employees of the Patent and Trademark Office shall be incapable, during the period of their appointments and for one year thereafter, of applying for a patent and of acquiring, directly or indirectly, except by inheritance or bequest, any patent or any right or interest in any patent, issued or to be issued by the Office. In patents applied for thereafter they shall not be entitled to any priority date earlier than one year after the termination of their appointment. (Amended January 2, 1975, Public Law 93–596, sec. 1, 88 Stat. 1949.)

§ 5. Repealed. (June 6, 1972, Public Law 92–310, Title II, sec. 208(a), 86 Stat. 203.)

§ 6. Duties of Commissioner

(a) The Commissioner, under the direction of the Secretary of Commerce, shall superintend or perform all duties required by law respecting the granting and issuing of patents and the registration of trademarks; shall have the authority to carry on studies, programs or exchanges of items or services regarding domestic and international patent and trademark law or the administration of the Patent and Trademark Office; and shall have charge of property belonging to the Patent and Trademark Office. He may, subject to the approval of the Secretary of Commerce, establish regulations, not inconsistent with law, for the conduct of proceedings in the Patent and Trademark Office.

(b) The Commissioner, under the direction of the Secretary of Commerce, may, in coordination with the Department of State, carry on programs and studies cooperatively with foreign patent offices and international intergovernmental organizations, or may authorize such programs and studies to be carried on, in connection with the performance of duties stated in subsection (a) of this section.

(c) The Commissioner, under the direction of the Secretary of Commerce, may, with the concurrence of the Secretary of State, transfer funds appropriated to the Patent and Trademark Office, not to exceed $100,000 in any year, to the Department of State for the purpose of making special payments to international intergovernmental organizations for studies and programs for advancing international cooperation concerning patents, trademarks, and related matters. These special payments may be in addition to any other payments or contributions to the international organization and shall not be subject to any limitations imposed by law on the amounts of such other payments or contributions by the Government of the United States. (Amended October 5, 1971, Public Law 92–132, 85 Stat. 364; January 2, 1975, Public Law 93–596, sec. 1, 88 Stat. 1949; August 27, 1982, Public Law 97–247, sec. 13, 96 Stat. 321.)

(d) Repealed. (August 27, 1982, Public Law 97–247, sec. 7, 96 Stat. 320.)

§ 7. Board of Appeals

The examiners-in-chief shall be persons of competent legal knowledge and scientific ability, who shall be appointed under the classified civil service. The Commissioner, the deputy commissioner, the assistant commissioners, and the examiners-in-chief shall constitute a Board of Appeals, which on written appeal of the applicant, shall review adverse decisions of examiners upon applications for patents. Each appeal shall be heard by at least three members of the Board of Appeals, the members hearing such appeal to be designated by the Commissioner. The Board of Appeals has sole power to grant rehearings.

Whenever the Commissioner considers it necessary to maintain the work of the Board of Appeals current, he may designate any patent examiner of the primary examiner grade or higher, having the requisite ability, to serve as examiner-in-chief for periods not exceeding six months each. An examiner so designated shall be qualified to act as a member of the Board of Appeals. Not more than one such primary examiner shall be a member of the Board of Appeals hearing an appeal. The Secretary of Commerce is authorized to fix the per annum rate of basic compensation of each designated examiner-in-chief in the Patent and Trademark Office at not in excess of the maximum scheduled rate provided for positions in grade 16 of the General Schedule of the Classification Act of 1949, as amended. The per annum rate of basic compensation of each designated examiner-in-chief shall be adjusted, at the close of the period for which he was designated to act as examiner-in-chief, to the per annum rate of basic compensation which he would have been receiving at the close of such period if such designation had not been made. (Amended September 6, 1958, Public Law 85–933, sec. 1, 72 Stat. 1793; September 23, 1959, Public Law 86–370, sec. 1(b), 73 Stat. 650; January 2, 1975, Public Law 93–596, sec. 1, 88 Stat. 1949; and January 2, 1975, Public Law 93–601, sec. 2, 88 Stat. 1956.)

§ 8. Library

The Commissioner shall maintain a library of scientific and other works and periodicals, both foreign and domestic, in the Patent and Trademark Office to aid the officers in the discharge of their duties. (Amended January 2, 1975, Public Law 93–596, sec. 1, 88 Stat. 1949.)

§ 9. Classification of patents

The Commissioner may revise and maintain the classification by subject matter of United States letters patent, and such other patents and printed publications as may be necessary or practicable, for the purpose of determining with readiness and accuracy the novelty of inventions for which applications for patent are filed.

§ 10. Certified copies of records

The Commissioner may furnish certified copies of specifications and drawings of patents issued by the Patent and Trademark Office, and of other records available either to the public or to the person applying therefore. (Amended January 2, 1975, Public Law 93–596, sec. 1, 88 Stat. 1949.)

§ 11. Publications

(a) The Commissioner may print, or cause to be printed, the following:

1. Patents, including specifications and drawings, together with copies of the same. The Patent and Trademark Office may print the headings of the drawings for patents for the purpose of photolithography.

2. Certificates of trade-mark registrations, including statements and drawings, together with copies of the same.

3. The Official Gazette of the United States Patent and Trademark Office.

4. Annual indexes of patents and patentees, and of trade-marks and registrants.

5. Annual volumes of decisions in patent and trade-mark cases.

6. Pamphlet copies of the patent laws and rules of practice, laws and rules relating to trade-marks, and circulars or other publications relating to the business of the Office.

(b) The Commissioner may exchange any of the publications specified in items 3, 4, 5, and 6 of subsection (a) of this section for publications desirable for the use of the Patent and Trademark Office. (Amended January 2, 1975, Public Law 93–596, sec. 1, 88 Stat. 1949.)

§ 12. Exchange of copies of patents with foreign countries

The Commissioner may exchange copies of specifications and drawings of United States patents for those of foreign countries.

§ 13. Copies of patents for public libraries

The Commissioner may supply printed copies of specifications and drawings of patents to public libraries in the United States which shall maintain such copies for the use of the public, at the rate for each year's issue established for this purpose in section 41(d) of this title. (Amended August 27, 1982, Public Law 97–247, sec. 15, 96 Stat. 321.)

§ 14. Annual report to Congress

The Commissioner shall report to Congress annually the moneys received and expended, statistics concerning the work of the Office, and other information relating to the Office as may be useful to the Congress or the public.

Chapter 2—Proceedings In The Patent And Trademark Office

Sec.
21. Filing date and day for taking action.
22. Printing of papers filed.
23. Testimony in Patent and Trademark Office cases.
24. Subpoenas, witnesses.
25. Declaration in lieu of oath.
26. Effect of defective execution.

§ 21. Filing date and day for taking action.

(a) The Commissioner may by rule prescribe that any paper or fee required to be filed in the Patent and Trademark Office will be considered filed in the Office on the date on which it was deposited with the United States Postal Service or would have been deposited with the United States Postal Service but for postal service interruptions or emergencies designated by the Commissioner.

(b) When the day, or the last day, for taking any action or paying any fee in the United States Patent and Trademark Office falls on Saturday, Sunday, or a federal holiday within the District of Columbia, the action may be taken, or the fee paid, on the next succeeding secular or business day. (Amended January 2, 1975, Public Law 93–596, sec. 1, 88 Stat. 1949; August 27, 1982, Public Law 97–247, sec. 12, 96 Stat. 321.)

§ 22. Printing of papers filed

The Commissioner may require papers filed in the Patent and Trademark Office to be printed or typewritten. (Amended January 2, 1975, Public Law 93–596, sec. 1, 88 Stat. 1949.)

§ 23. Testimony in Patent and Trademark Office cases

The Commissioner may establish rules for taking affidavits and depositions required in cases in the Patent and Trademark Office. Any officer authorized by law to take depositions to be used in the courts of the United States, or of the State where he resides, may take such affidavits and depositions. (Amended January 2, 1975, Public Law 93–596, sec. 1, 88 Stat. 1949.)

§ 24. Subpoenas, witnesses

The clerk of any United States court for the district wherein testimony is to be taken for use in any contested case in the Patent and Trademark Office, shall, upon the application of any party thereto, issue a subpoena for any witness residing or being within such district, commanding him to appear and testify before an officer in such district authorized to take depositions and affidavits, at the time and place stated in the subpoena. The provisions of the Federal Rules of Civil Procedure relating to the attendance of witnesses and to the production of documents and things shall apply to contested cases in the Patent and Trademark Office.

Every witness subpoenaed and in attendance shall be allowed the fees and traveling expenses allowed to witnesses attending the United States district courts.

A judge of a court whose clerk issued a subpoena may enforce obedience to the process or punish disobedience as in other like cases, on proof that a witness, served with such subpoena, neglected or refused to appear or to testify. No witness shall be deemed guilty of contempt for disobeying such subpoena unless his fees and traveling expenses in going to, and returning from, and one day's attendance at the place of examination, are paid or tendered him at the time of the service of the subpoena; nor for refusing to disclose any secret matter except upon appropriate order of the court which issued the subpoena. (Amended January 2, 1975, Public Law 93–596, sec. 1, 88 Stat. 1949.)

§ 25. Declaration in lieu of oath

(a) The Commissioner may by rule prescribe that any document to be filed in the Patent and Trademark Office and which is required by any law, rule, or other regulation to be under oath may be subscribed to by a written declaration in such form as the Commissioner may prescribe, such declaration to be in lieu of the oath otherwise required.

(b) Whenever such written declaration is used, the document must warn the declarant that willful false statements and the like are punishable by fine or imprisonment, or both (18 U.S.C. 1001). (New section added March 26, 1964, Public Law 88–292, sec. 1, 78 Stat. 171; amended January 2, 1975, Public Law 93–596, sec. 1, 88 Stat. 1949.)

Note.— 18 U.S.C. 1001 provides: "Whoever in any matter within the jurisdiction of any department or agency of the United States knowingly and willfully falsifies, conceals or covers up by any trick, scheme, or device a material fact, or makes any false, fictitious or fraudulent statements or representations, or makes or uses any false writing or document knowing the same to contain any false, fictitious or fraudulent statement or entry, shall be fined not more than $10,000 or imprisoned not more than five years, or both." (June 25, 1948, 62 Stat. 749)

§ 26. Effect of defective execution

Any document to be filed in the Patent and Trademark Office and which is required by any law, rule, or other regulation to be executed in a specified manner may be provisionally accepted by the Commissioner despite a defective execution, provided a properly executed document is submitted within such time as may be prescribed. (New section added March 26, 1964, Public Law 88–292, sec. 1, 78 Stat. 171; amended January 2, 1975, Public Law 93–596, sec. 1, 88 Stat. 1949.)

CHAPTER 3—PRACTICE BEFORE PATIENT AND TRADEMARK OFFICE

SEC.
31. Regulations for agents and attorneys.
32. Suspension or exclusion from practice.
33. Unauthorized representation as practitioner.

§ 31. Regulations for agents and attorneys

The Commissioner, subject to the approval of the Secretary of Commerce, may prescribe regulations governing the recognition and conduct of agents, attorneys, or other persons representing applicants or other parties before the Patent and Trademark Office, and may require them, before being recognized as representatives of applicants or other persons, to show that they are of good moral character and reputation and are possessed of the necessary qualifications to render to applicants or other persons, valuable service, advice, and assistance in the presentation or prosecution of their applications or other business before the Office. (Amended January 2, 1975, Public Law 93–596, sec. 1, 88 Stat. 1949.)

§ 32. Suspension or exclusion from practice

The Commissioner may, after notice and opportunity for a hearing, suspend or exclude, either generally or in any particular case, from further practice before the Patent and Trademark Office, any person, agent, or attorney shown to be incompetent or disreputable, or guilty of gross misconduct, or who does not comply with the regulations established under section 31 of this title, or who shall, by word, circular, letter, or advertising, with intent to defraud in any manner, deceive, mislead, or threaten any applicant or prospective applicant, or other person having immediate or prospective business before the Office. The reasons for any such suspension or exclusion shall be duly recorded. The United States District Court for the District of Columbia, under such conditions and upon such proceedings as it by its rules determines, may review the action of the Commissioner upon the petition of the person so refused recognition or so suspended or excluded. (Amended January 2, 1975, Public Law 93–596, sec. 1, 88 Stat. 1949.)

§ 33. Unauthorized representation as practitioner

Whoever, not being recognized to practice before the Patent and Trademark Office, holds himself out or permits himself to be held out as so recognized, or as being qualified to prepare or prosecute applications for patent, shall be fined not more than $1,000 for each offense. (Amended January 2, 1975, Public Law 93–596, sec. 1, 88 Stat. 1949.)

CHAPTER 4—PATENT FEES

SEC.
41. Patent fees.
42. Patent and Trademark Office funding.

§ 41. Patent fees

(a) The Commissioner shall charge the following fees:

1. On filing each application for an original patent, except in design or plant cases, $300; in addition, on filing or on presentation at any other time, $30 for each claim in independent form which is in excess of three, $10 for each claim (whether independent or dependent) which is in excess of twenty, and $100 for each application containing a multiple dependent claim. For the purpose of computing fees, a multiple dependent claim as referred to in section 112 of this title or any claim depending therefrom shall be considered as separate dependent claims in accordance with the number of claims to which reference is made. Errors in payment of the additional fees may be rectified in accordance with regulations of the Commissioner.

2. For issuing each original or reissue patent, except in design or plant cases, $500.

3. In design and plant cases:
   a. On filing each design application, $125.
   b. On filing each plant application, $200.
   c. On issuing each design patent, $175.
   d. On issuing each plant patent, $250.

4. On filing each application for the reissue of a patent, $300; in addition, on filing or on presentation at any other time, $30 for each claim in independent form which is in excess of the number of independent claims of the original patent, and $10 for each claim (whether independent or dependent) which is in excess of twenty and also in excess of the number of claims of the original patent. Errors in payment of the additional fees may be rectified in accordance with regulations of the Commissioner.

5. On filing each disclaimer, $50.

6. On filing an appeal from the examiner to the Board of Appeals, $115; in addition, on filing a brief in support of the appeal, $115, and on requesting an oral hearing before the Board of Appeals, $100.

7. On filing each petition for the revival of an unintentionally abandoned application for a patent or for the unintentionally delayed payment of the fee for issuing each patent, $500, unless the petition is filed under sections 133 or 151 of this title, in which case the fee shall be $50.

8. For petitions for one-month extensions of time to take actions required by the Commissioner in an application:
   a. On filing a first petition, $50.

    b. On filing a second petition, $100.

    c. On filing a third or subsequent petition, $200.

  (b) The Commissioner shall charge the following fees for maintaining a patent in force:

    1. Three years and six months after grant, $400.

    2. Seven years and six months after grant, $800.

    3. Eleven years and six months after grant, $1,200.

Unless payment of the applicable maintenance fee is received in the Patent and Trademark Office on or before the date the fee is due or within a grace period of six months thereafter, the patent will expire as of the end of such grace period. The Commissioner may require the payment of a surcharge as a condition of accepting within such six-month grace period the late payment of an applicable maintenance fee. No fee will be established for maintaining a design or plant patent in force.

Note.—Sec. 1 of Public Law 97–247, August 27, 1982, 96 Stat. 317, authorizes the appropriations of funds for the Patent and Trademark Office for fiscal years 1983–1985 and requires that such funds will be used to reduce by 50 percent the payment of fees under section 41(a) and (b) by independent inventors, nonprofit organizations, and small businesses, as defined by section 3 of the Small Business Act and applicable regulations.

(c)(1) The Commissioner may accept the payment of any maintenance fee required by subsection (b) of this section after the six-month grace period if the delay is shown to the satisfaction of the Commissioner to have been unavoidable. The Commissioner may require the payment of a surcharge as a condition of accepting payment of any maintenance fee after the six-month grace period. If the Commissioner accepts payment of a maintenance fee after the six-month grace period, the patent shall be considered as not having expired at the end of the grace period.

  (2) No patent, the term of which has been maintained as a result of the acceptance of a payment of a maintenance fee under this subsection, shall abridge or affect the right of any person or his successors in business who made, purchased or used after the six-month grace period but prior to the acceptance of a maintenance fee under this subsection anything protected by the patent, to continue the use of, or to sell to others to be used or sold, the specific thing so made, purchased, or used. The court before which such matter is in question may provide for the continued manufacture, use or sale of the thing made, purchased, or used as specified,

or for the manufacture, use or sale of which substantial preparation was made after the six-month grace period but before the acceptance of a maintenance fee under this subsection, and it may also provide for the continued practice of any process, practiced, or for the practice of which substantial preparation was made, after the six-month grace period but prior to the acceptance of a maintenance fee under this subsection, to the extent and under such terms as the court deems equitable for the protection of investments made or business commenced after the six-month grace period but before the acceptance of a maintenance fee under the subsection.

(d) The Commissioner will establish fees for all other processing, services, or materials related to patents not specified above to recover the estimated average cost to the Office of such processing, services, or materials. The yearly fee for providing a library specified in section 13 of this title with uncertified printed copies of the specifications and drawings for all patents issued in that year will be $50.

(e) The Commissioner may waive the payment of any fee for any service or material related to patents in connection with an occasional or incidental request made by a department or agency of the Government, or any officer thereof. The Commissioner may provide any applicant issued a notice under section 132 of this title with a copy of the specifications and drawings for all patents referred to in that notice without charge.

(f) The fees established in subsections (a) and (b) of this section may be adjusted by the Commissioner on October 1, 1985, and every third year thereafter, to reflect any fluctuations occurring during the previous three years in the Consumer Price Index, as determined by the Secretary of Labor. Changes of less than 1 per centum may be ignored.

(g) No fee established by the Commissioner under this section will take effect prior to sixty days following notice in the Federal Register. (As amended December 12, 1980, Public Law 96–517, sec. 2, 94 Stat. 3017; August 27, 1982, Public Law 97–247, sec. 3, 96 Stat. 317.)

§ 42. Patent and Trademark Office funding

(a) All fees for services performed by or materials furnished by the Patent and Trademark Office will be payable to the Commissioner.

(b) All fees paid to the Commissioner and all appropriations for defraying the costs of the activities of the Patent and Trademark Office will be credited to the Patent and Trademark Office Appropriation Account in the Treasury of the United States, the provisions of section 725e of title 31, United States Code, notwithstanding.

(c) Revenues from fees will be available to the Commissioner of Patents to carry out, to the extent provided for in appropriation Acts, the activities of the Patent and Trademark Office. Fees available to the Commissioner under section 31 of the Trademark Act of 1946, as amended (15 U.S.C. 1113), shall be used exclusively for the processing of trademark registrations and for other services and materials relating to trademarks.

(d) The Commissioner may refund any fee paid by mistake or any amount paid in excess of that required. (As amended November 14, 1975, Public Law 94–131, sec. 4, 89 Stat. 690; December 12, 1980, Public Law 96–517, sec. 3, 94 Stat. 3018; August 27, 1982, Public Law 97–247, sec. 3(g), 96 Stat. 319.)

PART II—PATENTABILITY OF INVENTIONS AND GRANT OF PATENTS

CHAPTER   SEC.
10. Patentability of Inventions 100
11. Application for Patent 111
12. Examination of applications 131
13. Review of Patent and Trademark Office Decisions 141
14. Issue of Patent 151
15. Plant Patents 161
16. Designs 171
17. Secrecy of Certain Inventions and Filing Applications
    Abroad 181

CHAPTER 10—PATENTABILITY OF INVENTIONS

SEC.
100. Definitions.
101. Inventions patentable.
102. Conditions for patentability; novelty and loss of right to patent.
103. Conditions for patentability; non-obvious subject matter.
104. Invention made abroad.

§ 100. Definitions

When used in this title unless the context otherwise indicates—

(a) The term "invention" means invention or discovery.

(b) The term "process" means process, art or method, and includes a new use of a known process, machine, manufacture, composition of matter, or material.

(c) The terms "United States" and "this country" mean the United States of America, its territories and possessions.

(d) The word "patentee" includes not only the patentee to whom the patent was issued but also the successors in title to the patentee.

§ 101. Inventions patentable

Whoever invents or discovers any new and useful process, machine, manufacture, or composition of matter, or any new and useful improvement thereof, may obtain a patent therefor, subject to the conditions and requirements of this title.

§ 102. Conditions for patentability; novelty and loss of right to patent

A person shall be entitled to a patent unless—

(a) the invention was known or used by others in this country, or patented or described in a printed publication in this or a foreign country, before the invention thereof by the applicant for patent, or

(b) the invention was patented or described in a printed publication in this or a foreign country or in public use or on sale in this country, more than one year prior to the date of the application for patent in the United States, or

(c) he has abandoned the invention, or

(d) the invention was first patented or caused to be patented, or was the subject of an inventor's certificate, by the applicant or his legal representatives or assigns in a foreign country prior to the date of the application for patent in this country on an application for patent or inventor's certificate filed more than twelve months before the filing of the application in the United States, or

(e) the invention was described in a patent granted on an application for patent by another filed in the United States before the invention thereof by the applicant for patent, or on an international application by another who has fulfilled the requirements of paragraphs (1), (2), and (4) of section 371(c) of this title before the invention thereof by the applicant for patent, or

(f) he did not himself invent the subject matter sought to be patented, or

(g) before the applicant's invention thereof the invention was made in this country by another who had not abandoned, suppressed, or concealed it. In determining priority of invention there shall be considered not only the respective dates of conception and reduction to practice of the invention, but also the reasonable diligence of one who was first to conceive and last to reduce to practice, from a time prior to conception by the other (Amended July 28, 1972, Public Law 92–358, sec. 2, 86 Stat. 501; November 14, 1975, Public Law 94–131, sec. 5, 89 Stat. 691.)

§ 103. Conditions for patentability; non-obvious subject matter

A patent may not be obtained though the invention is not identically disclosed or described as set forth in section 102 of this title, if the differences between the subject matter sought to be patented and the prior art are such that the subject matter as a whole would have been obvious at the time the invention was made to a person having ordinary skill in the art to which said subject matter pertains. Patentability shall not be negatived by the manner in which the invention was made.

§ 104. Invention made abroad

In proceedings in the Patent Office and in the courts, an applicant for a patent, or a patentee, may not establish a date of invention by reference to knowledge or use thereof, or other activity with respect thereto, in a foreign country, except as provided in sections 119 and 365 of this title. Where an invention was made by a person, civil or military, while domiciled in the United States and serving in a foreign country in connection with operations by or on behalf of the United States, he shall be entitled to the same rights of priority with respect to such inventions as if the same had been made in the United States. (Amended January 2, 1975, Public Law 93–596, sec. 1, 88 Stat. 1949; November 14, 1975, Public Law 94–131, sec. 6, 89 Stat. 691.)

CHAPTER 11—APPLICATION FOR PATENT

SEC.
111. Application for patent.
112. Specification.
113. Drawings.
114. Models, specimens.
115. Oath of applicant.

116. Inventors.
117. Death or incapacity of inventor.
118. Filing by other than inventor.
119. Benefit of earlier filing date in foreign country; right of priority.
120. Benefit of earlier filing date in the United States.
121. Divisional applications.
122. Confidential status of applications.

§ 111.   Application for patent

Application for patent shall be made, or authorized to be made, by the inventor, except as otherwise provided in this title, in writing to the Commissioner. Such application shall include (1) a specification as prescribed by section 112 of this title; (2) a drawing as prescribed by section 113 of this title; and (3) an oath by the applicant as prescribed by section 115 of this title. The application must be accompanied by the fee required by law. The fee and oath may be submitted after the specification and any required drawing are submitted, within such period and under such conditions, including the payment of a surcharge, as may be prescribed by the Commissioner. Upon failure to submit the fee and oath within such prescribed period, the application shall be regarded as abandoned, unless it is shown to the satisfaction of the Commissioner that the delay in submitting the fee and oath was unavoidable. The filing date of an application shall be the date on which the specification and any required drawing are received in the Patent and Trademark Office. (Amended August 27, 1982, Public Law 97–247, sec. 5, 96 Stat. 319.)

§ 112.   Specification

The specification shall contain a written description of the invention, and of the manner and process of making and using it, in such full, clear, concise, and exact terms as to enable any person skilled in the art to which it pertains, or with which it is most nearly connected, to make and use the same, and shall set forth the best mode contemplated by the inventor of carrying out his invention.

The specification shall conclude with one or more claims particularly pointing out and distinctly claiming the subject matter which the applicant regards as his invention. A claim may be written in independent or, if the nature of the case admits, in dependent or multiple dependent form.

Subject to the following paragraph, a claim in dependent form shall contain a reference to a claim previously set forth and then specify a further limitation of the subject matter claimed. A claim in dependent form shall be construed to incorporate by reference all the limitations of the claim to which it refers.

A claim in multiple dependent form shall contain a reference, in the alternative only, to more than one claim previously set forth and then specify a further limitation of the subject matter claimed. A multiple dependent claim shall not serve as a basis for any other multiple dependent claim. A multiple dependent claim shall be construed to incorporate by reference all the limitations of the particular claim in relation to which it is being considered.

An element in a claim for a combination may be expressed as a means or step for performing a specified function without the recital of structure, material, or acts in support thereof, and such claim shall be construed to cover the corresponding structure, material, or acts described in the specification and equivalents thereof. (Amended July 24, 1965, Public Law 89–83, sec. 9, 79 Stat. 261; November 14, 1975, Public Law 94–131, sec. 7, 89 Stat. 691.)

§ 113. Drawings

The applicant shall furnish a drawing where necessary for the understanding of the subject matter sought to be patented. When the nature of such subject matter admits of illustration by a drawing and the applicant has not furnished such a drawing, the Commissioner may require its submission within a time period of not less than two months from the sending of a notice thereof. Drawings submitted after the filing date of the application may not be used (i) to overcome any insufficiency of the specification due to lack of an enabling disclosure or otherwise inadequate disclosure therein, or (ii) to supplement the original disclosure thereof for the purpose of interpretation of the scope of any claim. (Amended November 14, 1975, Public Law 94–131, sec. 8, 89 Stat. 691.)

§ 114. Models, specimens

The Commissioner may require the applicant to furnish a model of convenient size to exhibit advantageously the several parts of his invention.

When the invention relates to a composition of matter, the Commissioner may require the applicant to furnish specimens or ingredients for the purpose of inspection or experiment.

§ 115.   Oath of applicant

The applicant shall make oath that he believes himself to be the original and first inventor of the process, machine, manufacture, or composition of matter, or improvement thereof, for which he solicits a patent; and shall state of what country he is a citizen. Such oath may be made before any person within the United States authorized by law to administer oaths, or, when made in a foreign country, before any diplomatic or consular officer of the United States authorized to administer oaths, or before any officer having an official seal and authorized to administer oaths in the foreign country in which the applicant may be, whose authority is proved by certificate of a diplomatic or consular officer of the United States, or apostille of an official designated by a foreign country which, by treaty or convention, accords like effect to apostilles of designated officials in the United States. Such oath is valid if it complies with the laws of the state or country where made. When the application is made as provided in this title by a person other than the inventor, the oath may be so varied in form that it can be made by him. (Amended August 27, 1982, Public Law 97–247, sec. 14(a), 96 Stat. 321.)

§ 116.   Inventors

When an invention is made by two or more persons jointly, they shall apply for patent jointly and each sign the application and make the required oath, except as otherwise provided in this title.

If a joint inventor refuses to join in an application for patent or cannot be found or reached after diligent effort, the application may be made by the other inventor on behalf of himself and the omitted inventor. The Commissioner, on proof of the pertinent facts and after such notice to the omitted inventor as he prescribes, may grant a patent to the inventor making the application, subject to the same rights which the omitted inventor would have had if he had been joined. The omitted inventor may subsequently join in the application.

Whenever through error a person is named in an application for patent as the inventor, or through an error an inventor is not named in an application and such error arose without any deceptive intention on his part, the Commissioner may permit the application to be amended accordingly, under such terms as he prescribes. (Amended August 27, 1982, Public Law 97–247, sec. 6(a), 96 Stat. 320.)

§ 117. Death or incapacity of inventor

Legal representatives of deceased inventors and of those under legal incapacity may make application for patent upon compliance with the requirements and on the same terms and conditions applicable to the inventor.

§ 118. Filing by other than inventor

Whenever an inventor refuses to execute an application for patent, or cannot be found or reached after diligent effort, a person to whom the inventor has assigned or agreed in writing to assign the invention or who otherwise shows sufficient proprietary interest in the matter justifying such action, may make application for patent on behalf of and as agent for the inventor on proof of the pertinent facts and a showing that such action is necessary to preserve the rights of the parties or to prevent irreparable damage; and the Commissioner may grant a patent to such inventor upon such notice to him as the Commissioner deems sufficient, and on compliance with such regulations as he prescribes.

§ 119. Benefit of earlier filing date in foreign country; right of priority

An application for patent for an invention filed in this country by any person who has, or whose legal representatives or assigns have, previously regularly filed an application for a patent for the same invention in a foreign country which affords similar privileges in the case of applications filed in the United States or to citizens of the United States, shall have the same effect as the same application would have if filed in this country on the date on which the application for patent for the same invention was first filed in such foreign country, if the application in this country is filed within twelve months from the earliest date on which such foreign application was filed; but no patent shall be granted on any application for patent for an invention which had been patented or described in a printed publication in any country more than one year before the date of the actual filing of the application in this country, or which had been in public use or on sale in this country more than one year prior to such filing.

No application for patent shall be entitled to this right of priority unless a claim therefor and a certified copy of the original foreign application, specification and drawings upon which it is based are filed in the Patent and Trademark Office before the patent is granted, or at such time during the pendency of the application as required by the Commissioner not earlier than six months after the filing of the application in this country. Such certification shall be made by the patent office of the foreign country in which filed and show the date of the application and of the filing of the specification and other papers. The Commissioner may require a translation of the papers filed if not in the English language and such other information as he deems necessary.

In like manner and subject to the same conditions and requirements, the right provided in this section may be based upon a subsequent regularly filed application in the same foreign country instead of the first filed foreign application, provided that any foreign application filed prior to such subsequent application has been withdrawn, abandoned, or otherwise disposed of, without having been laid open to public inspection and without leaving any rights outstanding, and has not served, nor thereafter shall serve, as a basis for claiming a right of priority.

Applications for inventors' certificates filed in a foreign country in which applicants have a right to apply, at their discretion, either for a patent or for an inventor's certificate shall be treated in this country in the same manner and have the same effect for purpose of the right of priority under this section as applications for patents, subject to the same conditions and requirements of this section as apply to applications for patents, provided such applicants are entitled to the benefits of the Stockholm Revision of the Paris Convention at the time of such filing. (Amended October 3, 1961, Public Law 87–333, sec. 1, 75 Stat. 748; July 28, 1972, Public Law 92–358, sec. 1, 86 Stat. 502; and January 2, 1975, Public Law 93–596, sec. 1, 88 Stat. 1949.)

§ 120. Benefit of earlier filing date in the United States

An application for patent for an invention disclosed in the manner provided by the first paragraph of section 112 of this title in an application previously filed in the United States, or as provided by section 363 of this title, by the same inventor shall have the same effect, as to such invention, as though filed on the date of the prior application, if filed before the patenting or abandonment of or termination of proceedings on the first application or on an application similarly entitled to the benefit of the filing date of the first application and if it contains or is amended to contain a specific reference to the earlier filed application. (Amended November 14, 1975, Public Law 94–131, sec. 9, 89 Stat. 691.)

§ 121. Divisional applications

If two or more independent and distinct inventions are claimed in one application, the Commissioner may require the application to be restricted to one of the inventions. If the other invention is made the subject of a divisional application which complies with the requirements of section 120 of this title it shall be entitled to the benefit of the filing date of the original application. A patent issuing on an application with respect to which a requirement for restriction under this section has been made, or on an application filed as a result of such a requirement, shall not be used as a reference either in the Patent and Trademark Office or in the courts against a divisional application or against the original application or any patent issued on either of them, if the divisional application is filed before the issuance of the patent on the other application. If a divisional application is directed solely to subject matter described and claimed in the original application as filed, the Commissioner may dispense with signing and execution by the inventor. The validity of a patent shall not be questioned for failure of the Commissioner to require the application to be restricted to one invention. (Amended January 2, 1975, Public Law 93–596, sec. 1, 88 Stat. 1949.)

§ 122. Confidential status of applications

Applications for patents shall be kept in confidence by the Patent and Trademark Office and no information concerning the same given without authority of the applicant or owner unless necessary to carry out the provisions of any Act of Congress or in such special circumstances as may be determined by the Commissioner. (Amended January 2, 1975, Public Law 93–596, sec. 1, 88 Stat. 1949.)

CHAPTER 12—EXAMINATION OF APPLICATION

SEC.
131. Examination of application.
132. Notice of rejection; reexamination.

133. Time for prosecuting application.
134. Appeal to the Board of Appeals.
135. Interferences.

§ 131. Examination of application

The Commissioner shall cause an examination to be made of the application and the alleged new invention; and if on such examination it appears that the applicant is entitled to a patent under the law, the Commissioner shall issue a patent therefor.

§ 132. Notice of rejection; reexamination

Whenever, on examination, any claim for a patent is rejected, or any objection or requirement made, the Commissioner shall notify the applicant thereof, stating the reasons for such rejection, or objection or requirement, together with such information and references as may be useful in judging of the propriety of continuing the prosecution of his application; and if after receiving such notice, the applicant persists in his claim for a patent, with or without amendment, the application shall be reexamined. No amendment shall introduce new matter into the disclosure of the invention.

§ 133. Time for prosecuting application

Upon failure of the applicant to prosecute the application within six months after any action therein, of which notice has been given or mailed to the applicant, or within such shorter time, not less than thirty days, as fixed by the Commissioner in such action, the application shall be regarded as abandoned by the parties thereto, unless it be shown to the satisfaction of the Commissioner that such delay was unavoidable.

§ 134. Appeal to the Board of Appeals

An applicant for a patent, any of whose claims has been twice rejected, may appeal from the decision of the primary examiner to the Board of Appeals, having once paid the fee for such appeal.

§ 135. Interferences

(a) Whenever an application is made for a patent which, in the opinion of the Commissioner, would interfere with any pending application, or with any unexpired patent, he shall give notice thereof to the applicants, or applicant and patentee, as the case may be. The question of priority of invention shall be determined by a board of patent interferences (consisting of three examiners of interferences) whose decision, if adverse to the claim of an applicant, shall constitute the final refusal by the Patent and Trademark Office of the claims involved, and the Commissioner may issue a patent to the applicant who is adjudged the prior inventor. A final judgment adverse to a patentee from which no appeal or other review has been or can be taken or had shall constitute cancellation of the claims involved from the patent, and notice thereof shall be endorsed on copies of the patent thereafter distributed by the Patent and Trademark Office.

(b) A claim which is the same as, or for the same or substantially the same subject matter as, a claim of an issued patent may not be made in any application unless such a claim is made prior to one year from the date on which the patent was granted.

(c) Any agreement or understanding between parties to an interference, including any collateral agreements referred to therein, made in connection with or in contemplation of the termination of the interference, shall be in writing and a true copy thereof filed in the Patent and Trademark Office before the termination of the interference as between the said parties to the agreement or understanding. If any party filing the same so requests, the copy shall be kept separate from the file of the interference, and made available only to Government agencies on written request, or to any person on a showing of good cause. Failure to file the copy of such agreement or understanding shall render permanently unenforceable such agreement or understanding and any patent of such parties involved in the interference or any patent subsequently issued on any application of such parties so involved. The Commissioner may, however, on a showing of good cause for failure to file within the time prescribed, permit the filing of the agreement or understanding during the six-month period subsequent to the termination of the interference as between the parties to the agreement or understanding.

The Commissioner shall give notice to the parties or their attorneys of record, a reasonable time prior to said termination, of the filing requirement of this section. If the Commissioner gives such notice at a later time, irrespective of the right to file such agreement or understanding within the six-month period on a showing of good cause, the parties may file such agreement or understanding within sixty days of the receipt of such notice.

Any discretionary action of the Commissioner under this subsection shall be reviewable under section 10 of the Administrative Procedure Act. (Amended October 15, 1962, Public Law 87–831, 76 Stat. 958; and January 2, 1975, Public Law 93–596, sec. 1, 88 Stat. 1949.)

CHAPTER 13—REVIEW OF PATENT AND TRADEMARK OFFICE DECISION

SEC.
141. Appeal to Court of Appeals for the Federal Circuit.
142. Notice of appeal.
143. Proceedings on appeal.
144. Decision on appeal.
145. Civil action to obtain patent.
146. Civil action in case of interference.

§ 141. Appeal to Court of Appeals for the Federal Circuit

An applicant dissatisfied with the decision of the Board of Appeals may appeal to the United States Court of Appeals for the Federal Circuit, thereby waiving his right to proceed under section 145 of this title. A party to an interference dissatisfied with the decision of the board of patent interferences on the question of priority may appeal to the United States Court of Appeals for the Federal Circuit, but such appeal shall be dismissed if any adverse party to such interference, within twenty days after the appellant has filed notice of appeal according to section 142 of this title, files notice with the Commissioner that he elects to have all further proceedings conducted as provided in section 146 of this title. Thereupon the appellant shall have thirty days thereafter within which to file a civil action under section 146, in default of which the decision appealed from shall govern the further proceedings in the case.

§ 142. Notice of appeal

When an appeal is taken to the United States Court of Appeals for the Federal Circuit, the appellant shall give notice thereof to the Commissioner, and shall file in the Patent and Trademark Office his reasons of appeal, specifically set forth in writing, within such time after the date of the decision appealed from, not less than sixty days, as the Commissioner appoints.

§ 143. Proceedings on appeal

The United States Court of Appeals for the Federal Circuit shall, before hearing such appeal, give notice of the time and place of the hearing to the Commissioner and the parties thereto. The Commissioner shall transmit to the court certified copies of all the necessary original papers and evidence in the case specified by the appellant and any additional papers and evidence specified by the appellee and in an ex parte case the Commissioner shall furnish the court with the grounds of the decision of the Patent and Trademark Office, in writing, touching all the points involved by the reasons of appeal.

§ 144. Decision on appeal

The United States Court of Appeals for the Federal Circuit on petition, shall hear and determine such appeal on the evidence produced before the Patent and Trademark Office, and the decision shall be confined to the points set forth in the reasons of appeal. Upon its determination the court shall return to the Commissioner a certificate of its proceedings and decision, which shall be entered of record in the Patent and Trademark Office and govern the further proceedings in the case.

§ 145. Civil action to obtain patent

An applicant dissatisfied with the decision of the Board of Appeals may unless appeal has been taken to the United States Court of Appeals for the Federal Circuit, have remedy by civil action against the Commissioner in the United States District Court for the District of Columbia if commenced within such time after such decision, not less than sixty days, as the Commissioner appoints. The court may adjudge that such applicant is entitled to receive a patent for his invention, as specified in any of his claims involved in the decision of the Board of Appeals, as the facts in the case may appear and such adjudication shall authorize the Commissioner to issue such patent on compliance with the requirements of law. All the expenses of the proceedings shall be paid by the applicant.

§ 146. Civil action in case of interference

Any party to an interference dissatisfied with the decision of the board of patent interferences on the question of priority, may have remedy by civil action, if commenced within such time after such decision, not less than sixty days, as the Commissioner appoints or as provided in section 141 of this title, unless he has appealed to the United States Court of Appeals for the Federal Circuit, and such appeal is pending or has been decided. In such suits the record in the Patent and Trademark Office shall be admitted on motion of either party upon the terms and conditions as to costs, expenses, and the further cross-examination of the witnesses as the court imposes, without prejudice to the right of the parties to take further testimony. The testimony and exhibits of the record in the Patent and Trademark Office when admitted shall have the same effect as if originally taken and produced in the suit.

Such suit may be instituted against the party in interest as shown by the records of the Patent and Trademark Office at the time of the decision complained of, but any party in interest may become a party to the action. If there be adverse parties residing in a plurality of districts not embraced within the same state, or an adverse party residing in a foreign country, the United States District Court for the District of Columbia shall have jurisdiction and may issue summons against the adverse parties directed to the marshal of any district in which any adverse party resides. Summons against adverse parties residing in foreign countries may be served by publication or otherwise as the court directs. The Commissioner shall not be a necessary party but he shall be notified of the filing of the suit by the clerk of the court in which it is filed and shall have the right to intervene. Judgment of the court in favor of the right of an applicant to a patent shall authorize the Commissioner to issue such patent on the filing in the Patent and Trademark Office of a certified copy of the judgment and on compliance with the requirements of law. (Amended January 2, 1975, Public Law 93–596, sec. 1, 88 Stat. 1949; April 2, 1982, Public Law 97–164, sec. 163, 96 Stat. 49.)

CHAPTER 14—ISSUE OF PATENT

SEC.
151. Issue of patent.
152. Issue of patent to assignee.
153. How issued.
154. Contents and term of patent.
155. Patent term extension.
155A. Patent term restoration.

§ 151. Issue of patent

If it appears that applicant is entitled to a patent under the law, a written notice of allowance of the application shall be given or mailed to the applicant. The notice shall specify a sum, constituting the issue fee or a portion thereof, which shall be paid within three months thereafter.

Upon payment of this sum the patent shall issue, but if payment is not timely made, the application shall be regarded as abandoned.

Any remaining balance of the issue fee shall be paid within three months from the sending of a notice thereof and, if not paid, the patent shall lapse at the termination of this three-month period. In calculating the amount of a remaining balance, charges for a page or less may be disregarded.

If any payment required by this section is not timely made, but is submitted with the fee for delayed payment and the delay in payment is shown to have been unavoidable, it may be accepted by the Commissioner as though no abandonment or lapse had ever occurred. (Amended July 24, 1965, Public Law 89–83, secs. 4 and 6, 79 Stat. 260; and January 2, 1975, Public Law 93–601, sec. 3, 88 Stat. 1956.)

§ 152. Issue of patent to assignee

Patents may be granted to the assignee of the inventor of record in the Patent and Trademark Office, upon the application made and the specification sworn to by the inventor, except as otherwise provided in this title. (Amended January 2, 1975, Public Law 93–596, sec. 1, 88 Stat. 1949.)

§ 153. How issued

Patents shall be issued in the name of the United States of America, under the seal of the Patent and Trademark Office, and shall be signed by the Commissioner or have his signature placed thereon and attested by an officer of the Patent and Trademark Office designated by the Commissioner, and shall be recorded in the Patent and Trademark Office. (Amended January 2, 1975, Public Law 93–596, sec. 1, 88 Stat. 1949.)

§ 154. Contents and term of patent

Every patent shall contain a short title of the invention and a grant to the patentee, his heirs or assigns, for the term of seventeen years, subject to the payment of issue fees as provided for in this title, of the right to exclude others from making, using, or selling the invention throughout the United States, referring to the specification for the particulars thereof. A copy of the specification and drawings shall be annexed to the patent and be a part thereof. (Amended July 24, 1965, Public Law 89–83, sec. 5, 79 Stat. 261; December 12, 1980, Public Law 96–517, sec. 4, 94 Stat. 3018.)

§ 155. Patent term extension

Notwithstanding the provisions of section 154, the term of a patent which encompasses within its scope a composition of matter or a process for using such composition shall be extended if such composition or process has been subjected to a regulatory review by the Federal Food and Drug Administration pursuant to the Federal Food, Drug and Cosmetic Act leading to the publication of regulation permitting the interstate distribution and sale of such composition or process and for which there has thereafter been a stay of regulation of approval imposed pursuant to Section 409 of the Federal Food, Drug and Cosmetic Act, which stay was in effect on January 1, 1981, by a length of time to be measured from the date such stay of regulation of approval was imposed until such proceedings are finally resolved and commercial marketing permitted. The patentee, his heirs, successors or assigns shall notify the Commissioner of Patents and Trademarks within 90 days of the date of enactment of this section or the date the stay of regulation of approval has been removed, whichever is later, of the number of the patent to be extended and the date the stay was imposed and the date commercial marketing was permitted. On receipt of such notice, the Commissioner shall promptly issue to the owner of record of the patent a certificate of extension, under seal, stating the fact and length of the extension and identifying the composition of matter or process for using such composition to which such extension is applicable. Such certificate shall be recorded in the official file of each patent extended and such certificate shall be considered as part of the original patent, and an appropriate notice shall be published in the Official Gazette of the Patent and Trademark Office. (Amended January 4, 1983, Public Law 97–414, 96 Stat. 2065.)

§ 155A. Patent term restoration

(a) Notwithstanding section 154 of this title, the term of each of the following patents shall be extended in accordance with this section:

(1) Any patent which encompasses within its scope a composition of matter which is a new drug product, if during the regula-

33

tory review of the product by the Federal Food and Drug Administration—

  (A) the Federal Food and Drug Administration notified the patentee, by letter dated February 20, 1976, that such product's new drug application was not approvable under section 505(b)(1) of the Federal Food, Drug and Cosmetic Act;

  (B) in 1977 the patentee submitted to the Federal Food and Drug Administration the results of a health effects test to evaluate the carcinogenic potential of such product;

  (C) the Federal Food and Drug Administration approved, by letter dated December 18, 1979, the new drug application for such application; and

  (D) the Federal Food and Drug Administration approved, by letter dated May 26, 1981, a supplementary application covering the facility for the production of such product.

(2) Any patent which encompasses within its scope a process for using the composition described in paragraph (1).

(b) The term of any patent described in subsection (a) shall be extended for a period equal to the period beginning February 20, 1976, and ending May 26, 1981, and such patent shall have the effect as if originally issued with such extended term.

(c) The patentee of any patent described in subsection (a) of this section shall, within ninety days after the date of enactment of this section, notify the Commissioner of Patents and Trademarks of the number of any patent so extended. On receipt of such notice, the Commissioner shall confirm such extension by placing a notice thereof in the official file of such patent and publishing an appropriate notice of such extension in the Official Gazette of the Patent and Trademark Office. (Added October 13, 1983, Public Law 98–127, sec. 4(a), 97 Stat. 832.)

CHAPTER 15—PLANT PATENTS

SEC.
161. Patents for plants.
162. Description, claim.
163. Grant.
164. Assistance of Department of Agriculture.

34

§ 161. Patents for plants

Whoever invents or discovers and asexually reproduces any distinct and new variety of plant, including cultivated sports, mutants, hybrids, and newly found seedlings, other than a tuber propagated plant or a plant found in an uncultivated state, may obtain a patent therefor, subject to the conditions and requirements of this title. (Amended September 3, 1954, 68 Stat. 1190.)

The provisions of this title relating to patents for inventions shall apply to patents for plants, except as otherwise provided.

§ 162. Description, claim

No plant patent shall be declared invalid for noncompliance with section 112 of this title if the description is as complete as is reasonably possible.

The claim in the specification shall be in formal terms to the plant shown and described.

§ 163. Grant

In the case of a plant patent the grant shall be of the right to exclude others from asexually reproducing the plant or selling or using the plant so reproduced.

§ 164. Assistance of Department of Agriculture.

The President may by Executive order direct the Secretary of Agriculture, in accordance with the requests of the Commissioner, for the purpose of carrying into effect the provisions of this title with respect to plants (1) to furnish available information of the Department of Agriculture, (2) to conduct through the appropriate bureau or division of the Department research upon special problems, or (3) to detail to the Commissioner officers and employees of the Department.

CHAPTER 16—DESIGNS

SEC.

171. Patents for designs.
172. Right of priority.
173. Term of design patent.

§ 171. Patents for designs

Whoever invents any new, original and ornamental design for an article of manufacture may obtain a patent therefor, subject to the conditions and requirements of this title.

The provisions of this title relating to patents for inventions shall apply to patents for designs, except as otherwise provided.

§ 172. Right of priority

The right of priority provided for by section 119 of this title and the time specified in section 102(d) shall be six months in the case of designs.

§ 173. Term of design patent

Patents for designs shall be granted for the term of fourteen years. (Amended August 27, 1982, Public Law 97–247, sec. 16, 96 Stat. 321.)

CHAPTER 17—SECRECY OF CERTAIN INVENTIONS AND FILING APPLICATIONS IN FOREIGN COUNTRIES

SEC.
181. Secrecy of certain inventions and withholding of patent.
182. Abandonment of invention for unauthorized disclosure.
183. Right of compensation.
184. Filing of application in foreign country.
185. Patent barred for filing without license.
186. Penalty.
187. Nonapplicability to certain persons.
188. Rules and regulations, delegation of power.

§ 181. Secrecy of certain inventions and withholding of patent

Whenever publication or disclosure by the grant of a patent on an invention in which the Government has a property interest might, in the opinion of the head of the interested Government agency, be detrimental to the national security, the Commissioner upon being so notified shall order that the invention be kept secret and shall withhold the grant of a patent therefor under the conditions set forth hereinafter.

Whenever the publication or disclosure of an invention by the granting of a patent, in which the Government does not have a property interest, might, in the opinion of the Commissioner, be detrimental to the national security, he shall make the application for patent in which such invention is disclosed available for inspection to the Atomic Energy Commission, the Secretary of Defense, and the chief officer of any other department or agency of the Government designated by the President as a defense agency of the United States.

Each individual to whom the application is disclosed shall sign a dated acknowledgment thereof, which acknowledgment shall be entered in the file of the application. If, in the opinion of the Atomic Energy Commission, the Secretary of a Defense Department, or the chief officer of another department or agency so designated, the publication or disclosure of the invention by the granting of a patent therefor would be detrimental to the national security, the Atomic Energy Commission, the Secretary of a Defense Department, or such other chief officer shall notify the Commissioner and the Commissioner shall order that the invention be kept secret and shall withhold the grant of a patent for such period as the national interest requires, and notify the applicant thereof. Upon proper showing by the head of the department or agency who caused the secrecy order to be issued that the examination of the application might jeopardize the national interest, the Commissioner shall thereupon maintain the application in a sealed condition and notify the applicant thereof. The owner of an application which has been placed under a secrecy order shall have a right to appeal from the order to the Secretary of Commerce under rules prescribed by him.

An invention shall not be ordered kept secret and the grant of a patent withheld for a period of more than one year. The Commissioner shall renew the order at the end thereof, or at the end of any renewal period, for additional periods of one year upon notification by the head of the department or the chief officer of the agency who caused the order to be issued that an affirmative determination has been made that the national interest continues so to require. An order in effect, or issued, during a time when the United States is at war, shall remain in effect for the duration of hostilities and one year following cessation of hostilities. An order in effect, or issued, during a national emergency declared by the President shall remain in effect for the duration of the national emergency and six months thereafter. The Commissioner may rescind any order upon notification by the heads of the departments and the chief officers of the agencies who caused the order to be issued that the publication or disclosure of the invention is no longer deemed detrimental to the national security.

§ 182.   Abandonment of invention for unauthorized disclosure

The invention disclosed in an application for patent subject to an order made pursuant to section 181 of this title may be held abandoned upon its being established by the Commissioner that in violation of said order the invention has been published or disclosed or that an application for a patent therefor has been filed in a foreign country by the inventor, his successors, assigns, or legal representatives, or anyone in privity with him or them, without the consent of the Commissioner. The abandonment shall be held to have occurred as of the time of violation. The consent of the Commissioner shall not be given without the concurrence of the heads of the departments and the chief officers of the agencies who caused the order to be issued. A holding of abandonment shall constitute forfeiture by the applicant, his successors, assigns, or legal representatives, or anyone in privity with him or them, of all claims against the United States based upon such invention.

§ 183. Right to compensation

An applicant, his successors, assigns, or legal representatives, whose patent is withheld as herein provided, shall have the right, beginning at the date the applicant is notified that, except for such order, his application is otherwise in condition for allowance, or February 1, 1952, whichever is later, and ending six years after a patent is issued thereon, to apply to the head of any department or agency who caused the order to be issued for compensation for the damage caused by the order of secrecy and/or for the use of the invention by the Government, resulting from his disclosure. The right to compensation for use shall begin on the date of the first use of the invention by the Government. The head of the department or agency is authorized, upon the presentation of a claim, to enter into an agreement with the applicant, his successors, assigns, or legal representatives, in full settlement for the damage and/or use. This settlement agreement shall be conclusive for all purposes notwithstanding any other provision of law to the contrary. If full settlement of the claim cannot be effected, the head of the department or agency may award and pay to such applicant, his successors, assigns, or legal representatives, a sum not exceeding 75 per centum of the sum which the head of the department or agency considers just compensation for the damage and/or use. A claimant may bring suit against the United States in the United States Claims Court or in the District Court of the United States for the district in which such claimant is a resident for an amount which when added to the award shall constitute just compensation for the damage and/or use of the invention by the Government. The owner of any patent issued upon an application that was subject to a secrecy order issued pursuant to section 181 of this title, who did not apply for compensation as above provided, shall have the right, after the date of issuance of such patent, to bring suit in the United States Claims Court for just compensation for the damage caused by reason of the order of secrecy and/or use by the Government of the invention resulting from his disclosure. The right to compensation for use shall begin on the date of the first use of the invention by the Government. In a suit under the provisions of this section the United States may avail itself of all defenses it may plead in an action under section 1498 of title 28. This section shall not confer a right of action on anyone or his successors, assigns, or legal representatives who, while in the full-time employment or service of the United States, discovered, invented, or developed the invention on which the claim is based. (Amended April 2, 1982, Public Law 97–164, sec. 160, 96 Stat. 48.)

§ 184. Filing of application in foreign country

Except when authorized by a license obtained from the Commissioner a person shall not file or cause or authorize to be filed in any foreign country prior to six months after filing in the United States an application for patent or for the registration of a utility model, industrial design, or model in respect of an invention made in this country. A license shall not be granted with respect to an invention subject to an order issued by the Commissioner pursuant to section 181 of this title without the concurrence of the head of the departments and the chief officers of the agencies who caused the order to be issued. The license may be granted retroactively where an application has been inadvertently filed abroad and the application does not disclose an invention within the scope of section 181 of this title.

The term "application" when used in this chapter includes applications and any modifications, amendments, or supplements thereto, or divisions thereof.

§ 185. Patent barred for filing without license

Notwithstanding any other provisions of law any person, and his successors, assigns, or legal representatives, shall not receive a United States patent for an invention if that person, or his successors, assigns, or legal representatives shall, without procuring the license prescribed in section 184 of this title, have made, or consented to or assisted another's making, application in a foreign country for a patent or for the registration of a utility model, industrial design, or model in respect of the invention. A United States patent issued to such person, his successors, assigns, or legal representatives shall be invalid.

§ 186. Penalty

Whoever, during the period or periods of time an invention has been ordered to be kept secret and the grant of a patent thereon withheld pursuant to section 181 of this title, shall, with knowledge of such order and without due authorization, willfully publish or disclose or authorize or cause to be published or disclosed the invention, or material information with respect thereto, or whoever, in violation of the provisions of section 184 of this title, shall file or cause or authorize to be filed in any foreign country an application for patent or for the registration of a utility model, industrial design, or model in respect of any invention made in the United States, shall, upon conviction, be fined not more than $10,000 or imprisoned for not more than two years, or both.

§ 187. Nonapplicability to certain persons

The prohibitions and penalties of this chapter shall not apply to any officer or agent of the United States acting within the scope of his authority, nor to any person acting upon his written instructions or permission.

§ 188. Rules and regulations, delegation of power

The Atomic Energy Commission, the Secretary of a defense department, the chief officer of any other department or agency of the Government designated by the President as a defense agency of the United States, and the Secretary of Commerce, may separately issue rules and regulations to enable the respective department or agency to carry out the provisions of this chapter, and may delegate any power conferred by this chapter.

CHAPTER [18] 38—PATENT RIGHTS IN INVENTIONS
MADE WITH FEDERAL ASSISTANCE

SEC.
200. Policy and objective.
201. Definitions.

202. Disposition of rights.

203. March-in rights.

204. Preference for United States industry.

205. Confidentiality.

206. Uniform clauses and regulations.

207. Domestic and foreign protection of federally owned inventions.

208. Regulations governing Federal licensing.

209. Restrictions on licensing of federally owned inventions.

210. Precedence of chapter.

211. Relationship to antitrust laws.

§ 200.   Policy and objective

It is the policy and objective of the Congress to use the patent system to promote the utilization of inventions arising from federally supported research or development; to encourage maximum participation of small business firms in federally supported research and development efforts; to promote collaboration between commercial concerns and nonprofit organizations, including universities; to ensure that inventions made by nonprofit organizations and small business firms are used in a manner to promote free competition and enterprise; to promote the commercialization and public availability of inventions made in the United States by United States industry and labor; to ensure that the Government obtains sufficient rights in federally supported inventions to meet the needs of the Government and protect the public against nonuse or unreasonable use of inventions; and to minimize the costs of administering policies in this area. (Added December 12, 1980, Public Law 96–517, sec. 6(a), 94 Stat. 3019.)

§ 201.   Definitions

As used in this chapter—

(a) The term "Federal agency" means any executive agency as defined in section 105 of title 5, United States Code, and the military departments as defined by section 102 of title 5, United States Code.

(b) The term "funding agreement" means any contract, grant, or cooperative agreement entered into between any Federal agency, other than the Tennessee Valley Authority, and any contractor for the performance of experimental, developmental, or research work funded in whole or in part by the Federal Government. Such term includes any assignment, substitution of parties, or subcontract of any type entered into for the performance of experimental, developmental, or research work under a funding agreement as herein defined.

(c) The term "contractor" means any person, small business firm, or nonprofit organization that is a party to a funding agreement.

(d) The term "invention" means any invention or discovery which is or may be patentable or otherwise protectable under this title.

(e) The term "subject invention" means any invention of the contractor conceived or first actually reduced to practice in the performance of work under a funding agreement.

(f) The term "practical application" means to manufacture in the case of a composition or product, to practice in the case of a process or method, or to operate in the case of a machine or system; and, in each case, under such conditions as to establish that the invention is being utilized and that its benefits are to the extent permitted by law or Government regulations available to the public on reasonable terms.

(g) The term "made" when used in relation to any invention means the conception or first actual reduction to practice of such invention.

(h) The term "small business firm" means a small business concern as defined at section 2 of Public Law 85–536 (15 U.S.C. 632) and implementing regulations of the Administrator of the Small Business Administration.

(i) The term "nonprofit organization" means universities and other institutions of higher education or an organization of the type described in section 501(c)(3) of the Internal Revenue Code of 1954 (26 U.S.C. 501(c)) and exempt from taxation under section 501(a) of the Internal Revenue Code (26 U.S.C. 501(a)) or any nonprofit scientific or educational organization qualified under a State nonprofit organization statute. (Added December 12, 1980, Public Law 96–517, sec. 6(a), 94 Stat. 3019.)

§ 202. Disposition of rights

(a) Each nonprofit organization or small business firm may, within a reasonable time after disclosure as required by paragraph (c)(1) of this section, elect to retain title to any subject invention: *Provided, however,* That a funding agreement may provide otherwise (i) when the funding agreement is for the operation of a Government-owned research or production facility, (ii) in exceptional circumstances when it is determined by the agency that restriction or elimination of the right to retain title to any subject invention will better promote the policy and objectives of this chapter or (iii) when it is determined by a Government authority which is authorized by statute or Executive order to conduct foreign intelligence or counter-intelligence activities that the restriction or elimination of the right to retain title to any subject invention is necessary to protect the security of such activities. The rights of the nonprofit organization or small business firm shall be subject to the provisions of paragraph (c) of this section and the other provisions of this chapter.

(b)(1) Any determination under (ii) of paragraph (a) of this section shall be in writing and accompanied by a written statement of facts justifying the determination. A copy of each such determination and justification shall be sent to the Comptroller General of the United States within thirty days after the award of the applicable funding agreement. In the case of determinations applicable to funding agreements with small business firms copies shall also be sent to the Chief Counsel for Advocacy of the Small Business Administration.

(2) If the Comptroller General believes that any pattern of determinations by a Federal agency is contrary to the policy and objectives of this chapter or that an agency's policies or practices are otherwise not in conformance with this chapter, the Comptroller General shall so advise the head of the agency. The head of the agency shall advise the Comptroller General in writing within one hundred and twenty days of what action, if any, the agency has taken or plans to take with respect to the matters raised by the Comptroller General.

(3) At least once each year, the Comptroller General shall transmit a report to the Committees on the Judiciary of the Senate and House of Representatives on the manner in which this chapter is being implemented by the agencies and on such other aspects of Government patent policies and practices with respect to federally funded inventions as the Comptroller General believes appropriate.

(c) Each funding agreement with a small business firm or nonprofit organization shall contain appropriate provisions to effectuate the following:

(1) A requirement that the contractor disclose each subject invention to the Federal agency within a reasonable time after it is made and that the Federal Government may receive title to any subject invention not reported to it within such time.

(2) A requirement that the contractor make an election to retain title to any subject invention within a reasonable time after disclosure and that the Federal Government may receive title to any subject invention in which the contractor does not elect to retain rights or fails to elect rights within such time.

(3) A requirement that a contractor electing rights file patent applications within reasonable times and that the Federal Government may receive title to any subject inventions in the United States or other countries in which the contractor has not filed patent applications on the subject invention within such times.

(4) With respect to any invention in which the contractor elects rights, the Federal agency shall have a nonexclusive, nontransferable, irrevocable, paid-up license to practice or have practiced for or on behalf of the United States any subject invention throughout the world, and may, if provided in the funding agreement, have additional rights to sublicense any foreign government or international organization pursuant to any existing or future treaty or agreement.

(5) The right of the Federal agency to require periodic reporting on the utilization or efforts at obtaining utilization that are being made by the contractor or his licensees or assignees: *Provided,* That any such information may be treated by the Federal agency as commercial and financial information obtained from a person and privileged and confidential and not subject to disclosure under section 552 of title 5 of the United States Code.

(6) An obligation on the part of the contractor, in the event a United States patent application is filed by or on its behalf or by any assignee of the contractor, to include within the specification of such application and any patent issuing thereon, a statement specifying that the invention was made with Government support and that the Government has certain rights in the invention.

(7) In the case of a nonprofit organization, (A) a prohibition upon the assignment of rights to a subject invention in the United States without the approval of the Federal agency, except where such assignment is made to an organization which has as one of its primary functions the management of inventions and which is not, itself, engaged in or does not hold a substantial interest in other organizations engaged in the manufacture or sale of products or the use of processes that might utilize the invention or be in competi-

44

tion with embodiments of the invention (provided that such assignee shall be subject to the same provisions as the contractor); (B) a prohibition against the granting of exclusive licenses under United States Patents or Patent Applications in a subject invention by the contractor to persons other than small business firms for a period in excess of the earlier of five years from first commercial sale or use of the invention or eight years from the date of the exclusive license excepting that time before regulatory agencies necessary to obtain premarket clearance unless, on a case-by-case basis, the Federal agency approves a longer exclusive license. If exclusive field of use licenses are granted, commercial sale or use in one field of use shall not be deemed commercial sale or use as to other fields of use, and a first commercial sale or use with respect to a product of the invention shall not be deemed to end the exclusive period to different subsequent products covered by the invention; (C) a requirement that the contractor share royalties with the inventor; and (D) a requirement that the balance of any royalties or income earned by the contractor with respect to subject inventions, after payment of expenses (including payments to inventors) incidental to the administration of subject inventions, be utilized for the support of scientific research or education.

(8) The requirements of sections 203 and 204 of this chapter.

(d) If a contractor does not elect to retain title to a subject invention in cases subject to this section, the Federal agency may consider and after consultation with the contractor grant requests for retention of rights by the inventor subject to the provisions of this Act and regulations promulgated hereunder.

(e) In any case when a Federal employee is a coinventor of any invention made under a funding agreement with a nonprofit organization or small business firm, the Federal agency employing such coinventor is authorized to transfer or assign whatever rights it may acquire in the subject invention from its employee to the contractor subject to the conditions set forth in this chapter.

(f)(1) No funding agreement with a small business firm or nonprofit organization shall contain a provision allowing a Federal agency to require the licensing to third parties of inventions owned by the contractor that are not subject inventions unless such provision has been approved by the head of the agency and a written justification has been signed by the head of the agency. Any such provision shall clearly state whether the licensing may be required in connection with the practice of a subject invention, a specifically identified work object, or both. The head of the agency may not delegate the authority to approve provisions or sign justifications required by this paragraph.

(2) A Federal agency shall not require the licensing of third parties under any such provision unless the head of the agency determines that the use of the invention by others is necessary for the practice of a subject invention or for the use of a work object of the funding agreement and that such action is necessary to achieve the practical application of the subject invention or work object. Any such determination shall be on the record after an opportunity for an agency hearing. Any action commenced for judicial review of such determination shall be brought within sixty days after notification of such determination. (Added December 12, 1980, Public Law 96–517, sec. 6(a), 94 Stat. 3020.)

§ 203. March-in rights

With respect to any subject invention in which a small business firm or nonprofit organization has acquired title under this chapter, the Federal agency under whose funding agreement the subject invention was made shall have the right, in accordance with such procedures as are provided in regulations promulgated hereunder to require the contractor, an assignee or exclusive licensee of a subject invention to grant a nonexclusive, partially exclusive, or exclusive license in any field of use to a responsible applicant or applicants, upon terms that are reasonable under the circumstances, and if the contractor, assignee, or exclusive licensee refuses such request, to grant such a license itself, if the Federal agency determines that such—

(a) action is necessary because the contractor or assignee has not taken, or is not expected to take within a reasonable time, effective steps to achieve practical application of the subject invention in such field of use;

(b) action is necessary to alleviate health or safety needs which are not reasonably satisfied by the contractor, assignee, or their licensees;

(c) action is necessary to meet requirements for public use specified by Federal regulations and such requirements are not reasonably satisfied by the contractor, assignee, or licensees; or

(d) action is necessary because the agreement required by section

46

204 has not been obtained or waived or because a licensee of the exclusive right to use or sell any subject invention in the United States is in breach of its agreement obtained pursuant to section 204. (Added December 12, 1980, Public Law 96–517, sec. 6(a), 94 Stat. 3022.)

§ 204. Preference for United States industry

Notwithstanding any other provision of this chapter, no small business firm or nonprofit organization which receives title to any subject invention and no assignee of any such small business firm or nonprofit organization shall grant to any person the exclusive right to use or sell any subject invention in the United States unless such person agrees that any products embodying the subject invention or produced through the use of the subject invention will be manufactured substantially in the United States. However, in individual cases, the requirement for such an agreement may be waived by the Federal agency under whose funding agreement the invention was made upon a showing by the small business firm, nonprofit organization, or assignee that reasonable but unsuccessful efforts have been made to grant licenses on similar terms to potential licensees that would be likely to manufacture substantially in the United States or that under the circumstances domestic manufacture is not commercially feasible. (Added December 12, 1980, Public Law 96–517, sec. 6(a), 94 Stat. 3023.)

§ 205. Confidentiality

Federal agencies are authorized to withhold from disclosure to the public information disclosing any invention in which the Federal Government owns or may own a right, title, or interest (including a nonexclusive license) for a reasonable time in order for a patent application to be filed. Furthermore, Federal agencies shall not be required to release copies of any document which is part of an application for patent filed with the United States Patent and Trademark Office or with any foreign patent office. (Added December 12, 1980, Public Law 96–517, sec. 6(a), 94 Stat. 3023.)

§ 206. Uniform clauses and regulations

The Office of Federal Procurement Policy, after receiving recommendations of the Office of Science and Technology Policy, may issue regulations which may be made applicable to Federal agencies implementing the provisions of sections 202 through 204 of this chapter and the Office of Federal Procurement Policy shall establish standard funding agreement provisions required under this chapter.

§ 207. Domestic and foreign protection of federally owned inventions

Each Federal agency is authorized to—

(1) apply for, obtain, and maintain patents or other forms of protection in the United States and in foreign countries on inventions in which the Federal Government owns a right, title, or interest;

(2) grant nonexclusive, exclusive, or partially exclusive licenses under federally owned patent applications, patents, or other forms of protection obtained, royalty-free or for royalties or other consideration, and on such terms and conditions, including the grant to the licensee of the right of enforcement pursuant to the provisions of chapter 29 of this title as determined appropriate in the public interest;

(3) undertake all other suitable and necessary steps to protect and administer rights to federally owned inventions on behalf of the Federal Government either directly or through contract; and

(4) transfer custody and administration, in whole or in part, to another Federal agency, of the right, title, or interest in any federally owned invention. (Added December 12, 1980, Public Law 96–517, sec. 6(a), 94 Stat. 3023.)

§ 208. Regulations governing Federal licensing

The Administrator of General Services is authorized to promulgate regulations specifying the terms and conditions upon which any federally owned invention, other than inventions owned by the Tennessee Valley Authority, may be licensed on a nonexclusive, partially exclusive, or exclusive basis. (Added December 12, 1980, Public Law 96–517, sec. 6(a), 94 Stat. 3024.)

§ 209. Restrictions on licensing of federally owned inventions

(a) No Federal agency shall grant any license under a patent or patent application on a federally owned invention unless the person requesting the license has supplied the agency with a plan for development and/or marketing of the invention, except that any such plan may be treated by the Federal agency as commercial and financial information obtained from a person and privileged and confidential and not subject to disclosure under section 552 of title 5 of the United States Code.

(b) A Federal agency shall normally grant the right to use or sell any federally owned invention in the United States only to a licensee that agrees that any products embodying the invention or produced through the use of the invention will be manufactured substantially in the United States.

(c)(1) Each Federal agency may grant exclusive or partially exclusive licenses in any invention covered by a federally owned domestic patent or patent application only if, after public notice and opportunity for filing written objections, it is determined that—

(A) the interests of the Federal Government and the public will best be served by the proposed license, in view of the applicant's intentions, plans, and ability to bring the invention to practical application or otherwise promote the invention's utilization by the public;

(B) the desired practical application has not been achieved, or is not likely expeditiously to be achieved, under any nonexclusive license which has been granted, or which may be granted, on the invention;

(C) exclusive or partially exclusive licensing is a reasonable and necessary incentive to call forth the investment of risk capital and expenditures to bring the invention to practical application or otherwise promote the invention's utilization by the public; and

(D) the proposed terms and scope of exclusivity are not greater than reasonably necessary to provide the incentive for bringing the invention to practical application or otherwise promote the invention's utilization by the public.

(2) A Federal agency shall not grant such exclusive or partially exclusive license under paragraph (1) of this subsection if it determines that the grant of such license will tend substantially to lessen competition or result in undue concentration in any section of the country in any line of commerce to which the technology to be licensed relates, or to create or maintain other situations inconsistent with the antitrust laws.

(3) First preference in the exclusive or partially exclusive licensing of federally owned inventions shall go to small business firms submitting plans that are determined by the agency to be within

the capabilities of the firms and equally likely, if executed, to bring the invention to practical application as any plans submitted by applicants that are not small business firms.

(d) After consideration of whether the interests of the Federal Government or United States industry in foreign commerce will be enhanced, any Federal agency may grant exclusive or partially exclusive licenses in any invention covered by a foreign patent application or patent, after public notice and opportunity for filing written objections, except that a Federal agency shall not grant such exclusive or partially exclusive license if it determines that the grant of such license will tend substantially to lessen competition or result in undue concentration in any section of the United States in any line of commerce to which the technology to be licensed relates, or to create or maintain other situations inconsistent with antitrust laws.

(e) The Federal agency shall maintain a record of determinations to grant exclusive or partially exclusive licenses.

(f) Any grant of a license shall contain such terms and conditions as the Federal agency determines appropriate for the protection of the interests of the Federal Government and the public, including provisions for the following:

(1) periodic reporting on the utilization or efforts at obtaining utilization that are being made by the licensee with particular reference to the plan submitted: *Provided,* That any such information may be treated by the Federal agency as commercial and financial information obtained from a person and privileged and confidential and not subject to disclosure under section 552 of title 5 of the United States Code;

(2) the right of the Federal agency to terminate such license in whole or in part if it determines that the licensee is not executing the plan submitted with its request for a license and the licensee cannot otherwise demonstrate to the satisfaction of the Federal agency that it has taken or can be expected to take within a reasonable time, effective steps to achieve practical application of the invention;

(3) the right of the Federal agency to terminate such license in whole or in part if the licensee is in breach of an agreement obtained pursuant to paragraph (b) of this section; and

(4) the right of the Federal agency to terminate the license in whole or in part if the agency determines that such action is necessary to meet requirements for public use specified by Federal regu-

lations issued after the date of the license and such requirements are not reasonably satisfied by the licensee. (Added December 12, 1980, Public Law 96–517, sec. 6(a), 94 Stat. 3024.)

§ 210.   Precedence of chapter

(a) This chapter shall take precedence over any other Act which would require a disposition of rights in subject inventions of small business firms or nonprofit organizations contractors in a manner that is inconsistent with this chapter, including but not necessarily limited to the following:

(1) section 10(a) of the Act of June 29, 1935, as added by title I of the Act of August 14, 1946 (7 U.S.C. 427i(a); 60 Stat. 1085);

(2) section 205(a) of the Act of August 14, 1946 (7 U.S.C. 1624(a); 60 Stat. 1090);

(3) section 501(c) of the Federal Mine Safety and Health Act of 1977 (30 U.S.C. 951(c); 83 Stat. 742);

(4) section 106(c) of the National Traffic and Motor Vehicle Safety Act of 1966 (15 U.S.C. 1395(c); 80 Stat. 721);

(5) section 12 of the National Science Foundation Act of 1950 (42 U.S.C. 1871(a); 82 Stat. 360);

(6) section 152 of the Atomic Energy Act of 1954 (42 U.S.C. 2182; 68 Stat. 943);

(7) section 305 of the National Aeronautics and Space Act of 1958 (42 U.S.C. 2457);

(8) section 6 of the Coal Research Development Act of 1960 (30 U.S.C. 666; 74 Stat. 337);

(9) section 4 of the Helium Act Amendments of 1960 (50 U.S.C. 167b; 74 Stat. 920);

(10) section 32 of the Arms Control and Disarmament Act of 1961 (22 U.S.C. 2572; 75 Stat. 634);

(11) subsection (e) of section 302 of the Appalachian Regional Development Act of 1965 (40 U.S.C. App. 302(e); 79 Stat. 5);

(12) section 9 of the Federal Nonnuclear Energy Research and Development Act of 1974 (42 U.S.C. 5901; 88 Stat. 1878);

(13) section 5(d) of the Consumer Product Safety Act (15 U.S.C. 2054(d); 86 Stat. 1211);

(14) section 3 of the Act of April 5, 1944 (30 U.S.C. 323; 58 Stat. 191);

(15) section 8001(c)(3) of the Solid Waste Disposal Act (42 U.S.C. 6981(c); 90 Stat. 2829);

(16) section 219 of the Foreign Assistance Act of 1961 (22 U.S.C. 2179; 83 Stat. 806);

(17) section 427(b) of the Federal Mine Health and Safety Act of 1977 (30 U.S.C. 937(b); 86 Stat. 155);

(18) section 306(d) of the Surface Mining and Reclamation Act of 1977 (30 U.S.C. 1226(d); 91 Stat. 455);

(19) section 21(d) of the Federal Fire Prevention and Control Act of 1974 (15 U.S.C. 2218(d); 88 Stat. 1548);

(20) section 6(b) of the Solar Photovoltaic Energy Research Development and Demonstration Act of 1978 (42 U.S.C. 5585(b); 92 Stat. 2516);

(21) section 12 of the Native Latex Commercialization and Economic Development Act of 1978 (7 U.S.C. 178(j); 92 Stat. 2533); and

(22) section 408 of the Water Resources and Development Act of 1978 (42 U.S.C. 7879; 92 Stat. 1360).

The Act creating this chapter shall be construed to take precedence over any future Act unless that Act specifically cites this Act and provides that it shall take precedence over this Act.

(b) Nothing in this chapter is intended to alter the effect of the laws cited in paragraph (a) of this section or any other laws with respect to the disposition of rights in inventions made in the performance of funding agreements with persons other than nonprofit organizations or small business firms.

(c) Nothing in this chapter is intended to limit the authority of agencies to agree to the disposition of rights in inventions made in the performance of work under funding agreements with persons other than nonprofit organizations or small business firms in accordance with the Statement of Government Patent Policy issued on August 23, 1971 (36 Fed.Reg. 16887), agency regulations, or other applicable regulations or to otherwise limit the authority of agencies to allow such persons to retain ownership of inventions. Any disposition of rights in inventions made in accordance with the Statement or implementing regulations, including any disposition occurring before enactment of this section, are hereby authorized.

(d) Nothing in this chapter shall be construed to require the disclosure of intelligence sources or methods or to otherwise affect the authority granted to the Director of Central Intelligence by statute or

Executive order for the protection of intelligence sources or methods. (Added December 12, 1980, Public Law 96–517, sec. 6(a), 94 Stat. 3026.)

§ 211. Relationship to antitrust laws

Nothing in this chapter shall be deemed to convey to any person immunity from civil or criminal liability, or to create any defenses to actions, under any antitrust law. (Added December 12, 1980, Public Law 96–517, sec. 6(a), 94 Stat. 3027.)

PART III—PATENTS AND PROTECTION OF PATENT RIGHTS

CHAPTER	SEC.
25. Amendment and Correction of Patents	251
26. Ownership and Assignment	261
27. Government Interests in Patents	266
28. Infringement of Patents	271
29. Remedies for Infringement of Patent and Other Actions	281

CHAPTER 25—AMENDMENT AND CORRECTION OF PATENTS

SEC.
251. Reissue of defective patents.
252. Effect of reissue.
253. Disclaimer.
254. Certificate of correction of Patent and Trademark Office mistake.
255. Certificate of correction of applicant's mistake.
256. Correction of named inventor.

§ 251. Reissue of defective patents

Whenever any patent is, through error without any deceptive intention, deemed wholly or partly inoperative or invalid, by reason of a defective specification or drawing, or by reason of the patentee claiming more or less than he had a right to claim in the patent, the Commissioner shall, on the surrender of such patent and the payment of the fee required by law, reissue the patent for the invention disclosed in the original patent, and in accordance with a new and amended application, for the unexpired part of the term of the original patent. No new matter shall be introduced into the application for reissue.

The Commissioner may issue several reissued patents for distinct and separate parts of the thing patented, upon demand of the applicant, and upon payment of the required fee for a reissue for each of such reissued patents.

The provisions of this title relating to applications for patent shall be applicable to applications for reissue of a patent, except that application for reissue may be made and sworn to by the assignee of the entire interest if the application does not seek to enlarge the scope of the claims of the original patent.

No reissued patent shall be granted enlarging the scope of the claims of the original patent unless applied for within two years from the grant of the original patent.

§ 252. Effect of reissue

The surrender of the original patent shall take effect upon the issue of the reissued patent, and every reissued patent shall have the same effect and operation in law, on the trial of actions for causes thereafter arising, as if the same had been originally granted in such amended form, but in so far as the claims or the original and reissued patents are identical, such surrender shall not affect any action then pending nor abate any cause of action then existing, and the reissued patent, to the extent that its claims are identical with the original patent, shall constitute a continuation thereof and have effect continuously from the date of the original patent.

No reissued patent shall abridge or affect the right of any person or his successors in business who made, purchased or used prior to the grant of a reissue anything patented by the reissued patent, to continue the use of, or to sell to others to be used or sold, the specific thing so made, purchased or used, unless the making, using or selling of such thing infringes a valid claim of the reissued patent which was in the original patent. The court before which such matter is in question may provide for the continued manufacture, use or sale of the thing made, purchased or used as specified, or for the manufacture, use or sale of which substantial preparation was made before the grant of the reissue, and it may also provide for the continued practice of any process patented by the reissue, practiced, or for the practice of which substantial preparation was made, prior to the grant of the reissue, to the extent and under such terms as the court deems equitable for the protection of investments made or business commenced before the grant of the reissue.

§ 253. Disclaimer

Whenever, without any deceptive intention, a claim of a patent is invalid the remaining claims shall not thereby be rendered invalid. A patentee, whether of the whole or any sectional interest therein, may, on payment of the fee required by law, make disclaimer of any complete claim, stating therein the extent of his interest in such patent. Such disclaimer shall be in writing and recorded in the Patent and Trademark Office; and it shall thereafter be considered as part of the original patent to the extent of the interest possessed by the disclaimant and by those claiming under him.

In like manner any patentee or applicant may disclaim or dedicate to the public the entire term, or any terminal part of the term, of the patent granted or to be granted. (Amended January 2, 1975, Public Law 93–596, sec. 1, 88 Stat. 1949.)

§ 254. Certificate of correction of Patent and Trademark Office mistake

Whenever a mistake in a patent, incurred through the fault of the Patent and Trademark Office, is clearly disclosed by the records of the Office, the Commissioner may issue a certificate of correction stating the fact and nature of such mistake, under seal, without charge, to be recorded in the records of patents. A printed copy thereof shall be attached to each printed copy of the patent, and such certificate shall be considered as part of the original patent. Every such patent, together with such certificate, shall have the same effect and operation in law on the trial of actions for causes thereafter arising as if the same had been originally issued in such corrected form. The Commissioner may issue a corrected patent without charge in lieu of and with like effect as a certificate of correction. (Amended January 2, 1975, Public Law 93–596, sec. 1, 88 Stat. 1949.)

§ 255. Certificate of correction of applicant's mistake

Whenever a mistake of a clerical or typographical nature, or of minor character, which was not the fault of the Patent and Trademark Office, appears in a patent and a showing has been made that such mistake occurred in good faith, the Commissioner may, upon payment of the required fee, issue a certificate of correction, if the correction does not involve such changes in the patent as would constitute new matter or would require reexamination. Such patent, together with the certificate, shall have the same effect and operation in law on the trial of actions for causes thereafter arising as if the same had been originally issued in such corrected form. (Amended January 2, 1975, Public Law 93–596, sec. 1, 88 Stat. 1949.)

§ 256. Correction of named inventor

Whenever through error a person is named in an issued patent as the inventor, or through error an inventor is not named in an issued patent and such error arose without any deceptive intention on his part, the Commissioner may, on application of all the parties and assignees, with proof of the facts and such other requirements as may be imposed, issue a certificate correcting such error.

The error of omitting inventors or naming persons who are not inventors shall not invalidate the patent in which such error occurred if it can be corrected as provided in this section. The court before which such matter is called in question may order correction of the patent on notice and hearing of all parties concerned and the Commissioner shall issue a certificate accordingly. (Amended August 27, 1982, Public Law 97–247, sec. 6(b), 96 Stat. 320.)

CHAPTER 26—OWNERSHIP AND ASSIGNMENT

Sec.
261. Ownership; assignment.
262. Joint owners.

§ 261. Ownership; assignment

Subject to the provisions of this title, patents shall have the attributes of personal property.

Applications for patent, patents, or any interest therein, shall be assignable in law by an instrument in writing. The applicant, patentee, or his assigns or legal representatives may in like manner grant and convey an exclusive right under his application for patent, or patents, to the whole or any specified part of the United States.

A certificate of acknowledgement under the hand and official seal of a person authorized to administer oaths within the United States, or, in a foreign country, of a diplomatic or consular officer of the United States or an officer authorized to administer oaths whose authority is proved by a certificate of a diplomatic or consular officer of the United States, or apostille of an official designated by a foreign country which, by treaty or convention, accords like effect to apostilles of designated officials in the United States, shall be prima facie evidence of the execution of an assignment, grant or conveyance of a patent or application for patent.

An assignment, grant or conveyance shall be void as against any subsequent purchaser or mortgagee for a valuable consideration, without notice, unless it is recorded in the Patent and Trademark Office within three months from its date or prior to the date of such subsequent purchase or mortgage. (Amended January 2, 1975, Public Law 93–596, sec. 1, 88 Stat. 1949; August 27, 1982, Public Law 97–247, sec. 14(b), 96 Stat. 321.)

§ 262. Joint owners

In the absence of any agreement to the contrary, each of the joint owners of a patent may make, use or sell the patented invention without the consent of and without accounting to the other owners.

CHAPTER 27—GOVERNMENT INTERESTS IN PATENTS

SEC.
266. [Repealed.]
267. Time for taking action in Government applications.

§ 266. Issue of patents without fees to Government employees

(Repealed July 24, 1965, Public Law 89–83, sec. 8, 79 Stat. 261.)

§ 267. Time for taking action in Government applications

Notwithstanding the provisions of sections 133 and 151 of this title, the Commissioner may extend the time for taking any action to three years, when an application has become the property of the United States and the head of the appropriate department or agency of the Government has certified to the Commissioner that the invention disclosed therein is important to the armament or defense of the United States.

CHAPTER 28—INFRINGEMENT OF PATENTS

SEC.
271. Infringement of patent.
272. Temporary presence in the United States.

§ 271. Infringement of patent

(a) Except as otherwise provided in this title, whoever without authority makes, uses or sells any patented invention, within the United States during the term of the patent therefor, infringes the patent.

(b) Whoever actively induces infringement of a patent shall be liable as an infringer.

(c) Whoever sells a component of a patented machine, manufacture, combination or composition, or a material or apparatus for use in practicing a patented process, constituting a material part of the invention, knowing the same to be especially made or especially adapted for use in an infringement of such patent, and not a staple article or commodity of commerce suitable for substantial noninfringing use, shall be liable as a contributory infringer.

(d) No patent owner otherwise entitled to relief for infringement or contributory infringement of a patent shall be denied relief or deemed guilty of misuse or illegal extension of the patent right by reason of his having done one or more of the following: (1) derived revenue from acts which if performed by another without his consent would constitute contributory infringement of the patent; (2) licensed or authorized another to perform acts which if performed without his consent would constitute contributory infringement of the patent; (3) sought to enforce his patent rights against infringement or contributory infringement.

§ 272. Temporary presence in the United States

The use of any invention in any vessel, aircraft or vehicle of any country which affords similar privileges to vessels, aircraft or vehicles of the United States, entering the United States temporarily or accidentally, shall not constitute infringement of any patent, if the invention is used exclusively for the needs of the vessel, aircraft or vehicle and is not sold in or used for the manufacture of anything to be sold in or exported from the United States.

CHAPTER 29—REMEDIES FOR INFRINGEMENT OF PATENT, AND OTHER ACTIONS

SEC.
281. Remedy for infringement of patent.
282. Presumption of validity; defenses.
283. Injunction.
284. Damages.
285. Attorney fees.
286. Time limitation on damages.
287. Limitation on damages; marking and notice.
288. Action for infringement of a patent containing an invalid claim.
289. Additional remedy for infringement of design patent.
290. Notice of patent suits.
291. Interfering patents.
292. False marking.

293. Nonresident patentee, service and notice.
294. Voluntary arbitration.

§ 281. Remedy for infringement of patent

A patentee shall have remedy by civil action for infringement of his patent.

§ 282. Presumption of validity; defenses

A patent shall be presumed valid. Each claim of a patent (whether in independent, dependent, or multiple dependent form) shall be presumed valid independently of the validity of other claims; dependent or multiple dependent claims shall be presumed valid even though dependent upon an invalid claim. The burden of establishing invalidity of a patent or any claim thereof shall rest on the party asserting such invalidity.

The following shall be defenses in any action involving the validity or infringement of a patent and shall be pleaded:

(1) Noninfringement, absence of liability for infringement, or unenforceability,

(2) Invalidity of the patent or any claim in suit on any ground specified in part II of this title as a condition for patentability,

(3) Invalidity of the patent or any claim in suit for failure to comply with any requirement of sections 112 or 251 of this title,

(4) Any other fact or act made a defense by this title.

In actions involving the validity or infringement of a patent the party asserting invalidity or noninfringement shall give notice in the pleadings or otherwise in writing to the adverse party at least thirty days before the trial, of the country, number, date, and name of the patentee of any patent, the title, date, and page numbers of any publication to be relied upon as anticipation of the patent in suit or, except in actions in the United States Claims Court, as showing the state of the art, and the name and address of any person who may be relied upon as the prior inventor or as having prior knowledge of or as having previously used or offered for sale the invention of the patent in suit. In the absence of such notice proof of the said matters may not be made at the trial except on such terms as the court requires. (Amended July 24, 1965, Public Law 89–83, sec. 10, 79 Stat. 261; November 24, 1975, Public Law 94–131, sec. 10, 89 Stat. 692.)

§ 283. Injunction

The several courts having jurisdiction of cases under this title may grant injunctions in accordance with the principles of equity to prevent the violation of any right secured by patent, on such terms as the court deems reasonable.

§ 284. Damages

Upon finding for the claimant the court shall award the claimant damages adequate to compensate for the infringement but in no event less than a reasonable royalty for the use made of the invention by the infringer, together with interest and costs as fixed by the court.

When the damages are not found by a jury, the court shall assess them. In either event the court may increase the damages up to three times the amount found or assessed.

The court may receive expert testimony as an aid to the determination of damages or of what royalty would be reasonable under the circumstances.

§ 285. Attorney fees

The court in exceptional cases may award reasonable attorney fees to the prevailing party.

§ 286. Time limitation on damages

Except as otherwise provided by law, no recovery shall be had for any infringement committed more than six years prior to the filing of the complaint or counterclaim for infringement in the action.

In the case of claims against the United States Government for use of a patented invention, the period before bringing suit, up to six years, between the date of receipt of a written claim for compensation by the department or agency of the Government having authority to settle such claim, and the date of mailing by the Government of a notice to the claimant that his claim has been denied shall not be counted as part of the period referred to in the preceding paragraph.

§ 287. Limitation on damages; marking and notice

Patentees, and persons making or selling any patented article for or under them, may give notice to the public that the same is patented, either by fixing thereon the word "patent" or the abbreviation "pat.", together with the number of the patent, or when, from the character of the article, this can not be done, by fixing to it, or to the package wherein one or more of them is contained, a label containing a like notice. In the event of failure so to mark, no damages shall be recovered by the patentee in any action for infringement, except on proof that the infringer was notified of the infringement and continued to infringe thereafter, in which event damages may be recovered only for infringement occurring after such notice. Filing of an action for infringement shall constitute such notice.

§ 288.   Action for infringement of a patent containing an invalid claim

Whenever, without deceptive intention, a claim of a patent is invalid, an action may be maintained for the infringement of a claim of the patent which may be valid. The patentee shall recover no costs unless a disclaimer of the invalid claim has been entered at the Patent and Trademark Office before the commencement of the suit. (Amended January 2, 1975, Public Law 93–596, sec. 1, 88 Stat. 1949.)

§ 289.   Additional remedy for infringement of design patent

Whoever during the term of a patent for a design, without license of the owner, (1) applies the patented design, or any colorable imitation thereof, to any article of manufacture for the purpose of sale, or (2) sells or exposes for sale any article of manufacture to which such design or colorable imitation has been applied shall be liable to the owner to the extent of his total profit, but not less than $250, recoverable in any United States district court having jurisdiction of the parties.

Nothing in this section shall prevent, lessen, or impeach any other remedy which an owner of an infringed patent has under the provisions of this title, but he shall not twice recover the profit made from the infringement.

§ 290.   Notice of patent suits

The clerks of the courts of the United States, within one month after the filing of an action under this title shall give notice thereof in writing to the Commissioner, setting forth so far as known the names and addresses of the parties, name of the inventor, and the designating number of the patent upon which the action has been brought. If any other patent is subsequently included in the action he shall give like notice thereof. Within one month after the decision is rendered or a judgment issued the clerk of the court shall give notice thereof to the Commissioner. The Commissioner shall, on receipt of such notices, enter the same in the file of such patent.

§ 291. Interfering patents

The owner of an interfering patent may have relief against the owner of another by civil action, and the court may adjudge the question of the validity of any of the interfering patents, in whole or in part. The provisions of the second paragraph of section 146 of this title shall apply to actions brought under this section.

§ 292. False marking

(a) Whoever, without the consent of the patentee, marks upon, or affixes to, or uses in advertising in connection with anything made, used, or sold by him, the name or any imitation of the name of the patentee, the patent number, or the words "patent," "patentee," or the like, with the intent of counterfeiting or imitating the mark of the patentee, or of deceiving the public and inducing them to believe that the thing was made or sold by or with the consent of the patentee; or

Whoever marks upon, or affixes to, or uses in advertising in connection with any unpatented article, the word "patent" or any word or number importing the same is patented, for the purpose of deceiving the public; or

Whoever marks upon, or affixes to, or uses in advertising in connection with any article, the words "patent applied for," "patent pending," or any word importing that an application for patent has been made, when no application for patent has been made, or if made, is not pending, for the purpose of deceiving the public—

Shall be fined not more than $500 for every such offense.

(b) Any person may sue for the penalty, in which event one-half shall go to the person suing and the other to the use of the United States.

§ 293. Nonresident patentee; service and notice

Every patentee not residing in the United States may file in the Patent and Trademark Office a written designation stating the name and address of a person residing within the United States on whom may be served process or notice of proceedings affecting the patent or rights thereunder. If the person designated cannot be found at the address given in the last designation, or if no person has been designated, the United States District Court for the District of Columbia shall have jurisdiction and summons shall be served by publication or otherwise as the court directs. The court shall have the same jurisdiction to take any action respecting the patent or rights thereunder that it would have if the patentee were personally within the jurisdiction of the court. (Amended January 2, 1975, Public Law 93–596, sec. 1, 88 Stat. 1949.)

§ 294.   Voluntary arbitration

(a) A contract involving a patent or any right under a patent may contain a provision requiring arbitration of any dispute relating to patent validity or infringement arising under the contract. In the absence of such a provision, the parties to an existing patent validity or infringement dispute may agree in writing to settle such dispute by arbitration. Any such provision or agreement shall be valid, irrevocable, and enforceable, except for any grounds that exist at law or in equity for revocation of a contract.

(b) Arbitration of such disputes, awards by arbitrators and confirmation of awards shall be governed by title 9, United States Code, to the extent such title is not inconsistent with this section. In any such arbitration proceeding, the defenses provided for under section 282 of this title shall be considered by the arbitrator if raised by any party to the proceeding.

(c) An award by an arbitrator shall be final and binding between the parties to the arbitration but shall have no force or effect on any other person. The parties to an arbitration may agree that in the event a patent which is the subject matter of an award is subsequently determined to be invalid or unenforceable in a judgment rendered by a court to competent jurisdiction from which no appeal can or has been taken, such award may be modified by any court of competent jurisdiction upon application by any party to the arbitration. Any such modification shall govern the rights and obligations between such parties from the date of such modification.

(d) When an award is made by an arbitrator, the patentee, his assignee or licensee shall give notice thereof in writing to the Commissioner. There shall be a separate notice prepared for each patent involved in such proceeding. Such notice shall set forth the names and addresses of the parties, the name of the inventor, and the name of the patent owner, shall designate the number of the patent, and shall contain a copy of the award. If an award is modified by a court, the party requesting such modification shall give notice of such modification to the Commissioner. The Commissioner shall, upon receipt of either notice, enter the same in the record of the prosecution of such patent. If the required notice is not filed with the Commissioner, any party to the proceeding may provide such notice to the Commissioner.

(e) The award shall be unenforceable until the notice required by subsection (d) is received by the Commissioner. (Added August 27, 1982, Public Law 97–247, sec. 17(b)(1), 96 Stat. 322.)

CHAPTER 30—PRIOR ART CITATIONS TO OFFICE AND REEXAMINATION OF PATENTS

SEC.
301. Citation of prior art.
302. Request for reexamination.
303. Determination of issue by Commissioner.
304. Reexamination order by Commissioner.
305. Conduct of reexamination proceedings.
306. Appeal.
307. Certificate of patentability, unpatentability, and claim cancellation.

§ 301. Citation of prior art

Any person at any time may cite to the Office in writing prior art consisting of patents or printed publications which that person believes to have a bearing on the patentability of any claim of a particular patent. If the person explains in writing the pertinency and manner of applying such prior art to at least one claim of the patent, the citation of such prior art and the explanation thereof will become a part of the official file of the patent. At the written request of the person citing the prior art, his or her identity will be excluded from the patent file and kept confidential. (Added December 12, 1980, Public Law 96–517, sec. 1, 94 Stat. 3015.)

§ 302. Request for reexamination

Any person at any time may file a request for reexamination by the Office of any claim of a patent on the basis of any prior art cited under the provisions of section 301 of this title. The request must be in writing and must be accompanied by payment of a reexamination fee established by the Commissioner of Patents pursuant to the provisions of section 41 of this title. The request must set forth the pertinency and manner applying cited prior art to every claim for which reexamination is requested. Unless the requesting person is the owner of the patent, the Commissioner promptly will send a copy of the request to the owner of record of the patent. (Added December 12, 1980, Public Law 96–517, sec. 1, 94 Stat. 3015.)

§ 303. Determination of issue by Commissioner

(a) Within three months following the filing of a request for reexamination under the provisions of section 302 of this title, the Commissioner will determine whether a substantial new question of patentability affecting any claim of the patent concerned is raised by the request, with or without consideration of other patents or printed publications. On his own initiative, and any time, the Commissioner may determine whether a substantial new question of patentability is raised by patents and publications discovered by him or cited under the provisions of section 301 of this title.

(b) A record of the Commissioner's determination under subsection (a) of this section will be placed in the official file of the patent, and a copy promptly will be given or mailed to the owner of record of the patent and to the person requesting reexamination, if any.

(c) A determination by the Commissioner pursuant to subsection (a) of this section that no substantial new question of patentability has been raised will be final and nonappealable. Upon such a determination, the Commissioner may refund a portion of the reexamination fee required under section 302 of this title. (Added December 12, 1980, Public Law 96–517, sec. 1, 94 Stat. 3015.)

§ 304. Reexamination order by Commissioner

If, in a determination made under the provisions of subsection 303(a) of this title, the Commissioner finds that a substantial new question of patentability affecting any claim of a patent is raised, the determination will include an order for reexamination of the patent for resolution of the question. The patent owner will be given a reasonable period, not less than two months from the date a copy of the determination is given or mailed to him, within which he may file a statement on such question, including any amendment to his patent and new claim or claims he may wish to propose, for consideration in the reexamination. If the patent owner files such a statement, he promptly will serve a copy of it on the person who has requested reexamination under the provisions of section 302 of this title. Within a period of two months from the date of service, that person may file and have considered in the reexamination a reply to any statement filed by the patent owner. That person promptly will serve on the patent owner a copy of any reply filed. (Added December 12, 1980, Public Law 96–517, sec. 1, 94 Stat. 3016.)

§ 305.   Conduct of reexamination proceedings

After the times for filing the statement and reply provided for by section 304 of this title have expired, reexamination will be conducted according to the procedures established for initial examination under the provisions of sections 132 and 133 of this title. In any reexamination proceeding under this chapter, the patent owner will be permitted to propose any amendment to his patent and a new claim or claims thereto, in order to distinguish the invention as claimed from the prior art cited under the provisions of section 301 of this title, or in response to a decision adverse to the patentability of a claim of a patent. No proposed amended or new claim enlarging the scope of a claim of the patent will be permitted in a reexamination proceeding under this chapter. All reexamination proceedings under this section, including any appeal to the Board of Appeals, will be conducted with special dispatch within the Office. (Added December 12, 1980, Public Law 96–517, sec. 1, 94 Stat. 3016.)

§ 306.   Appeal

The patent owner involved in a reexamination proceeding under this chapter may appeal under the provisions of section 134 of this title, and may seek court review under the provisions of sections 141 to 145 of this title, with respect to any decision adverse to the patentability of any original or proposed amended or new claim of the patent. (Added December 12, 1980, Public Law 96–517, sec. 1, 94 Stat. 3016.)

§ 307.   Certificate of patentability, unpatentability, and claim cancellation

(a) In a reexamination proceeding under this chapter, when the time for appeal has expired or any appeal proceeding has terminated, the Commissioner will issue and publish a certificate canceling any claim of the patent finally determined to be unpatentable, confirming any claim of the patent determined to be patentable, and incorporating in the patent any proposed amended or new claim determined to be patentable.

(b) Any proposed amended or new claim determined to be patentable and incorporated into a patent following a reexamination proceeding will have the same effect as that specified in section 252 of this title for reissued patents on the right of any person who made, purchased, or used anything patented by such proposed amended or new claim, or who made substantial preparation for the same, prior to issuance of a certificate under the provisions of subsection (a) of this section. (Added December 12, 1980, Public Law 96–517, sec. 1, 94 Stat. 3016.)

PART IV—PATENT COOPERATION TREATY

CHAPTER 35—DEFINITIONS

SEC.
351. Definitions.

§ 351. Definitions

When used in this part unless the context otherwise indicates—

(a) The term "treaty" means the Patent Cooperation Treaty done at Washington, on June 19, 1970, excluding chapter II thereof.

(b) The term "Regulations," when capitalized, means the Regulations under the treaty excluding part C thereof, done at Washington on the same date as the treaty. The term "regulations," when not capitalized, means the regulations established by the Commissioner under this title.

(c) The term "international application" means an application filed under the treaty.

(d) The term "international application originating in the United States means an international application filed in the Patent Office when it is acting as a Receiving Office under the treaty, irrespective of whether or not the United States has been designated in that international application.

(e) The term "international application designating the United States" means an international application specifying the United States as a country in which a patent is sought, regardless where such international application is filed.

(f) The term "Receiving Office" means a national patent office or intergovernmental organization which receives and processes international applications as prescribed by the treaty and the Regulations.

(g) The term "International Searching Authority" means a national patent office or intergovernmental organization as appointed under the treaty which processes international applications as prescribed by the treaty and the Regulations.

(h) The term "International Bureau" means the international intergovernmental organization which is recognized as the coordinating body under the treaty and the Regulations.

(i) Terms and expressions not defined in this part are to be taken in the sense indicated by the treaty and the Regulations. (Added November 14, 1975, Public Law 94–131, sec. 1, 89 Stat. 685.)

CHAPTER 36—INTERNATIONAL STAGE

SEC.
361. Receiving Office.
362. International Searching Authority.
363. International application designating the United States: Effect.
364. International stage: Procedure.
365. Right of priority; benefit of the filing date of a prior application.
366. Withdrawn international application.
367. Actions of other authorities: Review.
368. Secrecy of certain inventions; filing international applications in foreign countries.

§ 361. Receiving Office

(a) The Patent Office shall act as a Receiving Office for international applications filed by nationals or residents of the United States. In accordance with any agreement made between the United States and another country, the Patent Office may also act as a Receiving Office for international applications filed by residents or nationals of such country who are entitled to file international applications.

(b) The Patent Office shall perform all acts connected with the discharge of duties required of a Receiving Office, including the collection of international fees and their transmittal to the International Bureau.

(c) International applications filed in the Patent Office shall be in the English language.

(d) The basic fee portion of the international fee, and the transmittal and search fees prescribed under section 376(a) of this part, shall be paid on filing of an international application. Payment of designation fees may be made on filing and shall be made not later than one year from the priority date of the international application. (Added November 14, 1975, Public Law 94–131, sec. 1, 89 Stat. 686.)

§ 362. International Searching Authority

The Patent Office may act as an International Searching Authority with respect to international applications in accordance with the terms and conditions of an agreement which may be concluded with the International Bureau. (Added November 14, 1975, Public Law 94–131, sec. 1, 89 Stat. 686.)

§ 363. International application designating the United States: Effect

An international application designating the United States shall have the effect, from its international filing date under article 11 of the treaty, of a national application for patent regularly filed in the Patent Office except as otherwise provided in section 102(e) of this title. (Added November 14, 1975, Public Law 94–131, sec. 1, 89 Stat. 686.)

§ 364. International stage: Procedure

(a) International applications shall be processed by the Patent Office when acting as a Receiving Office or International Searching Authority, or both, in accordance with the applicable provisions of the treaty, the Regulations, and this title.

(b) An applicant's failure to act within prescribed time limits in connection with requirements pertaining to a pending international application may be excused upon a showing satisfactory to the Commissioner of unavoidable delay, to the extent not precluded by the treaty and the Regulations, and provided the conditions imposed by the treaty and the Regulations regarding the excuse of such failure to act are complied with. (Added November 14, 1975, Public Law 94–131, sec. 1, 89 Stat. 686.)

§ 365. Right of priority; benefit of the filing date of a prior application

(a) In accordance with the conditions and requirements of section 119 of this title, a national application shall be entitled to the right of priority based on a prior filed international application which designated at least one country other than the United States.

(b) In accordance with the conditions and requirement of the first paragraph of section 119 of this title and the treaty and the Regulations, an international application designating the United States shall be entitled to the right of priority based on a prior foreign application, or a prior international application designating at least one country other than the United States.

(c) In accordance with the conditions and requirements of section 120 of this title, an international application designating the United States shall be entitled to the benefit of the filing date of a prior national application or a prior international application designating the United States, and a national application shall be entitled to the benefit of the filing date of a prior international application designating the United States. If any claim for the benefit of an earlier filing date is based on a prior international application which designated but did not originate in the United States, the Commissioner may require the filing in the Patent Office of a certified copy of such application together with a translation thereof into the English language, if it was filed in another language. (Added November 14, 1975, Public Law 94–131, sec. 1, 89 Stat. 686.)

§ 366. Withdrawn international application

Subject to section 367 of this part, if an international application designating the United States is withdrawn or considered withdrawn, either generally or as to the United States, under the conditions of the treaty and the Regulations, before the applicant has complied with the applicable requirements prescribed by section 371(c) of this part, the designation of the United States shall have no effect and shall be considered as not having been made. However, such international application may serve as the basis for a claim of priority under section 365 (a) and (b) of this part, if it designated a country other than the United States. (Added November 14, 1975, Public Law 94–131, sec. 1, 89 Stat. 687.)

§ 367. Actions of other authorities: Review

(a) Where a Receiving Office other than the Patent Office has refused to accord an international filing date to an international application designating the United States or where it has held such application to be withdrawn either generally or as to the United States, the applicant may request review of the matter by the Commissioner, on compliance with the requirements of and within the time limits specified by the treaty and the Regulations. Such review may result in a determination that such application be considered as pending in the national stage.

(b) The review under subsection (a) of this section, subject to the same requirements and conditions, may also be requested in those instances where an international application designating the United States is considered withdrawn due to a finding by the International Bureau under article 12(3) of the treaty. (Added November 14, 1975, Public Law 94–131, sec. 1, 89 Stat. 687.)

§ 368. Secrecy of certain inventions; filing international applications in foreign countries

(a) International applications filed in the Patent Office shall be subject to the provisions of chapter 17 of this title.

(b) In accordance with article 27(8) of the treaty, the filing of an international application in a country other than the United States on the invention made in this country shall be considered to constitute the filing of an application in a foreign country within the meaning of chapter 17 of this title, whether or not the United States is designated in that international application.

(c) If a license to file in a foreign country is refused or if an international application is ordered to be kept secret and a permit refused, the Patent Office when acting as a Receiving Office or International Searching Authority, or both, may not disclose the contents of such application to anyone not authorized to receive such disclosure. (Added November 14, 1975, Public Law 94–131, sec. 1, 89 Stat. 687.)

CHAPTER 37—NATIONAL STAGE

Sec.
371. National stage: Commencement.
372. National stage: Requirements and procedure.
373. Improper applicant.
374. Publication of international application: Effect.
375. Patent issued on international application: Effect.
376. Fees.

§ 371. National stage: Commencement

(a) Receipt from the International Bureau of copies of international applications with amendments to the claims, if any, and international search reports is required in the case of all international applications designating the United States, except those filed in the Patent Office.

(b) Subject to subsection (f) of this section, the national stage shall commence with the expiration of the applicable time limit under article 22(1) or (2) of the treaty, at which time the applicant shall have complied with the applicable requirements specified in subsection (c) of this section.

(c) The applicant shall file in the Patent Office—

(1) the national fee prescribed under section 376(a)(4) of this part;

(2) a copy of the international application, unless not required under subsection (a) of this section or already received from the International Bureau, and a verified translation into the English language of the international application, if it was filed in another language;

(3) amendments, if any, to the claims in the international application, made under article 19 of the treaty, unless such amendments have been communicated to the Patent Office by the International Bureau, and a translation into the English language if such amendments were made in another language;

(4) an oath or declaration of the inventor (or other person authorized under chapter 11 of this title) complying with the requirements of section 115 of this title and with regulations prescribed for oaths or declarations of applicants.

(d) Failure to comply with any of the requirements of subsection (c) of this section, within the time limit provided by article 22(1) or (2) of the treaty shall result in abandonment of the international application.

(e) After an international application has entered the national stage, no patent may be granted or refused thereon before the expiration of the applicable time limit under article 28 of the treaty, except with the express consent of the applicant. The applicant may present amendments to the specification, claims, and drawings of the application after the national stage has commenced.

(f) At the express request of the applicant, the national stage of processing may be commenced at any time at which the application is in order for such purpose and the applicable requirements of subsection (c) of this section have been complied with. (Added November 14, 1975, Public Law 94–131, sec. 1, 89 Stat. 688.)

§ 372. National stage: Requirements and procedure

(a) All questions of substance and, within the scope of the requirements of the treaty and Regulations, procedure in an international application designating the United States shall be determined as in the case of national applications regularly filed in the Patent Office.

(b) In case of international applications designating but not originating in, the United States—

(1) the Commissioner may cause to be reexamined questions relating to form and contents of the application in accordance with the requirements of the treaty and the Regulations;

(2) the Commissioner may cause the question of unity of invention to be reexamined under section 121 of this title, within the scope of the requirements of the treaty and the Regulations.

(c) Any claim not searched in the international stage in view of a holding, found to be justified by the Commissioner upon review, that the international application did not comply with the requirement for unity of invention under the treaty and the Regulations, shall be considered canceled, unless payment of a special fee is made by the applicant. Such special fee shall be paid with respect to each claim not searched in the international stage and shall be submitted not later than one month after a notice was sent to the applicant informing him that the said holding was deemed to be justified. The payment of the special fee shall not prevent the Commissioner from requiring that the international application be restricted to one of the inventions claimed therein under section 121 of this title, and within the scope of the requirements of the treaty and the Regulations. (Added November 14, 1975, Public Law 94–131, sec. 1, 89 Stat. 689.)

§ 373. Improper applicant

An international application designating the United States, shall not be accepted by the Patent Office for the national stage if it was filed by anyone not qualified under chapter 11 of this title to be an applicant for the purpose of filing a national application in the United States. Such international applications shall not serve as the basis for the benefit of an earlier filing date under section 120 of this title in a subsequently filed application, but may serve as the basis for a claim of the right of priority under section 119 of this title, if the United States was not the sole country designated in such international application. (Added November 14, 1975, Public Law 94–131, sec. 1, 89 Stat. 689.)

§ 374. Publication of international application: Effect

The publication under the treaty of an international application shall confer no rights and shall have no effect under this title other than that of a printed publication. (Added November 14, 1975, Public Law 94–131, sec. 1, 89 Stat. 689.)

§ 375. Patent issued on international application: Effect

(a) A patent may be issued by the Commissioner based on an international application designating the United States, in accordance with the provisions of this title. Subject to section 102(e) of this title, such patent shall have the force and effect of a patent issued on a national application filed under the provisions of chapter 11 of this title.

(b) Where due to an incorrect translation the scope of a patent granted on an international application designating the United States, which was not originally filed in the English language, exceeds the scope of the international application in its original language, a court of competent jurisdiction may retroactively limit the scope of the patent, by declaring it unenforceable to the extent that it exceeds the scope of the international application in its original language. (Added November 14, 1975, Public Law 94–131, sec. 1, 89 Stat. 689.)

§ 376. Fees

(a) The required payment of the international fee, which amount is specified in the Regulations, shall be paid in United States currency. The Patent Office may also charge the following fees:

(1) A transmittal fee (see section 361(d));

(2) A search fee (see section 361(d));

(3) A supplemental search fee (to be paid when required);

(4) A national fee (see section 371(c));

(5) A special fee (to be paid when required; see section 372(c));

(6) Such other fees as established by the Commissioner.

(b) The amounts of fees specified in subsection (a) of this section, except the international fee, shall be prescribed by the Commissioner. He may refund any sum paid by mistake or in excess of the fees so specified, or if required under the treaty and the Regulations. The Commissioner may also refund any part of the search fee, where he determines such refund to be warranted. (Added November 14, 1975, Public Law 94–131, sec. 1, 89 Stat. 690.)

UNITED STATES CODE

TITLE 15, CHAPTER 22—TRADEMARKS

Subchapter I—Principal Register

Sec.

1051. Registration; application; payment of fees; designation of resident for service of process and notice.
1052. Trademarks registrable on principal register; concurrent registration.
1053. Service marks registrable.
1054. Collective marks and certification marks registrable.
1055. Use by related companies affecting validity and registration.
1056. Disclaimer of unregistrable matter.
1057. Certificates of registration.
    (a) Issuance and form.
    (b) Certificate as prima facie evidence.
    (c) Issuance to assignee.
    (d) Surrender, cancellation, or amendment by registrant.
    (e) Copies of Patent and Trademark Office records as evidence.
    (f) Correction of Patent and Trademark Office mistake.
    (g) Correction of applicant's mistake.
1058. Duration of registration; cancellation; affidavit of continued use; notice of Commissioner's action.
1059. Renewal of registration.
1060. Assignment of mark; execution; recording; purchaser without notice.
1061. Execution of acknowledgments and verifications.
1062. Publication; proceedings on refusal of registration; republication of marks registered under prior acts.
1063. Opposition to registration.
1064. Cancellation of registration.
1065. Incontestability of right to use mark under certain conditions.
1066. Interference; declaration by Commissioner.
1067. Interference, opposition, and proceedings for concurrent use registration or for cancellation; notice; Trademark Trial and Appeal Board.
1068. Same; action of Commissioner.
1069. Application of equitable principles in inter partes proceedings.
1070. Appeals to Trademark Trial and Appeal Board from decisions of examiners.
1071. Appeals to courts.
    (a) Persons entitled to appeal; Court of Appeals for the Federal Circuit; waiver of civil action; election of civil action by adverse party; procedure.

     (b) Civil action; persons entitled to; jurisdiction of court; status of Commissioner; procedure.

1072. Registration as constructive notice of claim of ownership.

SUBCHAPTER II—SUPPLEMENTAL REGISTER

1091. Marks registrable on supplemental register; application and proceedings for registration; nature of mark; mark used in foreign commerce.
1092. Publication; not subject to opposition; cancellation.
1093. Registration certificates for marks on principal and supplemental registers to be different.
1094. Provisions of chapter applicable to registrations on supplemental register.
1095. Registration on principal register not precluded.
1096. Registration on supplemental register not used to stop importations.

SUBCHAPTER III—GENERAL PROVISIONS

1111. Notice of registration; display with mark; recovery of profits and damages in infringement suit.
1112. Classification of goods and services; registration in plurality of classes.
1113. Fees and charges.
1114. Remedies; infringement; innocent infringement by printers and publishers.
1115. Same; registration on principal register as evidence of exclusive right to use mark; defenses.
1116. Same; injunctions; enforcement; notice to Commissioner.
1117. Same; recovery for violation of rights; profits, damages and costs.
1118. Same; destruction of infringing articles.
1119. Same; power of court over registration.
1120. Same; civil liability for false or fraudulent registration.
1121. Same; jurisdiction of Federal courts.
1122. Repealed.
1123. Rules and regulations for conduct of proceedings in Patent and Trademark Office.
1124. Importation of goods bearing infringing marks or names forbidden.
1125. False designations of origin and false descriptions forbidden.
1126. International conventions.
     (a) Register of marks communicated by international bureaus.
     (b) Benefits of section to persons whose country of origin is party to convention or treaty.
     (c) Prior registration in country of origin; country of origin defined.
     (d) Right of priority.

 (e) Registration on principal or supplemental register; copy of foreign registration.

 (f) Domestic registration independent of foreign registration.

 (g) Trade or commercial names of foreign nationals protected without registration.

 (h) Protection of foreign nationals against unfair competition.

 (i) Citizens or residents of United States entitled to benefits of section.

1127. Construction and definition; intent of chapter.

Subchapter I—Principal Register

SEC.

1051. Registration; application; payment of fees; designation of resident for service of process and notice
1052. Trademarks registrable on principal register; concurrent registration
1053. Service marks registrable
1054. Collective marks and certification marks registrable
1055. Use by related companies affecting validity and registration
1056. Disclaimer of unregistrable matter
1057. Certificates of registration—Issuance and form
1058. Duration of registration; cancellation; affidavit of continued use; notice of Commissioner's action
1059. Renewal of registration
1060. Assignment of mark; execution; recording; purchaser without notice
1061. Execution of acknowledgments and verifications
1062. Publication; proceedings on refusal of registration; republication of marks registered under prior acts
1063. Opposition to registration
1064. Cancellation of registration
1065. Incontestability of right to use mark under certain conditions
1066. Interference; declaration by Commissioner
1067. Interference, opposition, and proceedings for concurrent use registration or for cancellation; notice; Trademark Trial and Appeal Board
1068. Same; action of Commissioner
1069. Application of equitable principles in inter partes proceedings
1070. Appeals to Trademark Trial and Appeal Board from decisions of examiners
1071. Appeal to courts—Persons entitled to appeal; Court of Appeals for the Federal Circuit; waiver of civil action; election of civil action by adverse party; procedure
1072. Registration as constructive notice of claim of ownership

*§ 1051. Registration; application; payment of fees; designation of resident for service of process and notice [Section 1]

The owner of a trademark used in commerce may register his trademark under this chapter on the principal register established:

(a) By filing in the Patent and Trademark Office—

(1) a written application, in such form as may be prescribed by

---

*[*Ed. Note:* Following each official section cite and caption, in brackets, is a reference to the unofficial, but often referred to, section citation. Thus, for example, 15 U.S.C. 1125(a) is also section 43(a) of the Trademark (Lanham) Act of 1946, as amended.]

the Commissioner, verified by the applicant, or by a member of the firm or an officer of the corporation or association applying, specifying applicant's domicile and citizenship, the date of applicant's first use of the mark, the date of applicant's first use of the mark in commerce, the goods in connection with which the mark is used and the mode or manner in which the mark is used in connection with such goods, and including a statement to the effect that the person making the verification believes himself, or the firm, corporation, or association in whose behalf he makes the verification, to be the owner of the mark sought to be registered, that the mark is in use in commerce, and that no other person, firm, corporation, or association, to the best of his knowledge and belief, has the right to use such mark in commerce either in the identical form thereof or in such near resemblance thereto as to be likely, when applied to the goods of such other person, to cause confusion, or to cause mistake, or to deceive: *Provided,* That in the case of every application claiming concurrent use the applicant shall state exceptions to his claim of exclusive use, in which he shall specify, to the extent of his knowledge, any concurrent use by others, the goods in connection with which and the areas in which each concurrent use exists, the periods of each use, and the goods and area for which the applicant desires registration;

(2) a drawing of the mark; and

(3) such number of specimens or facsimiles of the mark as actually used as may be required by the Commissioner.

(b) By paying into the Patent and Trademark Office the filing fee.

(c) By complying with such rules or regulations, not inconsistent with law, as may be prescribed by the Commissioner.

(d) If the applicant is not domiciled in the United States he shall designate by a written document filed in the Patent and Trademark Office the name and address or some person resident in the United States on whom may be served notices or process in proceedings affecting the mark. Such notices or process may be served upon the person so designated by leaving with him or mailing to him a copy thereof at the address specified in the last designation so filed. If the person so designated cannot be found at the address given in the last designation, such notice or process may be served upon the Commissioner. (July 5, 1946, c. 540, Title I, sec. 1, 60 Stat. 427; October 9, 1962, Public Law 87–772, sec. 1, 76 Stat. 769; January 2, 1975, Public Law 93–596, sec. 1, 88 Stat. 1949.)

§ 1052. Trademarks registrable on principal register; concurrent registration [Section 2]

No trademark by which the goods of the applicant may be distinguished from the goods of others shall be refused registration on the principal register on account of its nature unless it—

(a) Consists of or comprises immoral, deceptive, or scandalous matter; or matter which may disparage or falsely suggest a connection with persons, living or dead, institutions, beliefs, or national symbols, or bring them into contempt, or disrepute.

(b) Consists of or comprises the flag or coat of arms or other insignia of the United States, or of any State or municipality, or of any foreign nation, or any simulation thereof.

(c) Consists of or comprises a name, portrait, or signature identifying a particular living individual except by his written consent, or the name, signature, or portrait of a deceased President of the United States during the life of his widow, if any, except by the written consent of the widow.

(d) Consists of or comprises a mark which so resembles a mark registered in the Patent and Trademark Office or a mark or trade name previously used in the United States by another and not abandoned, as to be likely, when applied to the goods of the applicant, to cause confusion, or to cause mistake, or to deceive: *Provided,* That when the Commissioner determines that confusion, mistake, or deception is not likely to result from the continued use by more than one person of the same or similar marks under conditions and limitations as to the mode or place of use of the marks or the goods in connection with which such marks are used, concurrent registrations may be issued to such persons when they have become entitled to use such marks as a result of their concurrent lawful use in commerce prior to (i) the earliest of the filing dates of the applications pending or of any registration issued under this chapter; or (ii) July 5, 1947, in the case of registrations previously issued under the Act of March 3, 1881, or February 20, 1905, and continuing in full force and effect on that date; or (iii) July 5, 1947, in the case of applications filed under the Act of February 20, 1905, and registered after July 5, 1947. Concurrent registrations may also be issued by the Commissioner when a court of competent jurisdiction has finally determined that more than one person is entitled to use the same or similar marks in commerce. In issuing concurrent registrations, the Commissioner shall prescribe conditions and limitations as to the mode or place of use of the mark or the goods in connection with which such mark is registered to the respective persons.

(e) Consists of a mark which, (1) when applied to the goods of the applicant is merely descriptive or deceptively misdescriptive of them, or (2) when applied to the goods of the applicant is primarily geographically descriptive or deceptively misdescriptive of them, except as indications of regional origin may be registrable under section 1054 of this title, or (3) is primarily merely a surname.

(f) Except as expressly excluded in paragraphs (a)–(d) of this section, nothing in this chapter shall prevent the registration of a mark used by the applicant which has become distinctive of the applicant's goods in commerce. The Commissioner may accept as prima facie evidence that the mark has become distinctive, as applied to the applicant's goods in commerce, proof of substantially exclusive and continuous use thereof as a mark by the applicant in commerce for the five years next preceding the date of the filing of the application for its registration. (July 5, 1946, c. 540, Title I, sec. 2, 60 Stat. 428; October 9, 1962, Public Law 87–772, sec. 2, 76 Stat. 769; January 2, 1975, Public Law 93–596, sec. 1, 88 Stat. 1949.)

§ 1053.   Service marks registrable [Section 3]

Subject to the provisions relating to the registration of trademarks, so far as they are applicable, service marks used in commerce shall be registrable, in the same manner and with the same effect as are trademarks, and when registered they shall be entitled to the protection provided in this chapter in the case of trademarks, except when used so as to represent falsely that the owner thereof makes or sells the goods on which such mark is used. The Commissioner may establish a separate register for such service marks. Applications and procedure under this section shall conform as nearly as practicable to those prescribed for the registration of trademarks. (July 5, 1946, c. 540, Title I, sec. 3, 60 Stat. 429.)

§ 1054.   Collective marks and certification marks registrable [Section 4]

Subject to the provisions relating to the registration of trademarks, so far as they are applicable, collective and certification marks, including indications of regional origin used in commerce, shall be registrable under this chapter, in the same manner and with the same effect as are trademarks, by persons, and nations, States, municipalities, and the like, exercising legitimate control over the use of the marks sought to be registered, even though not possessing an industrial or commercial establishment, and when registered they shall be entitled to the protection provided in this chapter in the case of trademarks, except when used so as to represent falsely that the owner or a user thereof makes or sells the goods or performs the services on or in connection with which such mark is used. The Commissioner may establish a separate register for such collective marks and certification marks. Applications and procedure under this section shall conform as nearly as practicable to those prescribed for the registration of trademarks. (July 5, 1946, c. 540, Title I, sec. 4, 60 Stat. 429.)

§ 1055. Use by related companies affecting validity and registration [Section 5]

Where a registered mark or a mark sought to be registered is or may be used legitimately by related companies, such use shall inure to the benefit of the registrant or applicant for registration, and such use shall not affect the validity of such mark or of its registration, provided such mark is not used in such manner as to deceive the public. (July 5, 1946, c. 540, Title I, sec. 5, 60 Stat. 429.)

§ 1056. Disclaimer of unregistrable matter [Section 6]

(a) The Commissioner may require the applicant to disclaim an unregistrable component of a mark otherwise registrable. An applicant may voluntarily disclaim a component of a mark sought to be registered.

(b) No disclaimer, including those made under paragraph (d) of section 1057 of this title shall prejudice or affect the applicant's or registrant's rights then existing or thereafter arising in the disclaimed matter, or his right of registration on another application if the disclaimed matter be or shall have become distinctive of his goods or services. (July 5, 1946, c. 540, Title I, sec. 6, 60 Stat. 429; October 9, 1962, Public Law 87–772, sec. 3, 76 Stat. 769.)

§ 1057. Certificates of registration—Issuance and form [Section 7]

(a) Certificates of registration of marks registered upon the principal register shall be issued in the name of the United States of America, under the seal of the Patent and Trademark Office, and shall be signed by the Commissioner or have his signature placed thereon, and a record thereof shall be kept in the Patent and Trademark Office. The registration shall reproduce the mark, and state that the mark is registered on the principal register under this chapter, the date of the first use of the mark, the date of the first use of the mark in commerce, the particular goods or services for which it is registered, the number and date of the registration, the term thereof, the date on which the application for registration was received in the Patent and Trademark Office, and any conditions and limitations that may be imposed in the registration.

Certificate as prima facie evidence

(b) A certificate of registration of a mark upon the principal register provided by this chapter shall be prima facie evidence of the validity of the registration, registrant's ownership of the mark, and of registrant's exclusive right to use the mark in commerce in connection with the goods or services specified in the certificate, subject to any conditions and limitations stated therein.

Issuance to assignee

(c) A certificate of registration of a mark may be issued to the assignee of the applicant, but the assignment must first be recorded in the Patent and Trademark Office. In case of change of ownership the Commissioner shall, at the request of the owner and upon a proper showing and the payment of the fee provided in this chapter, issue to such assignee a new certificate of registration of the said mark in the name of such assignee, and for the unexpired part of the original period.

Surrender, cancellation, or amendment by registrant

(d) Upon application of the registrant the Commissioner may permit any registration to be surrendered for cancellation, and upon cancellation appropriate entry shall be made in the records of the Patent and Trademark Office. Upon application of the registrant and payment of the prescribed fee, the Commissioner for good cause may permit any registration to be amended or to be disclaimed in part: *Provided,* That the amendment or disclaimer does not alter materially the character of the mark. Appropriate entry shall be made in the records of the Patent and Trademark Office and upon the certificate of registration or, if said certificate is lost or destroyed, upon a certified copy thereof.

Copies of Patent and Trademark Office records as evidence

(e) Copies of any records, books, papers, or drawings belonging to the Patent and Trademark Office relating to marks, and copies of registrations, when authenticated by the seal of the Patent and Trademark Office and certified by the Commissioner, or in his name by an employee of the Office duly designated by the Commissioner, shall be evidence in all cases wherein the originals would be evidence; and any person making application therefor and paying the fee required by law shall have such copies.

Correction of Patent and Trademark Office mistake

(f) Whenever a material mistake in a registration, incurred through the fault of the Patent and Trademark Office, is clearly disclosed by the records of the Office a certificate stating the fact and nature of such mistake, shall be issued without charge and recorded and a printed copy thereof shall be attached to each printed copy of the registration and such corrected registration shall thereafter have the same effect as if the same had been originally issued in such corrected form, or in the discretion of the Commissioner a new certificate of registration may be issued without charge. All certificates of correction heretofore issued in accordance with the rules of the Patent and Trademark Office and the registrations to which they are attached shall have the same force and effect as if such certificates and their issue had been specifically authorized by statute.

Correction of applicant's mistake

(g) Whenever a mistake has been made in a registration and a showing has been made that such mistake occurred in good faith through the fault of the applicant, the Commissioner is authorized to issue a certificate of correction or, in his discretion, a new certificate upon the payment of the required fee: *Provided,* That the correction does not involve such changes in the registration as to require republication of the mark. (July 5, 1946, c. 540, Title I, sec. 7, 60 Stat. 430; August 17, 1950, c. 733, 64 Stat. 459; October 9, 1962, Public Law 87–772, sec. 4, 76 Stat. 769.)

§ 1058. Duration of registration; cancellation; affidavit of continued use; notice of Commissioner's action [Section 8]

(a) Each certificate of registration shall remain in force for twenty years: *Provided,* That the registration of any mark under the provisions of this chapter shall be canceled by the Commissioner at the end of six years following its date, unless within one year next preceding the expiration of such six years the registrant shall file in the Patent and Trademark Office an affidavit showing that said mark is in use in commerce or showing that its nonuse is due to special circumstances which excuse such nonuse and is not due to any intention to abandon the mark. Special notice of the requirement for such affidavit shall be attached to each certificate of registration.

(b) Any registration published under the provisions of subsection (c) of section 1062 of this title shall be canceled by the Commissioner at the end of six years after the date of such publication unless within one year next preceding the expiration of such six years the registrant shall file in the Patent and Trademark Office an affidavit showing that said mark is in use in commerce or showing that its nonuse is due to special circumstances which excuse such nonuse and is not due to any intention to abandon the mark.

(c) The Commissioner shall notify any registrant who files either of the above-prescribed affidavits of his acceptance or refusal thereof and, if a refusal, the reasons therefor. (As amended January 2, 1975, Public Law 93–596, sec. 1, 88 Stat. 1949; August 27, 1982, Public Law 97–247, sec. 8, 96 Stat. 320.)

§ 1059. Renewal of registration [Section 9]

(a) Each registration may be renewed for periods of twenty years from the end of the expiring period upon payment of the prescribed fee and the filing of a verified application therefor, setting forth those goods or services recited in the registration on or in connection with which the mark is still in use in commerce and having attached thereto a specimen or facsimile showing current use of the mark, or showing that any nonuse is due to special circumstances which excuse such nonuse and it is not due to any intention to abandon the mark. Such application may be made at any time within six months before the expiration of the period for which the registration was issued or renewed, or it may be made within three months after such expiration on payment of the additional fee herein prescribed.

(b) If the Commissioner refuses to renew the registration, he shall notify the registrant of his refusal and the reasons therefor.

(c) An applicant for renewal not domiciled in the United States shall be subject to and comply with the provisions of section 1051(d) of this title. (July 5, 1946, c. 540, Title I, sec. 9, 60 Stat. 431; October 9, 1962, Public Law 87–772, sec. 5, 76 Stat. 770.)

§ 1060. Assignment of mark; execution; recording; purchaser without notice [Section 10]

A registered mark or a mark for which application to register has been filed shall be assignable with the goodwill of the business in which the mark is used, or with that part of the goodwill of the business connected with the use of and symbolized by the mark, and in any such assignment it shall not be necessary to include the goodwill of the business connected with the use of and symbolized by any other mark used in the business or by the name or style under which the business is conducted. Assignments shall be by instruments in writing duly executed. Acknowledgment shall be prima facie evidence of the execution of an assignment and when recorded in the Patent and Trademark Office the record shall be prima facie evidence of execution. An assignment shall be void as against any subsequent purchaser for a valuable consideration without notice, unless it is recorded in the Patent and Trademark Office within three months after the date thereof or prior to such subsequent purchase. A separate record of assignments submitted for recording hereunder shall be maintained in the Patent and Trademark Office.

An assignee not domiciled in the United States shall be subject to and comply with the provisions of section 1051(d) of this title. (As amended January 2, 1975, Public Law 93–596, sec. 1, 88 Stat. 1949.)

§ 1061. Execution of acknowledgments and verifications
[Section 11]

Acknowledgments and verifications required under this chapter may be made before any person within the United States authorized by law to administer oaths, or, when made in a foreign country, before any diplomatic or consular officer of the United States or before any official authorized to administer oaths in the foreign country concerned whose authority is proved by a certificate of a diplomatic or consular officer of the United States, or apostille of an official designated by a foreign country which, by treaty or convention, accords like effect to apostilles of designated officials in the United States, and shall be valid if they comply with the laws of the state or country where made. (July 5, 1946, c. 540, Title I, sec. 11, 60 Stat. 432. Amended August 27, 1982, Public Law 97–247, sec. 14(c), 96 Stat. 321.)

§ 1062. Publication; proceedings on refusal of registration; republication of marks registered under prior acts [Section 12]

(a) Upon the filing of an application for registration and payment of the fee provided in this chapter, the Commissioner shall refer the application to the examiner in charge of the registration of marks, who shall cause an examination to be made and, if on such examination it shall appear that the applicant is entitled to registration, the Commissioner shall cause the mark to be published in the Official Gazette of the Patent and Trademark Office: *Provided,* That in the case of an applicant claiming concurrent use, or in the case of an application to be placed in an interference as provided for in section 1066 of this title, the mark, if otherwise registrable, may be published subject to the determination of the rights of the parties to such proceedings.

(b) If the applicant is found not entitled to registration, the examiner shall advise the applicant thereof and of the reasons therefor. The applicant shall have a period of six months in which to reply or amend his application, which shall then be re-examined. This procedure may be repeated until (1) the examiner finally refuses registration of the mark or (2) the applicant fails for a period of six months to reply or amend or appeal, whereupon the application shall be deemed to have been abandoned, unless it can be shown to the satisfaction of the Commissioner that the delay in responding was unavoidable, whereupon such time may be extended.

(c) A registrant of a mark registered under the provisions of the Act of March 3, 1881, or the Act of February 20, 1905, may, at any time prior to the expiration of the registration thereof, upon the payment of the prescribed fee file with the Commissioner an affidavit setting forth those goods stated in the registration on which said mark is in use in commerce and that the registrant claims the benefits of this chapter for said mark. The Commissioner shall publish notice thereof with a reproduction of said mark in the Official Gazette, and notify the registrant of such publication and of the requirement for the affidavit of use or nonuse as provided for in subsection (b) of section 1058 of this title. Marks published under this subsection shall not be subject to the provisions of section 1063 of this title. (July 5, 1946, c. 540, Title I, sec. 12, 60 Stat. 432; October 9, 1962, Public Law 87–772, sec. 7, 76 Stat. 770.)

§ 1063. Opposition to registration [Section 13]

Any person who believes that he would be damaged by the registration of a mark upon the principal register may, upon payment of the required fee, file an opposition in the Patent and Trademark

Office, stating the grounds therefor, within thirty days after the publication under subsection (a) of section 1062 of this title of the mark sought to be registered. Upon written request prior to the expiration of the thirty-day period, the time for filing opposition shall be extended for an additional thirty days, and further extensions of time for filing opposition may be granted by the Commissioner for good cause when requested prior to the expiration of an extension. The Commissioner shall notify the applicant of each extension of the time for filing opposition. An opposition may be amended under such conditions as may be prescribed by the Commissioner. (As amended January 2, 1975, Public Law 93–596, sec. 1, 88 Stat. 1949; January 2, 1975, Public Law 93–600, sec. 1, 88 Stat. 1955; August 27, 1982, Public Law 97–247, sec. 9(a), 96 Stat. 320.)

§ 1064.　Cancellation of registration [Section 14]

A petition to cancel a registration of a mark, stating the grounds relied upon, may, upon payment of the prescribed fee, be filed by any person who believes that he is or will be damaged by the registration of a mark on the principal register established by this chapter, or under the Act of March 3, 1881, or the Act of February 20, 1905—

(a) within five years from the date of the registration of the mark under this chapter; or

(b) within five years from the date of publication under section 1062(c) of this title of a mark registered under the Act of March 3, 1881, or the Act of February 20, 1905; or

(c) at any time if the registered mark becomes the common descriptive name of an article or substance, or has been abandoned, or its registration was obtained fraudulently or contrary to the provisions of section 1054 of this title or of subsections (a), (b), or (c) of section 1052 of this title for a registration hereunder, or contrary to similar prohibitory provisions of said prior Acts for a registration thereunder, or if the registered mark is being used by, or with the permission of, the registrant so as to misrepresent the source of the goods or services in connection with which the mark is used; or

(d) at any time if the mark is registered under the Act of March 3, 1881, or the Act of February 20, 1905, and has not been published under the provisions of subsection (c) of section 1062 of this title; or

(e) at any time in the case of a certification mark on the ground that the registrant (1) does not control, or is not able legitimately to exercise control over, the use of such mark, or (2) engages in the production or marketing of any goods or services to which the certification mark is applied, or (3) permits the use of the certification mark for purposes other than to certify, or (4) discriminately refuses to certify or to continue to certify the goods or services of any person who maintains the standards or conditions which such mark certifies: *Provided,* That the Federal Trade Commission may apply to cancel on the grounds specified in subsections (c) and (e) of this section any mark registered on the principal register established by this chapter, and the prescribed fee shall not be required. (July 5, 1946, c. 540, Title I, sec. 14, 60 Stat. 433; October 9, 1962, Public Law 87–772, sec. 9, 76 Stat. 771; August 27, 1982, Public Law 97–247, sec. 9(b), 96 Stat. 320.)

§ 1065. Incontestability of right to use mark under certain conditions [Section 15]

Except on a ground for which application to cancel may be filed at any time under subsections (c) and (e) of section 1064 of this title, and except to the extent, if any, to which the use of a mark registered on the principal register infringes a valid right acquired under the law of any State or Territory by use of a mark or trade name continuing from a date prior to the date of registration under this chapter of such registered mark, the right of the registrant to use such registered mark in commerce for the goods or services on or in connection with which such registered mark has been in continuous use for five consecutive years subsequent to the date of such registration and is still in use in commerce, shall be incontestable: *Provided,* That—

(1) there has been no final decision adverse to registrant's claim of ownership of such mark for such goods or services, or to registrant's right to register the same or to keep the same on the register; and

(2) there is no proceeding involving said rights pending in the Patent and Trademark Office or in a court and not finally disposed of; and

(3) an affidavit is filed with the Commissioner within one year after the expiration of any such five-year period setting forth those goods or services stated in the registration on or in connection with which such mark has been in continuous use for such five consecutive years and is still in use in commerce, and the other matters specified in subsections (1) and (2) of this section; and

(4) no incontestable right shall be acquired in a mark which is

the common descriptive name of any article or substance, patented or otherwise.

Subject to the conditions above specified in this section, the incontestable right with reference to a mark registered under this chapter shall apply to a mark registered under the Act of March 3, 1881, or the Act of February 20, 1905, upon the filing of the required affidavit with the Commissioner within one year after the expiration of any period of five consecutive years after the date of publication of a mark under the provisions of subsection (c) of section 1062 of this title.

The Commissioner shall notify any registrant who files the above-prescribed affidavit of the filing thereof. (As amended January 2, 1975, Public Law 93–596, sec. 1, 88 Stat. 1949; August 27, 1982, Public Law 97–247, sec. 10, 96 Stat. 320.)

§ 1066.   Interference; declaration by Commissioner [Section 16]

Upon petition showing extraordinary circumstances, the Commissioner may declare that an interference exists when application is made for the registration of a mark which so resembles a mark previously registered by another, or for the registration of which another has previously made application, as to be likely when applied to the goods or when used in connection with the services of the applicant to cause confusion or mistake or to deceive. No interference shall be declared between an application and the registration of a mark the right to the use of which has become incontestable. (July 5, 1946, c. 540, Title I, sec. 16, 60 Stat. 434; October 9, 1962, Public Law 87–772, sec. 11, 76 Stat. 771; August 27, 1982, Public Law 97–247, sec. 11, 96 Stat. 321.)

§ 1067.   Interference, opposition, and proceedings for concurrent use registration or for cancellation; notice; Trademark Trial and Appeal Board [Section 17]

In every case of interference, opposition to registration, application to register as a lawful concurrent user, or application to cancel the registration of a mark, the Commissioner shall give notice to all parties and shall direct a Trademark Trial and Appeal Board to determine and decide the respective rights of registration.

The Trademark Trial and Appeal Board shall include the Commissioner, the Deputy Commissioner, the Assistant Commissioners, and members appointed by the Commissioner. Employees of the Patent and Trademark Office and other persons, all of whom shall be competent in trademark law, shall be eligible for appointment as members. Each case shall be heard by at least three members of the Board, the members hearing such case to be designated by the Commissioner. (As amended January 2, 1975, Public Law 93–596, sec. 1, 88 Stat. 1949; October 15, 1980, Public Law 96–455, sec. 1, 94 Stat. 2024.)

§ 1068.   Same; action of Commissioner [Section 18]

In such proceedings the Commissioner may refuse to register the opposed mark, may cancel or restrict the registration of a registered mark, or may refuse to register any or all of several interfering marks, or may register the mark or marks for the person or persons entitled thereto, as the rights of the parties under this chapter may be established in the proceedings: *Provided,* That in the case of the registration of any mark based on concurrent use, the Commissioner shall determine and fix the conditions and limitations provided for in subsection (d) of section 1052 of this title. (July 5, 1946, c. 540, Title I, sec. 18, 60 Stat. 435.)

§ 1069.   Application of equitable principles in inter partes proceedings [Section 19]

In all inter partes proceedings equitable principles of laches, estoppel, and acquiescence, where applicable may be considered and applied. The provisions of this section shall also govern proceedings heretofore begun in the Patent and Trademark Office and not finally determined. (As amended January 2, 1975, Public Law 93–596, sec. 1, 88 Stat. 1949.)

§ 1070.   Appeals to Trademark Trial and Appeal Board from decisions of examiners [Section 20]

An appeal may be taken to the Trademark Trial and Appeal Board from any final decision of the examiner in charge of the registration of marks upon the payment of the prescribed fee. (July 5, 1946, c. 540, Title I, sec. 20, 60 Stat. 435; August 8, 1958, Public Law 85–609, sec. 1(b), 72 Stat. 540.)

§ 1071.   Appeal to courts—Persons entitled to appeal; Court of Appeals for the Federal Circuit; waiver of civil action; election of civil action by adverse party; procedure [Section 21]

(a)(1) An applicant for registration of a mark, party to an interference proceeding, party to an opposition proceeding, party to an application to register as a lawful concurrent user, party to a cancellation proceeding, a registrant who has filed an affidavit as provided in section 1058 of this title, or an applicant for renewal, who is dissatisfied with the decision of the Commissioner or Trademark Trial and Appeal Board, may appeal to the United States Court of Appeals for the Federal Circuit thereby waiving his right to proceed under subsection (b) of this section: *Provided,* That such appeal shall be dismissed if any adverse party to the proceeding, other than the Commissioner, shall, within twenty days after the appellant has filed notice of appeal according to subsection (a)(2) of this section, files notice with the Commissioner that he elects to have all further proceedings conducted as provided in subsection (b) of this section. Thereupon the appellant shall have thirty days thereafter within which to file a civil action under said subsection (b) of this section, in default of which the decision appealed from shall govern the further proceedings in the case.

(2) Such an appeal to the United States Court of Appeals for the Federal Circuit shall be taken by filing a notice of appeal with the Commissioner, within sixty days after the date of the decision appealed from or such longer time after said date as the Commissioner appoints. The notice of such appeal shall specify the party or parties taking the appeal, shall designate the decision or part thereof appealed from, and shall state that the appeal is taken to said court.

(3) The court shall, before hearing such appeal, give notice of the time and place of the hearing to the Commissioner and the parties thereto. The Commissioner shall transmit to the court certified copies of all the necessary original papers and evidence in the case specified by the appellant and any additional papers and evidence specified by the appellee, and in an ex parte case the Commissioner shall furnish the court with a brief explaining the grounds of the decision of the Patent and Trademark Office, touching all the points involved in the appeal.

(4) The court shall decide such appeal on the evidence produced before the Patent and Trademark Office. The court shall return to the Commissioner a certificate of its proceedings and decision, which shall be entered of record in the Patent and Trademark Office and govern further proceedings in the case.

(b)(1) Whenever a person authorized by subsection (a) of this section to appeal to the United States Court of Appeals for the Federal Circuit is dissatisfied with the decision of the Commissioner or Trademark Trial and Appeal Board, said person may, unless appeal has been taken to said Court of Appeals for the Federal Circuit, have remedy by a civil action if commenced within such time after such decision, not less than sixty days, as the Commissioner appoints or as provided in subsection (a) of this section. The court may adjudge that an applicant is entitled to a registration upon the application involved, that a registration involved should be canceled, or such other matter as the issues in the proceeding require, as the facts in the case may appear. Such adjudication shall authorize the Commissioner to take any necessary action, upon compliance with the requirements of law.

(2) The Commissioner shall not be made a party to an inter partes proceeding under this subsection, but he shall be notified of the filing of the complaint by the clerk of the court in which it is filed and shall have the right to intervene in the action.

(3) In all cases where there is no adverse party, a copy of the complaint shall be served on the Commissioner; and all the expenses of the proceedings shall be paid by the party bringing them, whether the final decision is in his favor or not. In suits brought hereunder, the record in the Patent and Trademark Office shall be admitted on motion of any party, upon such terms and conditions as to costs, expenses, and the further cross-examination of the witnesses as the court imposes, without prejudice to the right of any party to take further testimony. The testimony and exhibits of the record in the Patent and Trademark Office, when admitted, shall have the same effect as if originally taken and produced in the suit.

(4) Where there is an adverse party, such suit may be instituted against the party in interest as shown by the records of the Patent and Trademark Office at the time of the decision complained of, but any party in interest may become a party to the action. If there be adverse parties residing in a plurality of districts not embraced within the same State, or an adverse party residing in a foreign country, the United States District Court for the District of Columbia shall have jurisdiction and may issue summons against the adverse parties directed to the marshal of any district in which any

adverse party resides. Summons against adverse parties residing in foreign countries may be served by publication or otherwise as the court directs. (As amended January 2, 1975, Public Law 93–596, sec. 1, 88 Stat. 1949; January 2, 1975, Public Law 93–600, sec. 2, 88 Stat. 1955; April 2, 1982, Public Law 97–164, sec. 162, 96 Stat. 49.)

§ 1072.   Registration as constructive notice of claim of ownership
[Section 22]

Registration of a mark on the principal register provided by this chapter or under the Act of March 3, 1881, or the Act of February 20, 1905, shall be constructive notice of the registrant's claim of ownership thereof. (July 5, 1946, c. 540, Title I, sec. 22, 60 Stat. 435.)

SUBCHAPTER II—THE SUPPLEMENTAL REGISTER

SEC.
1091. Marks registrable on supplemental register; application and proceedings for registration; nature of mark; mark used in foreign commerce
1092. Publication; not subject to opposition; cancellation
1093. Registration certificates for marks on principal and supplemental registers to be different
1094. Provisions of chapter applicable to registrations on supplemental register
1095. Registration on principal register not precluded
1096. Registration on supplemental register not used to stop importations

§ 1091.   Marks registrable on supplemental register; application and proceedings for registration; nature of mark; mark used in foreign commerce [Section 23]

In addition to the principal register, the Commissioner shall keep a continuation of the register provided in paragraph (b) of section 1 of the Act of March 19, 1920, entitled "An Act to give effect to certain provisions of the convention for the protection of trademarks and commercial names, made and signed in the city of Buenos Aires, in the Argentine Republic, August 20, 1910, and for other purposes," to be called the supplemental register. All marks capable of distinguishing applicant's goods or services and not registrable on the principal register provided in this chapter, except those declared to be unregistrable under paragraphs (a)–(d) of section 1052 of this title, which have been in lawful use in commerce by the proprietor thereof, upon or in connection with any goods or services for the year preceding the filing of the application may be registered on the supplemental register upon the payment of the prescribed fee and compliance with the provisions of section 1051 of this title so far as they are applicable.

Upon the filing of an application for registration on the supplemental register and payment of the fee herein provided the Commissioner shall refer the application to the examiner in charge of the registration of marks, who shall cause an examination to be made and if on such examination it shall appear that the applicant is entitled to registration, the registration shall be granted. If the applicant is found not entitled to registration the provisions of subsection (b) of section 1062 of this title shall apply.

For the purposes of registration on the supplemental register, a mark may consist of any trade-mark, symbol, label, package, configuration of goods, name, word, slogan, phrase, surname, geographical name, numeral, or device or any combination of any of the foregoing, but such mark must be capable of distinguishing the applicant's goods or services.

Upon a proper showing by the applicant that he requires domestic registration as a basis for foreign protection of his mark, the Commissioner may waive the requirement of a full year's use and may grant registration forthwith. (July 5, 1946, c. 540, Title II, sec. 23, 60 Stat. 435; Oct. 9, 1962, Public Law 87—772, sec. 13, 76 Stat. 773.)

§ 1092.   Publication; not subject to opposition; cancellation [Section 24]

Marks for the supplemental register shall not be published for or be subject to opposition, but shall be published on registration in the Official Gazette of the Patent and Trademark Office. Whenever any person believes that he is or will be damaged by the registration of a mark on this register he may at any time, upon payment of the prescribed fee and the filing of a verified petition stating the ground therefor, apply to the Commissioner to cancel such registration. The Commissioner shall refer such application to the Trademark Trial and Appeal Board which shall give notice thereof to the registrant. If it is found after a hearing before the Board that the registrant was not entitled to register the mark at the time of his application for registration thereof, or that the mark is not used by the registrant or has been abandoned, the registration shall be canceled by the Commissioner. (As amended January 2, 1975, Public Law 93–596, sec. 1, 88 Stat. 1949.)

§ 1093. Registration certificates for marks on principal and supplemental registers to be different [Section 25]

The certificates of registration for marks registered on the supplemental register shall be conspicuously different from certificates issued for marks registered on the principal register. (July 5, 1946, c. 540, Title II, sec. 25, 60 Stat. 436.)

§ 1094. Provisions of chapter applicable to registrations on supplemental register [Section 26]

The provisions of this chapter shall govern so far as applicable applications for registration and registrations on the supplemental register as well as those on the principal register, but applications for and registrations on the supplemental register shall not be subject to or receive the advantages of sections 1052(e), 1052(f), 1057(b), 1062(a), 1063 to 1068, inclusive, 1072, 1115 and 1124 of this title. (July 5, 1946, c. 540, Title II, sec. 26, 60 Stat. 436.)

§ 1095. Registration on principal register not precluded [Section 27]

Registration of a mark on the supplemental register, or under the Act of March 19, 1920, shall not preclude registration by the registrant on the principal register established by this chapter. (July 5, 1946, c. 540, Title II, sec. 27, 60 Stat. 436.)

§ 1096. Registration on supplemental register not used to stop importations [Section 28]

Registration on the supplemental register or under the Act of March 19, 1920, shall not be filed in the Department of the Treasury or be used to stop importations. (July 5, 1946, c. 540, Title II, sec. 28, 60 Stat. 436.)

SUBCHAPTER III—GENERAL PROVISIONS

SEC.
1111. Notice of registration; display with mark; recovery of profits and damages in infringement suit

1112. Classification of goods and services; registration in plurality of classes

1113. Fees

1114. Remedies; infringement; innocent infringement by printers and publishers

1115. Registration on principal register as evidence of exclusive right to use mark; defenses

1116. Injunctions; enforcement; notice to Commissioner

1117. Recovery for violation of rights; profits, damages and costs; attorney fees

1118. Destruction of infringing articles

1119. Power of court over registration

1120. Civil liability for false or fraudulent registration

1121. Jurisdiction of Federal courts

1122. Repealed

1123. Rules and regulations for conduct of proceedings in Patent and Trademark Office

1124. Importation of goods bearing infringing marks or names forbidden

1125. False designations of origin and false descriptions forbidden

1126. International conventions

1127. Construction and definitions; intent of chapter

§ 1111. Notice of registration; display with mark; recovery of profits and damages in infringement suit [Section 29]

Notwithstanding the provisions of section 1072 of this title, a registrant of a mark registered in the Patent and Trademark Office, may give notice that his mark is registered by displaying with the mark as used the words "Registered in U.S. Patent and Trademark Office" or "Reg. U.S. Pat. & Tm. Off." or the letter R enclosed within a circle, thus ®; and in any suit for infringement under this chapter by such a registrant failing to give such notice of registration, no profits and no damages shall be recovered under the provisions of this chapter unless the defendant had actual notice of the registration. (As amended January 2, 1975, Public Law 93–596, sec. 1, 2, 88 Stat. 1949.)

§ 1112. Classification of goods and services; registration in plurality of classes [Section 30]

The Commissioner may establish a classification of goods and services, for convenience of Patent and Trademark Office administration, but not to limit or extend the applicant's rights. The applicant may file an application to register a mark for any or all of the goods and services upon or in connection with which he is actually using the mark: *Provided,* That when such goods or services fall within a plurality of classes, a fee equaling the sum of the fees for filing an application in each class shall be paid, and the Commissioner may issue a single certificate of registration for such mark. (As amended January 2, 1975, Public Law 93–596, sec. 1, 88 Stat. 1949.)

§ 1113.   Fees [Section 31]

(a) The Commissioner will establish fees for the filing and processing of an application for the registration of a trademark or other mark and for all other services performed by and materials furnished by the Patent and Trademark Office related to trademarks and other marks. However, no fee for the filing or processing of an application for the registration of a trademark or other mark or for the renewal or assignment of a trademark or other mark will be adjusted more than once every three years. No fee established under this section will take effect prior to sixty days following notice in the Federal Register.

(b) The Commissioner may waive the payment of any fee for any service or material related to trademarks or other marks in connection with an occasional request made by a department or agency of the Government, or any officer thereof. The Indian Arts and Crafts Board will not be charged any fee to register Government trademarks of genuineness and quality for Indian products or for products of particular Indian tribes and groups. (As amended July 24, 1965, Public Law 89–83, sec. 3, 79 Stat. 260; January 2, 1975, Public Law 93–596, sec. 1, 88 Stat. 1949; August 27, 1982, Public Law 97–247, sec. 3, 96 Stat. 319; September 8, 1982, Public Law 97–256, sec. 103, 96 Stat. 816.)

§ 1114.   Remedies; infringement; innocent infringement by printers and publishers [Section 32]

(a) Any person who shall, without the consent of the registrant—

(1) use in commerce any reproduction, counterfeit, copy, or colorable imitation of a registered mark in connection with the sale, offering for sale, distribution, or advertising of any goods or services on or in connection with which such use is likely to cause confusion, or to cause mistake, or to deceive; or

(2) reproduce, counterfeit, copy, or colorably imitate a registered mark and apply such reproduction, counterfeit, copy, or colorable imitation to labels, signs, prints, packages, wrappers, receptacles or advertisements intended to be used in commerce

upon or in connection with the sale, offering for sale, distribution, or advertising of goods or services on or in connection with which such use is likely to cause confusion, or to cause mistake, or to deceive.

shall be liable in a civil action by the registrant for the remedies hereinafter provided. Under subsection (b) of this section, the registrant shall not be entitled to recover profits or damages unless the acts have been committed with knowledge that such imitation is intended to be used to cause confusion, or to cause mistake, or to deceive.

(b) Notwithstanding any other provision of this chapter, the remedies given to the owner of the right infringed shall be limited as follows: (a) Where an infringer is engaged solely in the business of printing the mark for others and establishes that he was an innocent infringer the owner of the right infringed shall be entitled as against such infringer only to an injunction against future printing; (b) where the infringement complained of is contained in or is part of paid advertising matter in a newspaper, magazine, or other similar periodical the remedies of the owner of the right infringed as against the publisher or distributor of such newspaper, magazine, or other similar periodical shall be confined to an injunction against the presentation of such advertising matter in future issues of such newspapers, magazines, or other similar periodical: *Provided,* That these limitations shall apply only to innocent infringers; (c) injunction relief shall not be available to the owner of the right infringed in respect of an issue of a newspaper, magazine, or other similar periodical containing infringing matter when restraining the dissemination of such infringing matter in any particular issue of such periodical would delay the delivery of such issue after the regular time therefor, and such delay would be due to the method by which publication and distribution of such periodical is customarily conducted in accordance with sound business practice, and not to any method or device adopted for the evasion of this section or to prevent or delay the issuance of an injunction or restraining order with respect to such infringing matter. (July 5, 1946, c. 540, Title VI, sec. 32, 60 Stat. 437; October 9, 1962, Public Law 87–772, sec. 17, 76 Stat. 773.)

§ 1115. **Registration on principal register as evidence of exclusive right to use mark; defenses** [Section 33]

(a) Any registration issued under the Act of March 3, 1881, or the

Act of February 20, 1905, or of a mark registered on the principal register provided by this chapter and owned by a party to an action shall be admissible in evidence and shall be prima facie evidence of registrant's exclusive right to use the registered mark in commerce on the goods or services specified in the registration subject to any conditions or limitations stated therein, but shall not preclude an opposing party from proving any legal or equitable defense or defect which might have been asserted if such mark had not been registered.

(b) If the right to use the registered mark has become incontestable under section 1065 of this title, the registration shall be conclusive evidence of the registrant's exclusive right to use the registered mark in commerce on or in connection with the goods or services specified in the affidavit filed under the provisions of said section 1065 subject to any conditions or limitations stated therein except when one of the following defenses or defects is established:

(1) That the registration or the incontestable right to use the mark was obtained fraudulently; or

(2) That the mark has been abandoned by the registrant; or

(3) That the registered mark is being used, by or with the permission of the registrant or a person in privity with the registrant, so as to misrepresent the source of the goods or services in connection with which the mark is used; or

(4) That the use of the name, term, or device charged to be an infringement is a use, otherwise than as a trade or service mark, of the party's individual name in his own business, or of the individual name of anyone in privity with such party, or of a term or device which is descriptive of and used fairly and in good faith only to describe to users the goods or services of such party, or their geographic origin; or

(5) That the mark whose use by a party is charged as an infringement was adopted without knowledge of the registrant's prior use and has been continuously used by such party or those in privity with him from a date prior to registration of the mark under this chapter or publication of the registered mark under subsection (c) of section 1062 of this title: *Provided, however,* That this defense or defect shall apply only for the area in which such continuous prior use is proved; or

(6) That the mark whose use is charged as an infringement was registered and used prior to the registration under this chapter or

publication under subsection (c) of section 1062 of this title of the registered mark of the registrant, and not abandoned: *Provided, however,* That this defense or defect shall apply only for the area in which the mark was used prior to such registration or such publication of the registrant's mark; or

(7) That the mark has been or is being used to violate the antitrust laws of the United States. (July 5, 1946, c. 540, Title VI, sec. 33, 60 Stat. 438; October 9, 1962, Public Law 87–772, sec. 18, 76 Stat. 774.)

§ 1116. Injunctions; enforcement; notice to Commissioner [Section 34]

The several courts vested with jurisdiction of civil actions arising under this chapter shall have power to grant injunctions, according to the principles of equity and upon such terms as the court may deem reasonable, to prevent the violation of any right of the registrant of a mark registered in the Patent and Trademark Office. Any such injunction may include a provision directing the defendant to file with the court and serve on the plaintiff within thirty days after the service on the defendant of such injunction, or such extended period as the court may direct, a report in writing under oath setting forth in detail the manner and form in which the defendant has complied with the injunction. Any such injunction granted upon hearing, after notice to the defendant, by any district court of the United States, may be served on the parties against whom such injunction is granted anywhere in the United States where they may be found, and shall be operative and may be enforced by proceedings to punish for contempt, or otherwise, by the court by which such injunction was granted, or by any other United States district court in whose jurisdiction the defendant may be found.

The said courts shall have jurisdiction to enforce said injunction, as provided in this chapter, as fully as if the injunction had been granted by the district court in which it is sought to be enforced. The clerk of the court or judge granting the injunction shall, when required to do so by the court before which application to enforce said injunction is made, transfer without delay to said court a certified copy of all papers on file in his office upon which said injunction was granted.

It shall be the duty of the clerks of such courts within one month after the filing of any action, suit, or proceeding arising under the provisions of this chapter to give notice thereof in writing to the Commissioner setting forth in order so far as known the names and addresses of the litigants and the designating number or numbers of the registration or registrations upon which the action, suit, or proceeding has been brought, and in the event any other registration be subsequently included in the action, suit, or proceeding by amendment, answer, or other pleading, the clerk shall give like notice thereof to the Commissioner, and within one month after the decision is rendered, appeal taken or a decree issued the clerk of the court shall give notice thereof to the Commissioner, and it shall be the duty of the Commissioner on receipt of such notice forthwith to endorse the same upon the file wrapper of the said registration or registrations and to incorporate the same as a part of the contents of said file wrapper. (July 5, 1946, c. 540, Title VI, sec. 34, 60 Stat. 439; January 2, 1975, Public Law 93–596, sec. 1, 88 Stat. 1949.)

§ 1117. Recovery for violation of rights; profits, damages and costs; attorney fees [Section 35]

When a violation of any right of the registrant of a mark registered in the Patent and Trademark Office shall have been established in any civil action arising under this chapter, the plaintiff shall be entitled, subject to the provisions of sections 1111 and 1114 of this title, and subject to the principles of equity, to recover (1) defendant's profits, (2) any damages sustained by the plaintiff, and (3) the costs of the action. The court shall assess such profits and damages or cause the same to be assessed under its direction. In assessing profits the plaintiff shall be required to prove defendant's sales only; defendant must prove all elements of cost or deduction claimed. In assessing damages the court may enter judgment, according to the circumstances of the case, for any sum above the amount found as actual damages, not exceeding three times such amount. If the court shall find that the amount of the recovery based on profits is either inadequate or excessive the court may in its discretion enter judgment for such sum as the court shall find to be just, according to the circumstances of the case. Such sum in either of the above circumstances shall constitute compensation and not a penalty. The court in exceptional cases may award reasonable attorney fees to the prevailing party. (July 5, 1946, c. 540, Title VI, sec. 35, 60 Stat. 439; October 9, 1962, Public Law 87–772, sec. 19, 76 Stat. 774; January 2, 1975, Public Law 93–

596, sec. 1, 88 Stat. 1949; January 2, 1975, Public Law 93–600, sec. 3, 88 Stat. 1955.)

§ 1118.   Destruction of infringing articles [Section 36]

In any action arising under this chapter, in which a violation of any right of the registrant of a mark registered in the Patent and Trademark Office shall have been established, the court may order that all labels, signs, prints, packages, wrappers, receptacles, and advertisements in the possession of the defendant, bearing the registered mark or any reproduction, counterfeit, copy, or colorable imitation thereof, and all plates, molds, matrices, and other means of making the same, shall be delivered up and destroyed. (July 5, 1946, c. 540, Title VI, sec. 36, 60 Stat. 440; January 2, 1975, Public Law 93–596, sec. 1, 88 Stat. 1949.)

§ 1119.   Power of court over registration [Section 37]

In any action involving a registered mark the court may determine the right to registration, order the cancelation of registrations, in whole or in part, restore canceled registrations, and otherwise rectify the register with respect to the registrations of any party to the action. Decrees and orders shall be certified by the court to the Commissioner, who shall make appropriate entry upon the records of the Patent and Trademark Office, and shall be controlled thereby. (July 5, 1946, c. 540, Title VI, sec. 37, 60 Stat. 440; January 2, 1975, Public Law 93–596, sec. 1, 88 Stat. 1949.)

§ 1120.   Civil liability for false or fraudulent registration [Section 38]

Any person who shall procure registration in the Patent and Trademark Office of a mark by a false or fraudulent declaration or representation, oral or in writing, or by any false means, shall be liable in a civil action by any person injured thereby for any damages sustained in consequence thereof. (July 5, 1946, c. 540, Title VI, sec. 38, 60 Stat. 440; January 2, 1975, Public Law 93–596, sec. 1, 88 Stat. 1949.)

§ 1121.   Jurisdiction of Federal courts [Section 39]

The district and territorial courts of the United States shall have original jurisdiction and the courts of appeal of the United States (other than the United States Court of Appeals for the Federal Circuit) shall have appellate jurisdiction, of all actions arising under this chapter, without regard to the amount in controversy or to diversity or lack of diversity of the citizenship of the parties. (July 5, 1946, c. 540, Title VI, sec. 39, 60 Stat. 440; June 25, 1948, c. 646, secs. 1, 32(a), 62 Stat. 870, 991; May 24, 1949, c. 139, sec. 127, 63 Stat. 107; April 2, 1982, Title I, sec. 148, 96 Stat. 46.)

(a) No State or other jurisdiction of the United States or any political subdivision or any agency thereof may require alteration of a registered mark, or require that additional trademarks, servicemarks, trade names, or corporate names that may be associated with or incorporated into the registered mark be displayed in the mark in a manner differing from the display of such additional trademarks, servicemarks, trade names, or corporate names contemplated by the registered mark as exhibited in the certificate of registration issued by the United States Patent and Trademark Office. (October 12, 1982, Public Law 97–296, 96 Stat. 1316.)

§ 1122. Repealed.

May 24, 1949, c. 139, sec. 142, 63 Stat. 109 [Section 40]

§ 1123. Rules and regulations for conduct of proceedings in Patent and Trademark Office [Section 41]

The Commissioner shall make rules and regulations, not inconsistent with law, for the conduct of proceedings in the Patent and Trademark Office under this chapter. (July 5, 1946, c. 540, Title VI, sec. 41, 60 Stat. 440; January 2, 1975, Public Law 93–596, sec. 1, 88 Stat. 1949.)

§ 1124. Importation of goods bearing infringing marks or names forbidden [Section 42]

Except as provided in subsection (d) of section 526 of the Tariff Act of 1930 [19 USCS § 1526(d)], no article of imported merchandise which shall copy or simulate the name of the [any] domestic manufacture, or manufacturer, or trader, or of any manufacturer or trader located in any foreign country which, by treaty, convention, or law affords similar privileges to citizens of the United States, or which shall copy or simulate a trademark registered in accordance with the provisions of this Act [15 USCS §§ 1051 et seq.] or shall bear a name or mark calculated to induce the public to believe that the article is manufactured in the United States, or that it is manufactured in any foreign country or locality other than the country or locality in which it is in fact manufactured, shall be admitted to entry at any customhouse of the United States; and, in order to aid the officers of the customs in enforcing this prohibition, any domestic manufacturer or trader, and any foreign manufacturer or trader, who is entitled under the provisions of a treaty, conviction, declaration, or agreement between the United States and any foreign country to the advantages afforded by law to citizens of the United States in respect to trademarks and commercial names, may require his name and residence, and the name of the locality in which his goods are manufactured, and a copy of the certificate of registration of his trademark, issued in accordance with the provisions of this Act [15 USCS §§ 1051 et seq.], to be recorded in books which shall be kept for this purpose in the Department of the Treasury, under such regulations as the Secretary of the Treasury shall prescribe, and may furnish to the Department facsimiles of his name, the name of the locality in which his goods are manufactured, or of his registered trademark, and thereupon the Secretary of the Treasury shall cause one or more copies of the same to be transmitted to each collector or other proper officer of customs. (As amended October 3, 1978, Public Law 95–410, Title II, sec. 211(b), 92 Stat. 903.)

§ 1125. False designations of origin and false descriptions forbidden [Section 43]

(a) Any person who shall affix, apply, or annex, or use in connection with any goods or services, or any container or containers for goods, a false designation of origin, or any false description or representation, including words or other symbols tending falsely to describe or represent the same, and shall cause such goods or services to enter into commerce, and any person who shall with knowledge of the falsity of such designation of origin or description or representation cause or procure the same to be transported or used in commerce or deliver the same to any carrier to be transported or used, shall be liable to a civil action by any person doing business in the locality falsely indicated as that of origin or in the region in which said locality is situated, or by any person who believes that he is or is likely to be damaged by the use of any such false description or representation.

(b) Any goods marked or labeled in contravention of the provisions of this section shall not be imported into the United States or admitted to entry at any customhouse of the United States. The

105

owner, importer, or consignee of goods refused entry at any custom-house under this section may have any recourse by protest or appeal that is given under the customs revenue laws or may have the remedy given by this chapter in cases involving goods refused entry or seized. (July 5, 1946, c. 540, Title VIII, sec. 43, 60 Stat. 441.)

§ 1126. International conventions [Section 44]

Register of marks communicated by international bureaus

(a) The Commissioner shall keep a register of all marks communicated to him by the international bureaus provided for by the conventions for the protection of industrial property, trademarks, trade and commercial names, and the repression of unfair competition to which the United States is or may become a party, and upon the payment of the fees required by such conventions and the fees herein prescribed may place the marks so communicated upon such register. This register shall show a facsimile of the mark or trade or commercial name; the name, citizenship, and address of the registrant; the number, date, and place of the first registration of the mark, including the dates on which application for such registration was filed and granted and the term of such registration; a list of goods or services to which the mark is applied as shown by the registration in the country of origin, and such other data as may be useful concerning the mark. This register shall be a continuation of the register provided in section 1(a) of the Act of March 19, 1920.

Benefits of section to persons whose country of origin is party to convention or treaty

(b) Any person whose country of origin is a party to any convention or treaty relating to trademarks, trade or commercial names, or the repression of unfair competition, to which the United States is also a party, or extends reciprocal rights to nationals of the United States by law, shall be entitled to the benefits of this section under the conditions expressed herein to the extent necessary to give effect to any provision of such convention, treaty or reciprocal law, in addition to the rights to which any owner of a mark is otherwise entitled by this chapter.

Prior registration in country of origin; country of origin defined

(c) No registration of a mark in the United States by a person described in subsection (b) of this section shall be granted until such mark has been registered in the country of origin of the applicant, unless the applicant alleges use in commerce.

For the purposes of this section, the country of origin of the applicant is the country in which he has a bona fide and effective industrial or commercial establishment, or if he has not such an establishment the country in which he is domiciled, or if he has not a domicile in any of the countries described in subsection (b) of this section, the country of which he is a national.

Right of priority

(d) An application for registration of a mark under sections 1051, 1052, 1053, 1054 or 1091 of this title, filed by a person described in subsection (b) of this section who has previously duly filed an application for registration of the same mark in one of the countries described in subsection (b) of this section shall be accorded the same force and effect as would be accorded to the same application if filed in the United States on the same date on which the application was first filed in such foreign country: *Provided,* That—

(1) the application in the United States is filed within six months from the date on which the application was first filed in the foreign country;

(2) the application conforms as nearly as practicable to the requirements of this chapter, but use in commerce need not be alleged;

(3) the rights acquired by third parties before the date of the filing of the first application in the foreign[1] country shall in no way be affected by a registration obtained on an application filed under this subsection;

(4) nothing in this subsection shall entitle the owner of a registration granted under this section to sue for acts committed prior to the date on which his mark was registered in this country unless the registration is based on use in commerce.

In like manner and subject to the same conditions and requirements, the right provided in this section may be based upon a subsequent regularly filed application in the same foreign country, instead of the first filed foreign application: *Provided,* That any foreign application filed prior to such subsequent application has been withdrawn, abandoned, or otherwise disposed of, without having been laid open to public inspection and without leaving any rights outstanding, and has not served, nor thereafter shall serve, as a basis for claiming a right of priority.

(e) A mark duly registered in the country of origin of the foreign applicant may be registered on the principal register if eligible, otherwise on the supplemental register in this chapter provided. The application therefor shall be accompanied by a certification or a certified copy of the registration in the country of origin of the applicant.

Domestic registration independent of foreign registration

(f) The registration of a mark under the provisions of subsections (c), (d), and (e) of this section by a person described in subsection (b) of this section shall be independent of the registration in the country of origin and the duration, validity, or transfer in the United States of such registration shall be governed by the provisions of this chapter.

Trade or commercial names of foreign nationals
protected without registration

(g) Trade names or commercial names of persons described in subsection (b) of this section shall be protected without the obligation of filing or registration whether or not they form parts of marks.

Protection of foreign nationals against unfair competition

(h) Any person designated in subsection (b) of this section as entitled to the benefits and subject to the provisions of this chapter shall be entitled to effective protection against unfair competition, and the remedies provided in this chapter for infringement of marks shall be available so far as they may be appropriate in repressing acts of unfair competition.

Citizens or residents of United States entitled to benefits of section

(i) Citizens or residents of the United States shall have the same benefits as are granted by this section to persons described in subsection (b) of this section. (July 5, 1946, c. 540, Title IX, sec. 44, 60 Stat. 441; October 3, 1961, Public Law 87–333, sec. 2, 75 Stat. 748; October 9, 1962, Public Law 87–772, sec. 20, 76 Stat. 774.)

§ 1127. Construction and definitions; intent of chapter [Section 45]

In the construction of this chapter, unless the contrary is plainly apparent from the context—

The United States includes and embraces all territory which is under its jurisdiction and control.

The word "commerce" means all commerce which may lawfully be regulated by Congress.

The term "principal register" refers to the register provided for by sections 1051 to 1072 of this title, and the term "supplemental register" refers to the register provided for by sections 1091 to 1096 of this title.

The term "person" and any other word or term used to designate the applicant or other entitled to a benefit or privilege or rendered liable under the provisions of this chapter includes a juristic person as well as a natural person. The term "juristic person" includes a firm, corporation, union, association, or other organization capable of suing and being sued in a court of law.

The terms "applicant" and "registrant" embrace the legal representatives, predecessors, successors and assigns of such applicant or registrant.

The term "Commissioner" means the Commissioner of Patents and Trademarks.

The term "related company" means any person who legitimately controls or is controlled by the registrant or applicant for registration in respect to the nature and quality of the goods or services in connection with which the mark is used.

The terms "trade name" and "commercial name" include individual names and surnames, firm names and trade names used by manufacturers, industrialists, merchants, agriculturists, and others to identify their businesses, vocations, or occupations; the names or titles lawfully adopted and used by persons, firms, associations, corporations, companies, unions, and any manufacturing, industrial, commercial, agricultural, or other organizations engaged in trade or commerce and capable of suing and being sued in a court of law.

The term "trademark" includes any word, name, symbol, or device or any combination thereof adopted and used by a manufacturer or merchant to identify his goods and distinguish them from those manufactured or sold by others.

The term "service mark" means a mark used in the sale or advertising of services to identify the services of one person and distinguish them from the services of others. Titles, character names and other distinctive features of radio or television programs may be registered as service marks notwithstanding that they, or the programs, may advertise the goods of the sponsor.

The term "certification mark" means a mark used upon or in connection with the products or services of one or more persons other than the owner of the mark to certify regional or other origin, material, mode of manufacture, quality, accuracy or other characteristics

109

of such goods or services or that the work or labor on the goods or services was performed by members of a union or other organization.

The term "collective mark" means a trademark or service mark used by the members of a cooperative, an association or other collective group or organization and includes marks used to indicate membership in a union, an association or other organization.

The term "mark" includes any trademark, service mark, collective mark, or certification mark entitled to registration under this chapter whether registered or not.

For the purposes of this chapter a mark shall be deemed to be used in commerce (a) on goods when it is placed in any manner on the goods or their containers or the displays associated therewith or on the tags or labels affixed thereto and the goods are sold or transported in commerce and (b) on services when it is used or displayed in the sale or advertising of services and the services are rendered in commerce, or the services are rendered in more than one State or in this and a foreign country and the person rendering the services is engaged in commerce in connection therewith.

A mark shall be deemed to be "abandoned"—

(a) When its use has been discontinued with intent not to resume. Intent not to resume may be inferred from circumstances. Nonuse for two consecutive years shall be prima facie abandonment.

(b) When any course of conduct of the registrant, including acts of omission as well as commission, causes the mark to lose its significance as an indication of origin.

The term "colorable imitation" includes any mark which so resembles a registered mark as to be likely to cause confusion or mistake or to deceive.

The term "registered mark" means a mark registered in the United States Patent and Trademark Office under this chapter or under the Act of March 3, 1881, or the Act of February 20, 1905, or the Act of March 19, 1920. The phrase "marks registered in the Patent and Trademark Office" means registered marks.

The term "Act of March 3, 1881", "Act of February 20, 1905", or "Act of March 19, 1920," means the respective Act as amended.

A "counterfeit" is a spurious mark which is identical with, or substantially indistinguishable from, a registered mark.

Words used in the singular include the plural and vice versa.

The intent of this chapter is to regulate commerce within the control of Congress by making actionable the deceptive and misleading use of marks in such commerce; to protect registered marks used in such commerce from interference by State, or territorial legislation; to protect persons engaged in such commerce against unfair competition; to prevent fraud and deception in such commerce by the use of reproductions, copies, counterfeits, or colorable imitations of registered marks; and to provide rights and remedies stipulated by treaties and conventions respecting trademarks, trade names, and unfair competition entered into between the United States and foreign nations. (July 5, 1946, c. 540, Title X, sec. 45, 60 Stat. 443; October 9, 1962, Public Law 87–772, sec. 21, 76 Stat. 774; January 2, 1975, Public Law 93–596, sec. 1, 88 Stat. 1949.)

UNITED STATES CODE

TITLE 17—COPYRIGHTS

Chapter 1—Subject Matter and Scope of Copyright

Sec.
101. Definitions.
102. Subject matter of copyright: In general.
103. Subject matter of copyright: Compilations and derivative works.
104. Subject matter of copyright: National origin.
105. Subject matter of copyright: United States Government works.
106. Exclusive rights in copyrighted works.
107. Limitations on exclusive rights: Fair use.
108. Limitations on exclusive rights: Reproduction by libraries and archives.
109. Limitations on exclusive rights: Effect of transfer of particular copy or phonorecord.
110. Limitations on exclusive rights: Exemption of certain performances and displays.
111. Limitations on exclusive rights: Secondary transmissions.
112. Limitations on exclusive rights: Ephemeral recordings.
113. Scope of exclusive rights in pictorial, graphic, and sculptural works.
114. Scope of exclusive rights in sound recordings.
115. Scope of exclusive rights in nondramatic musical works: Compulsory license for making and distributing phonorecords.
116. Scope of exclusive rights in nondramatic musical works: Public performances by means of coin-operated phonorecord players.
117. Limitations on exclusive rights: Computer programs.
118. Scope of exclusive rights: Use of certain works in connection with noncommercial broadcasting.

Chapter 2—Copyright Ownership and Transfer

Sec.
201. Ownership of copyright.
202. Ownership of copyright as distinct from ownership of material object.
203. Termination of transfers and licenses granted by the author.
204. Execution of transfers of copyright ownership.
205. Recordation of transfers and other documents.

Chapter 3—Duration of Copyright

Sec.
301. Preemption with respect to other laws.

302. Duration of copyright: Works created on or after January 1, 1978.
303. Duration of copyright: Works created but not published or copyrighted before January 1, 1978.
304. Duration of copyright: Subsisting copyrights.
305. Duration of copyright: Terminal date.

CHAPTER 4—COPYRIGHT NOTICE, DEPOSIT, AND REGISTRATION

SEC.
401. Notice of copyright: Visually perceptible copies.
402. Notice of copyright: Phonorecords of sound recordings.
403. Notice of copyright: Publications incorporating United States Government works.
404. Notice of copyright: Contributions to collective works.
405. Notice of copyright: Omission of notice.
406. Notice of copyright: Error in name or date.
407. Deposit of copies or phonorecords for Library of Congress.
408. Copyright registration in general.
409. Application for copyright registration.
410. Registration of claim and issuance of certificate.
411. Registration as prerequisite to infringement suit.
412. Registration as prerequisite to certain remedies for infringement.

CHAPTER 5—COPYRIGHT INFRINGEMENT AND REMEDIES

SEC.
501. Infringement of copyright.
502. Remedies for infringement: Injunctions.
503. Remedies for infringement: Impounding and disposition of infringing articles.
504. Remedies for infringement: Damage and profits.
505. Remedies for infringement: Costs and attorney's fees.
506. Criminal offenses.
507. Limitations on actions.
508. Notification of filing and determination of actions.
509. Seizure and forfeiture.
510. Remedies for alteration of programing by cable systems.

CHAPTER 6—MANUFACTURING REQUIREMENTS AND IMPORTATION

SEC.
601. Manufacture, importation, and public distribution of certain copies.
602. Infringing importation of copies or phonorecords.
603. Importation prohibitions: Enforcement and disposition of excluded articles.

Chapter 7—Copyright Office

Sec.
701. The Copyright Office: General responsibilities and organization.
702. Copyright Office regulations.
703. Effective date of actions in Copyright Office.
704. Retention and disposition of articles deposited in Copyright office.
705. Copyright Office records: Preparation, maintenance, public inspection, and searching.
706. Copies of Copyright Office records.
707. Copyright Office forms and publications.
708. Copyright Office fees.
709. Delay in delivery caused by disruption of postal or other services.
710. Reproductions for use of the blind and physically handicapped: Voluntary licensing forms and procedures.

Chapter 8—Copyright Royalty Tribunal

Sec.
801. Copyright Royalty Tribunal: Establishment and purpose.
802. Membership of the Tribunal.
803. Procedures of the Tribunal.
804. Institution and conclusion of proceedings.
805. Staff of the Tribunal.
806. Administrative support of the Tribunal.
807. Deduction of costs of proceedings.
808. Reports.
809. Effective date of final determinations.
810. Judicial review.

Chapter 1—Subject Matter and Scope of Copyright

Sec.
101. Definitions.
102. Subject matter of copyright: In general.
103. Subject matter of copyright: Compilations and derivative works.
104. Subject matter of copyright: National origin.
105. Subject matter of copyright: United States Government works.
106. Exclusive rights in copyrighted works.
107. Limitations on exclusive rights: Fair use.
108. Limitations on exclusive rights: Reproduction by libraries and archives.
109. Limitations on exclusive rights: Effect of transfer of particular copy or phonorecord.
110. Limitations on exclusive rights: Exemption of certain performances and displays.
111. Limitations on exclusive rights: Secondary transmissions.

112. Limitations on exclusive rights: Ephemeral recordings.
113. Scope of exclusive rights in pictorial, graphic, and sculptural works.
114. Scope of exclusive rights in sound recordings.
115. Scope of exclusive rights in nondramatic musical works: Compulsory license for making and distributing phonorecords.
116. Scope of exclusive rights in nondramatic musical works: Public performances by means of coin-operated phonorecord players.
117. Scope of exclusive rights: Use in conjunction with computers and similar information systems.
118. Scope of exclusive rights: Use of certain works in connection with noncommercial broadcasting.

§ 101. Definitions

As used in this title, the following terms and their variant forms mean the following:

An "anonymous work" is a work on the copies or phonorecords of which no natural person is identified as author.

"Audiovisual works" are works that consist of a series of related images which are intrinsically intended to be shown by the use of machines or devices such as projectors, viewers, or electronic equipment, together with accompanying sounds, if any, regardless of the nature of the material objects, such as films or tapes, in which the works are embodied.

The "best edition" of a work is the edition, published in the United States at any time before the date of deposit, that the Library of Congress determines to be most suitable for its purposes.

A person's "children" are that person's immediate offspring, whether legitimate or not, and any children legally adopted by that person.

A "collective work" is a work, such as a periodical issue, anthology, or encyclopedia, in which a number of contributions, constituting separate and independent works in themselves, are assembled into a collective whole.

A "compilation" is a work formed by the collection and assembling of preexisting materials or of data that are selected, coordinated, or arranged in such a way that the resulting work as a whole constitutes an original work of authorship. The term "compilation" includes collective works.

"Copies" are material objects, other than phonorecords, in which a work is fixed by any method now known or later developed, and from which the work can be perceived, reproduced, or otherwise communicated, either directly or with the aid of a machine or device. The term "copies" includes the material object, other than a phonorecord, in which the work is first fixed.

"Copyright owner", with respect to any one of the exclusive rights comprised in a copyright, refers to the owner of that particular right.

A work is "created" when it is fixed in a copy or phonorecord for the first time; where a work is prepared over a period of time, the portion of it that has been fixed at any particular time constitutes the work as of that time, and where the work has been prepared in different versions, each version constitutes a separate work.

A "derivative work" is a work based upon one or more preexisting works, such as a translation, musical arrangement, dramatization, fictionalization, motion picture version, sound recording, art reproduction, abridgment, condensation, or any other form in which a work may be recast, transformed, or adapted. A work consisting of editorial revisions, annotations, elaborations, or other modifications which, as a whole, represent an original work of authorship, is a "derivative work".

A "device", "machine", or "process" is one now known or later developed.

To "display" a work means to show a copy of it, either directly or by means of a film, slide, television image, or any other device or process or, in the case of a motion picture or other audiovisual work, to show individual images nonsequentially.

A work is "fixed" in a tangible medium of expression when its embodiment in a copy or phonorecord, by or under the authority of the author, is sufficiently permanent or stable to permit it to be perceived, reproduced, or otherwise communicated for a period of more than transitory duration. A work consisting of sounds, images, or both, that are being transmitted, is "fixed" for purposes of this title if a fixation of the work is being made simultaneously with its transmission.

The terms "including" and "such as" are illustrative and not limitative.

A "joint work" is a work prepared by two or more authors with the intention that their contributions be merged into inseparable or interdependent parts of a unitary whole.

116

"Literary works" are works, other than audiovisual works, expressed in words, numbers, or other verbal or numerical symbols or indicia, regardless of the nature of the material objects, such as books, periodicals, manuscripts, phonorecords, film, tapes, disks, or cards, in which they are embodied.

"Motion pictures" are audiovisual works consisting of a series of related images which, when shown in succession, impart an impression of motion, together with accompanying sounds, if any.

To "perform" a work means to recite, render, play, dance, or act it, either directly or by means of any device or process or, in the case of a motion picture or other audiovisual work, to show its images in any sequence or to make the sounds accompanying it audible.

"Phonorecords" are material objects in which sounds, other than those accompanying a motion picture or other audiovisual work, are fixed by any method now known or later developed, and from which the sounds can be perceived, reproduced, or otherwise communicated, either directly or with the aid of a machine or device. The term "phonorecords" includes the material object in which the sounds are first fixed.

"Pictorial, graphic, and sculptural works" include two-dimensional and three-dimensional works of fine, graphic, and applied art, photographs, prints and art reproductions, maps, globes, charts, technical drawings, diagrams, and models. Such works shall include works of artistic craftsmanship insofar as their form but not their mechanical or utilitarian aspects are concerned; the design of a useful article, as defined in this section, shall be considered a pictorial, graphic, or sculptural work only if, and only to the extent that, such design incorporates pictorial, graphic, or sculptural features that can be identified separately from, and are capable of existing independently of, the utilitarian aspects of the article.

A "pseudonymous work" is a work on the copies or phonorecords of which the author is identified under a fictitious name.

"Publication" is the distribution of copies or phonorecords of a work to the public by sale or other transfer of ownership, or by rental, lease, or lending. The offering to distribute copies or phonorecords to a group of persons for purposes of further distribution, public performance or public display, constitutes publication. A public performance or display of a work does not of itself constitute publication.

To perform or display a work "publicly" means—

(1) to perform or display it at a place open to the public or at any place where a substantial number of persons outside of a normal circle of a family and its social acquaintances is gathered; or

(2) to transmit or otherwise communicate a performance or display of the work to a place specified by clause (1) or to the public, by means of any device or process, whether the members of the public capable of receiving the performance or display receive it in the same place or in separate places and at the same time or at different times.

"Sound recordings" are works that result from the fixation of a series of musical, spoken, or other sounds, but not including the sounds accompanying a motion picture or other audiovisual work, regardless of the nature of the material objects, such as disks, tapes, or other phonorecords, in which they are embodied.

"State" includes the District of Columbia and the Commonwealth of Puerto Rico, and any territories to which this title is made applicable by an Act of Congress.

A "transfer of copyright ownership" is an assignment, mortgage, exclusive license, or any other conveyance, alienation, or hypothecation of a copyright or of any of the exclusive rights comprised in a copyright, whether or not it is limited in time or place of effect, but not including a nonexclusive license.

A "transmission program" is a body of material that, as an aggregate has been produced for the sole purpose of transmission to the public in sequence and as a unit.

To "transmit" a performance or display is to communicate it by any device or process whereby images or sounds are received beyond the place from which they are sent.

The "United States", when used in a geographical sense, comprises the several States, the District of Columbia and the Commonwealth of Puerto Rico, and the organized territories under the jurisdiction of the United States Government.

A "useful article" is an article having an intrinsic utilitarian function that is not merely to portray the appearance of the article or to convey information. An article that is normally a part of a useful article is considered a "useful article".

The author's "widow" or "widower" is the author's surviving spouse under the law of the author's domicile at the time of his or her death, whether or not the spouse has later remarried.

A "work of the United States Government" is a work prepared by an officer or employee of the United States Government as part of that person's official duties.

A "work made for hire" is—

(1) a work prepared by an employee within the scope of his or her employment; or

(2) a work specially ordered or commissioned for use as a contribution to a collective work, as a part of a motion picture or other audiovisual work, as a translation, as a supplementary work, as a compilation, as an instructional text, as a test, as answer material for a test, or as an atlas, if the parties expressly agree in a written instrument signed by them that the work shall be considered a work made for hire. For the purpose of the foregoing sentence, a "supplementary work" is a work prepared for publication as a secondary adjunct to a work by another author for the purpose of introducing, concluding, illustrating, explaining, revising, commenting upon, or assisting in the use of the other work, such as forewords, afterwords, pictorial illustrations, maps, charts, tables, editorial notes, musical arrangements, answer material for tests, bibliographies, appendixes, and indexes, and an "instructional text" is a literary, pictorial, or graphic work prepared for publication and with the purpose of use in systematic instructional activities.

A "computer program" is a set of statements or instructions to be used directly or indirectly in a computer in order to bring about a certain result. (Added December 12, 1980, Public Law 96–517, sec. 10(a), 94 Stat. 3028.)

§ 102. Subject matter of copyright: In general

(a) Copyright protection subsists, in accordance with this title, in original works of authorship fixed in any tangible medium of expression, now known or later developed, from which they can be perceived, reproduced, or otherwise communicated, either directly or with the aid of a machine or device. Works of authorship include the following categories:

(1) literary works;

(2) musical works, including any accompanying words;

(3) dramatic works, including any accompanying music;

(4) pantomimes and choreographic works;

(5) pictorial, graphic, and sculptural works;

(6) motion pictures and other audiovisual works; and

(7) sound recordings.

(b) In no case does copyright protection for an original work of authorship extend to any idea, procedure, process, system, method of operation, concept, principle, or discovery, regardless of the form in which it is described, explained, illustrated, or embodied in such work.

§ 103. Subject matter of copyright: Compilations and derivative works

(a) The subject matter of copyright as specified by section 102 includes compilations and derivative works, but protection for a work employing preexisting material in which copyright subsists does not extend to any part of the work in which such material has been used unlawfully.

(b) The copyright in a compilation or derivative work extends only to the material contributed by the author of such work, as distinguished from the preexisting material employed in the work, and does not imply any exclusive right in the preexisting material. The copyright in such work is independent of, and does not affect or enlarge the scope, duration, ownership, or subsistence of, any copyright protection in the preexisting material.

§ 104. Subject matter of copyright: National origin

(a) Unpublished Works—The works specified by sections 102 and 103, while unpublished, are subject to protection under this title without regard to the nationality or domicile of the author.

(b) Published Works—The works specified by sections 102 and 103, when published, are subject to protection under this title if—

(1) on the date of first publication, one or more of the authors is a national or domiciliary of the United States, or is a national, domiciliary, or sovereign authority of a foreign nation that is a party to a copyright treaty to which the United States is also a party, or is a stateless person, wherever that person may be domiciled; or

(2) the work is first published in the United States or in a foreign nation that, on the date of first publication, is a party to the Universal Copyright Convention; or

(3) the work is first published by the United Nations or any of its specialized agencies, or by the Organization of American States; or

(4) the work comes within the scope of a Presidential proclamation. Whenever the President finds that a particular foreign nation extends, to works by authors who are nationals or domiciliaries of the United States or to works that are first published in the United States, copyright protection on substantially the same basis as that on which the foreign nation extends protection to works of its own nationals and domiciliaries and works first published in that nation, the President may by proclamation extend protection under this title to works of which one or more of the authors is, on the date of first publication, a national, domiciliary, or sovereign authority of that nation, or which was first published in that nation. The President may revise, suspend, or revoke any such proclamation or impose any conditions or limitations on protection under a proclamation.

§ 105. Subject matter of copyright: United States Government works

Copyright protection under this title is not available for any work of the United States Government, but the United States Government is not precluded from receiving and holding copyrights transferred to it by assignment, bequest, or otherwise.

§ 106. Exclusive rights in copyrighted works

Subject to sections 107 through 118, the owner of copyright under this title has the exclusive right to do and to authorize any of the following:

(1) to reproduce the copyrighted work in copies or phono-records;

(2) to prepare derivative works based upon the copyrighted work;

(3) to distribute copies or phonorecords of the copyrighted work to the public by sale or other transfer of ownership, or by rental, lease, or lending;

(4) in the case of literary, musical, dramatic, and choreographic works, pantomimes, and motion pictures and other audiovisual works, to perform the copyrighted work publicly; and

(5) in the case of literary, musical, dramatic, and choreographic works, pantomimes, and pictorial, graphic, or sculptural works, including the individual images of a motion picture or other audiovisual work, to display the copyrighted work publicly.

§ 107. Limitations on exclusive rights: Fair use

Notwithstanding the provisions of section 106, the fair use of a copyrighted work, including such use by reproduction in copies or phonorecords or by any other means specified by that section, for purposes such as criticism, comment, news reporting, teaching (including multiple copies for classroom use), scholarship, or research, is not an infringement of copyright. In determining whether the use made of a work in any particular case is a fair use the factors to be considered shall include—

(1) the purpose and character of the use, including whether such use is of a commercial nature or is for nonprofit educational purposes;

(2) the nature of the copyrighted work;

(3) the amount and substantiality of the portion used in relation to the copyrighted work as a whole; and

(4) the effect of the use upon the potential market for or value of the copyrighted work.

§ 108. Limitations on exclusive rights: Reproduction by libraries and archives

(a) Notwithstanding the provisions of section 106, it is not an infringement of copyright for a library or archives, or any of its employees acting within the scope of their employment, to reproduce no more than one copy or phonorecord of a work, or to distribute such copy or phonorecord, under the conditions specified by this section, if—

(1) the reproduction or distribution is made without any purpose of direct or indirect commercial advantage;

(2) the collections of the library or archives are (i) open to the public, or (ii) available not only to researchers affiliated with the library or archives or with the institution of which it is a part, but also to other persons doing research in a specialized field; and

(3) the reproduction or distribution of the work includes a notice of copyright.

(b) The rights of reproduction and distribution under this section apply to a copy or phonorecord of an unpublished work duplicated in facsimile form solely for purposes of preservation and security or for deposit for research use in another library or archives of the type described by clause (2) of subsection (a), if the copy or phonorecord reproduced is currently in the collections of the library or archives.

(c) The right of reproduction under this section applies to a copy or phonorecord of a published work duplicated in facsimile form solely for the purpose of replacement of a copy or phonorecord that is damaged, deteriorating, lost, or stolen, if the library or archives has, after a reasonable effort, determined that an unused replacement cannot be obtained at a fair price.

(d) The rights of reproduction and distribution under this section apply to a copy, made from the collection of a library or archives where the user makes his or her request or from that of another library or archives, of no more than one article or other contribution to a copyrighted collection or periodical issue, or to a copy or phonorecord of a small part of any other copyrighted work, if—

   (1) the copy or phonorecord becomes the property of the user, and the library or archives has had no notice that the copy or phonorecord would be used for any purpose other than private study, scholarship, or research; and

   (2) the library or archives displays prominently, at the place where orders are accepted, and includes on its order form, a warning of copyright in accordance with requirements that the Register of Copyrights shall prescribe by regulation.

(e) The rights of reproduction and distribution under this section apply to the entire work, or to a substantial part of it, made from the collection of a library or archives where the user makes his or her request or from that of another library or archives, if the library or archives has first determined, on the basis of a reasonable investigation, that a copy or phonorecord of the copyrighted work cannot be obtained at a pair price, if—

   (1) the copy or phonorecord becomes the property of the user, and the library or archives has had no notice that the copy or phonorecord would be used for any purpose other than private study, scholarship, or research; and

(2) the library or archives displays prominently, at the place where orders are accepted, and includes on its order form, a warning of copyright in accordance with requirements that the Register of Copyrights shall prescribe by regulation.

(f) Nothing in this section—

(1) shall be construed to impose liability for copyright infringement upon a library or archives or its employees for the unsupervised use of reproducing equipment located on its premises: *Provided,* That such equipment displays a notice that the making of a copy may be subject to the copyright law;

(2) excuses a person who uses such reproducing equipment or who requests a copy or phonorecord under subsection (d) from liability for copyright infringement for any such act, or for any later use of such copy or phonorecord, if it exceeds fair use as provided by section 107;

(3) shall be construed to limit the reproduction and distribution by lending of a limited number of copies and excerpts by a library or archives of an audiovisual news program, subject to clauses (1), (2), and (3) of subsection (a); or

(4) in any way affects the right of fair use as provided by section 107, or any contractual obligations assumed at any time by the library or archives when it obtained a copy or phonorecord of a work in its collections.

(g) The rights of reproduction and distribution under this section extend to the isolated and unrelated reproduction or distribution of a single copy or phonorecord of the same material on separate occasions, but do not extend to cases where the library or archives, or its employee—

(1) is aware or has substantial reason to believe that it is engaging in the related or concerted reproduction or distribution of multiple copies or phonorecords of the same material, whether made on one occasion or over a period of time, and whether intended for aggregate use by one or more individuals or for separate use by the individual members of a group; or

(2) engages in the systematic reproduction or distribution of single or multiple copies or phonorecords of material described in subsection (d): *Provided,* That nothing in this clause prevents a library or archives from participating in interlibrary arrangements that do not have, as their purpose or effect, that the library or archives receiving such copies or phonorecords for distribution

124

does so in such aggregate quantities as to substitute for a subscription to or purchase of such work.

(h) The rights of reproduction and distribution under this section do not apply to a musical work, a pictorial, graphic or sculptural work, or a motion picture or other audiovisual work other than an audiovisual work dealing with news, except that no such limitation shall apply with respect to rights granted by subsections (b) and (c), or with respect to pictorial or graphic works published as illustrations, diagrams, or similar adjuncts to works of which copies are reproduced or distributed in accordance with subsections (d) and (e).

(i) Five years from the effective date of this Act, and at five-year intervals thereafter, the Register of Copyrights, after consulting with representatives of authors, book and periodical publishers, and other owners of copyrighted materials, and with representatives of library users and librarians, shall submit to the Congress a report setting forth the extent to which this section has achieved the intended statutory balancing of the rights of creators, and the needs of users. The report should also describe any problems that may have arisen, and present legislative or other recommendations, if warranted.

§ 109. **Limitations on exclusive rights: Effect of transfer of particular copy or phonorecord**

(a) Notwithstanding the provisions of section 106(3), the owner of a particular copy or phonorecord lawfully made under this title, or any person authorized by such owner, is entitled, without the authority of the copyright owner, to sell or otherwise dispose of the possession of that copy or phonorecord.

(b) Notwithstanding the provisions of section 106(5), the owner of a particular copy lawfully made under this title, or any person authorized by such owner, is entitled, without the authority of the copyright owner, to display that copy publicly, either directly or by the projection of no more than one image at a time, to viewers present at the place where the copy is located.

(c) The privileges prescribed by subsections (a) and (b) do not, unless authorized by the copyright owner, extend to any person who has acquired possession of the copy or phonorecord from the copyright owner, by rental, lease, loan, or otherwise, without acquiring ownership of it.

§ 110. Limitations on exclusive rights: Exemption of certain performances and displays

Notwithstanding the provisions of section 106, the following are not infringements of copyright:

(1) performance or display of a work by instructors or pupils in the course of face-to-face teaching activities of a nonprofit educational institution, in a classroom or similar place devoted to instruction, unless, in the case of a motion picture or other audiovisual work, the performance, or the display of individual images, is given by means of a copy that was not lawfully made under this title, and that the person responsible for the performance knew or had reason to believe was not lawfully made;

(2) performance of a nondramatic literary or musical work or display of a work, by or in the course of a transmission, if—

(A) the performance or display is a regular part of the systematic instructional activities of a governmental body or a nonprofit educational institution; and

(B) the performance or display is directly related and of material assistance to the teaching content of the transmission; and

(C) the transmission is made primarily for—

(i) reception in classrooms or similar places normally devoted to instruction, or

(ii) reception by persons to whom the transmission is directed because their disabilities or other special circumstances prevent their attendance in classrooms or similar places normally devoted to instruction, or

(iii) reception by officers or employees of governmental bodies as a part of their official duties or employment;

(3) performance of a nondramatic literary or musical work or of a dramatical-musical work of a religious nature, or display of a work, in the course of services at a place of worship or other religious assembly;

(4) performance of a nondramatic literary or musical work otherwise than in a transmission to the public, without any purpose of direct or indirect commercial advantage and without payment of any fee or other compensation for the performance to any of its performers, promoters, or organizers, if—

(A) there is no direct or indirect admission charge; or

(B) the proceeds, after deducting the reasonable costs of producing the performance, are used exclusively for educational, religious, or charitable purposes and not for private financial gain, except where the copyright owner has served notice of objection to the performance under the following conditions;

    (i) the notice shall be in writing and signed by the copyright owner or such owner's duly authorized agent; and

    (ii) the notice shall be served on the person responsible for the performance at least seven days before the date of the performance, and shall state the reasons for the objection; and

    (iii) the notice shall comply, in form, content, and manner of service, with requirements that the Register of Copyrights shall prescribe by regulation;

(5) communication of a transmission embodying a performance or display of a work by the public reception of the transmission on a single receiving apparatus of a kind commonly used in private homes, unless—

    (A) a direct charge is made to see or hear the transmission; or

    (B) the transmission thus received is further transmitted to the public;

(6) performance of a nondramatic musical work by a governmental body or a nonprofit agricultural or horticultural organization, in the course of an annual agricultural or horticultural fair or exhibition conducted by such body or organization; the exemption provided by this clause shall extend to any liability for copyright infringement that would otherwise be imposed on such body or organization, under doctrines of vicarious liability or related infringement, for a performance by a concessionnaire, business establishment, or other person at such fair or exhibition, but shall not excuse any such person from liability for the performance;

(7) performance of a nondramatic musical work by a vending establishment open to the public at large without any direct or indirect admission charge, where the sole purpose of the performance is to promote the retail sale of copies or phonorecords of the work, and the performance is not transmitted beyond the place where the establishment is located and is within the immediate area where the sale is occurring;

(8) performance of a nondramatic literary work, by or in the course of a transmission specifically designed for and primarily directed to blind or other handicapped persons who are unable to read normal printed material as a result of their handicap, or deaf or other handicapped persons who are unable to hear the aural

signals accompanying a transmission of visual signals, if the performance is made without any purpose of direct or indirect commercial advantage and its transmission is made through the facilities of: (i) a governmental body; or (ii) a noncommercial educational broadcast station (as defined in section 397 of title 47); or (iii) a radio subcarrier authorization (as defined in 47 CFR 73.293–73.295 and 73.593–73.595); or (iv) a cable system (as defined in section 111(f)).

(9) performance on a single occasion of a dramatic literary work published at least ten years before the date of the performance, by or in the course of a transmission specifically designed for and primarily directed to blind or other handicapped persons who are unable to read normal printed material as a result of their handicap, if the performance is made without any purpose of direct or indirect commercial advantage and its transmission is made through the facilities of a radio subcarrier authorization referred to in clause (8) (iii), *Provided,* That the provisions of this clause shall not be applicable to more than one performance of the same work by the same performers or under the auspices of the same organization.

(10) notwithstanding paragraph 4 above, the following is not an infringement of copyright: performance of a nondramatic literary or musical work in the course of a social function which is organized and promoted by a nonprofit veterans' organization or a nonprofit fraternal organization to which the general public is not invited, but not including the invitees of the organizations, if the proceeds from the performance, after deducting the reasonable costs of producing the performance, are used exclusively for charitable purposes and not for financial gain. For purposes of this section the social functions of any college or university fraternity or sorority shall not be included unless the social function is held solely to raise funds for a specific charitable purpose. (Added October 25, 1982, Public Law 97–366, sec. 3, 96 Stat. 1759.)

§ 111. **Limitations on exclusive rights: Secondary transmissions**

(a) *Certain Secondary Transmissions Exempted*—The secondary transmission of a primary transmission embodying a performance or display of a work is not an infringement of copyright if—

(1) the secondary transmission is not made by a cable system, and consists entirely of the relaying, by the management of a

hotel, apartment house, or similar establishment, of signals transmitted by a broadcast station licensed by the Federal Communications Commission, within the local service area of such station, to the private lodgings of guests or residents of such establishment, and no direct charge is made to see or hear the secondary transmission; or

(2) the secondary transmission is made solely for the purpose and under the conditions specified by clause (2) of section 110; or

(3) the secondary transmission is made by any carrier who has no direct or indirect control over the content or selection of the primary transmission or over the particular recipients of the secondary transmission, and whose activities with respect to the secondary transmission consist solely of providing wires, cables, or other communications channels for the use of others: *Provided,* That the provisions of this clause extend only to the activities of said carrier with respect to secondary transmissions and do not exempt from liability the activities of others with respect to their own primary or secondary transmissions; or

(4) the secondary transmission is not made by a cable system but is made by a governmental body, or other nonprofit organization, without any purpose of direct or indirect commercial advantage, and without charge to the recipients of the secondary transmission other than assessments necessary to defray the actual and reasonable costs of maintaining and operating the secondary transmission service.

(b) *Secondary Transmission of Primary Transmission to Controlled Group*—Notwithstanding the provisions of subsections (a) and (c), the secondary transmission to the public of a primary transmission embodying a performance or display of a work is actionable as an act of infringement under section 501, and is fully subject to the remedies provided by sections 502 through 506 and 509, if the primary transmission is not made for reception by the public at large but is controlled and limited to reception by particular members of the public: *Provided,* however, That such secondary transmission is not actionable as an act of infringement if—

(1) the primary transmission is made by a broadcast station licensed by the Federal Communications Commission; and

(2) the carriage of the signals comprising the secondary transmission is required under the rules, regulations, or authorizations of the Federal Communications Commission; and

(3) the signal of the primary transmitter is not altered or changed in any way by the secondary transmitter.

(c) *Secondary Transmissions by Cable Systems—*

(1) Subject to the provisions of clauses (2), (3), and (4) of this subsection, secondary transmissions to the public by a cable system of a primary transmission made by a broadcast station licensed by the Federal Communications Commission or by an appropriate governmental authority of Canada or Mexico and embodying a performance or display of a work shall be subject to compulsory licensing upon compliance with the requirements of subsection (d) where the carriage of the signals comprising the secondary transmission is permissible under the rules, regulations, or authorizations of the Federal Communications Commission.

(2) Notwithstanding the provisions of clause (1) of this subsection, the willful or repeated secondary transmission to the public by a cable system of a primary transmission made by a broadcast station licensed by the Federal Communications Commission or by an appropriate governmental authority of Canada or Mexico and embodying a performance or display of a work is actionable as an act of infringement under section 501, and is fully subject to the remedies provided by sections 502 through 506 and 509, in the following cases:

(A) where the carriage of the signals comprising the secondary transmission is not permissible under the rules, regulations, or authorizations of the Federal Communications Commission; or

(B) where the cable system has not recorded the notice specified by subsection (d) and deposited the statement of account and royalty fee required by subsection (d).

(3) Notwithstanding the provisions of clause (1) of this subsection and subject to the provisions of subsection (e) of this section, the secondary transmission to the public by a cable system of a primary transmission made by a broadcast station licensed by the Federal Communications Commission or by an appropriate governmental authority of Canada or Mexico and embodying a performance or display of a work is actionable as an act of infringement under section 501, and is fully subject to the remedies provided by sections 502 through 506 and sections 509 and 510, if the content of the particular program in which the performance or display is embodied, or any commercial advertising or station

announcements transmitted by the primary transmitter during, or immediately before or after, the transmission of such program, is in any way willfully altered by the cable system through changes, deletions, or additions, except for the alteration, deletion, or substitution of commercial advertisements performed by those engaged in television commercial advertising market research: *Provided,* That the research company has obtained the prior consent of the advertiser who has purchased the original commercial advertisement, the television station broadcasting that commercial advertisement, and the cable system performing the secondary transmission: *And provided further,* That such commercial alteration, deletion, or substitution is not performed for the purpose of deriving income from the sale of that commercial time.

(4) Notwithstanding the provisions of clause (1) of this subsection, the secondary transmission to the public by a cable system of a primary transmission made by a broadcast station licensed by an appropriate governmental authority of Canada or Mexico and embodying a performance or display of a work is actionable as an act of infringement under section 501, and is fully subject to the remedies provided by sections 502 through 506 and section 509, if (A) with respect to Canadian signals, the community of a cable system is located more than 150 miles from the United States-Canadian border and is also located south of the forty-second parallel of latitude, or (B) with respect to Mexican signals, the secondary transmission is made by a cable system which received the primary transmission by means other than direct interception of a free space radio wave emitted by such broadcast television station, unless prior to April 15, 1976, such cable system was actually carrying, or was specifically authorized to carry, the signal of such foreign station on the system pursuant to the rules, regulations, or authorizations of the Federal Communications Commission.

(d) *Compulsory License for Secondary Transmissions by Cable Systems*—

(1) For any secondary transmission to be subject to compulsory licensing under subsection (c), the cable system shall, at least one month before the date of the commencement of operations of the cable system or within one hundred and eighty days after the enactment of this Act, whichever is later, and thereafter within thirty days after each occasion on which the ownership or control or the signal carriage complement of the cable system changes, record in the Copyright Office a notice including a statement of

the identity and address of the person who owns or operates the secondary transmission service or has power to exercise primary control over it, together with the name and location of the primary transmitter or primary transmitters whose signals are regularly carried by the cable system, and thereafter, from time to time, such further information as the Register of Copyrights, after consultation with the Copyright Royalty Tribunal (if and when the Tribunal has been constituted), shall prescribe by regulation to carry out the purpose of this clause.

(2) A cable system whose secondary transmissions have been subject to compulsory licensing under subsection (c) shall, on a semiannual basis, deposit with the Register of Copyrights, in accordance with requirements that the Register shall, after consultation with the Copyright Royalty Tribunal (if and when the Tribunal has been constituted), prescribe by regulation—

(A) a statement of account, covering the six months next preceding, specifying the number of channels on which the cable system made secondary transmissions to its subscribers, the names and locations of all primary transmitters whose transmissions were further transmitted by the cable system, the total number of subscribers, the gross amounts paid to the cable system for the basic service of providing secondary transmissions of primary broadcast transmitters, and such other data as the Register of Copyrights may, after consultation with the Copyright Royalty Tribunal (if and when the Tribunal has been constituted), from time to time prescribe by regulation. Such statement shall also include a special statement of account covering any nonnetwork television programming that was carried by the cable system in whole or in part beyond the local service area of the primary transmitter, under rules, regulations, or authorizations of the Federal Communications Commission permitting the substitution or addition of signals under certain circumstances, together with logs showing the times, dates, stations, and programs involved in such substituted or added carriage; and

(B) except in the case of a cable system whose royalty is specified in subclause (C) or (D), a total royalty fee for the period covered by the statement, computed on the basis of specified percentages of the gross receipts from subscribers to the cable service during said period for the basic service of providing secondary transmissions of primary broadcast transmitters, as follows:

(i) 0.675 of 1 per centum of such gross receipts for the privilege of further transmitting any nonnetwork programming of a primary transmitter in whole or in part beyond the local service area of such primary transmitter, such amount to be applied against the fee, if any, payable pursuant to paragraphs (ii) through (iv);

(ii) 0.675 of 1 per centum of such gross receipts for the first distant signal equivalent;

(iii) 0.425 of 1 per centum of such gross receipts for each of the second, third, and fourth distant signal equivalents;

(iv) 0.2 of 1 per centum of such gross receipts for the fifth distant signal equivalent and each additional distant signal equivalent thereafter; and

in computing the amounts payable under paragraph (ii) through (iv), above, any fraction of a distant signal equivalent shall be computed at its fractional value and, in the case of any cable system located partly within and partly without the local service area of a primary transmitter, gross receipts shall be limited to those gross receipts derived from subscribers located without the local service area of such primary transmitter; and

(C) if the actual gross receipts paid by subscribers to a cable system for the period covered by the statement for the basic service of providing secondary transmissions of primary broadcast transmitters total $80,000 or less, gross receipts of the cable system for the purpose of this subclause shall be computed by subtracting from such actual gross receipts the amount by which $80,000 exceeds such actual gross receipts, except that in no case shall a cable system's gross receipts be reduced to less than $3,000. The royalty fee payable under this subclause shall be 0.5 of 1 per centum, regardless of the number of distant signal equivalents, if any; and

(D) if the actual gross receipts paid by subscribers to a cable system for the period covered by the statement, for the basic service of providing secondary transmissions of primary broadcast transmitters, are more than $80,000 but less than $160,000, the royalty fee payable under this subclause shall be (i) 0.5 of 1 per centum of any gross receipts up to $80,000; and (ii) 1 per centum of any gross receipts in excess of $80,000 but less than $160,000, regardless of the number of distant signal equivalents, if any.

(3) The Register of Copyrights shall receive all fees deposited under this section and, after deducting the reasonable costs incurred by the Copyright Office under this section, shall deposit the balance in the Treasury of the United States, in such manner as the Secretary of the Treasury directs. All funds held by the Secretary of the Treasury shall be invested in interest-bearing United States securities for later distribution with interest by the Copyright Royalty Tribunal as provided by this title. The Register shall submit to the Copyright Royalty Tribunal, on a semiannual basis, a compilation of all statements of account covering the relevant six-month period provided by clause (2) of this subsection.

(4) The royalty fees thus deposited shall, in accordance with the procedures provided by clause (5), be distributed to those among the following copyright owners who claim that their works were the subject of secondary transmissions by cable systems during the relevant semiannual period:

(A) any such owner whose work was included in a secondary transmission made by a cable system of a nonnetwork television program in whole or in part beyond the local service area of the primary transmitter; and

(B) any such owner whose work was included in a secondary transmission identified in a special statement of account deposited under clause (2)(A); and

(C) any such owner whose work was included in nonnetwork programing consisting exclusively of aural signals carried by a cable system in whole or in part beyond the local service area of the primary transmitter of such programs.

(5) The royalty fees thus deposited shall be distributed in accordance with the following procedures:

(A) During the month of July in each year, every person claiming to be entitled to compulsory license fees for secondary transmissions shall file a claim with the Copyright Royalty Tribunal, in accordance with requirements that the Tribunal shall prescribe by regulation. Notwithstanding any provisions of the antitrust laws, for purposes of this clause any claimants may agree among themselves as to the proportionate division of compulsory licensing fees among them, may lump their claims together and file them jointly or as a single claim, or may designate a common agent to receive payment on their behalf.

(B) After the first day of August of each year, the Copyright Royalty Tribunal shall determine whether there exists a controversy concerning the distribution of royalty fees. If the Tribunal determines that no such controversy exists, it shall, after deducting its reasonable administrative costs under this section, distribute such fees to the copyright owners entitled, or to their designated agents. If the Tribunal finds the existence of a controversy, it shall, pursuant to chapter 8 of this title, conduct a proceeding to determine the distribution of royalty fees.

(C) During the pendency of any proceeding under this subsection, the Copyright Royalty Tribunal shall withhold from distribution an amount sufficient to satisfy all claims with respect to which a controversy exists, but shall have discretion to proceed to distribute any amounts that are not in controversy.

(e) *Nonsimultaneous Secondary Transmissions by Cable Systems*—

(1) Notwithstanding those provisions of the second paragraph of subsection (f) relating to nonsimultaneous secondary transmissions by a cable system, any such transmissions are actionable as an act of infringement under section 501, and are fully subject to the remedies provided by sections 502 through 506 and sections 509 and 510, unless—

(A) the program on the videotape is transmitted no more than one time to the cable system's subscribers; and

(B) the copyrighted program, episode, or motion picture videotape, including the commercials contained within such program, episode, or picture, is transmitted without deletion or editing; and

(C) an owner or officer of the cable system (i) prevents the duplication of the videotape while in the possession of the system, (ii) prevents unauthorized duplication while in the possession of the facility making the videotape for the system if the system owns or controls the facility, or takes reasonable precautions to prevent such duplication if it does not own or control the facility, (iii) takes adequate precautions to prevent duplication while the tape is being transported, and (iv) subject to clause (2), erases or destroys, or causes the erasure or destruction of, the videotape; and

(D) within forty-five days after the end of each calendar quarter, an owner or officer of the cable system executes an affidavit attesting (i) to the steps and precautions taken to prevent duplication of the videotape, and (ii) subject to clause (2), to the erasure or destruction of all videotapes made or used during such quarter; and

(E) such owner or officer places or causes each such affidavit, and affidavits received pursuant to clause (2) (C), to be placed in a file, open to public inspection, at such system's main office in the community where the transmission is made or in the nearest community where such system maintains an office; and

(F) the nonsimultaneous transmission is one that the cable system would be authorized to transmit under the rules, regulations, and authorizations of the Federal Communications Commission in effect at the time of the nonsimultaneous transmission if the transmission had been made simultaneously, except that this subclause shall not apply to inadvertent or accidental transmissions.

(2) If a cable system transfers to any person a videotape of a program nonsimultaneously transmitted by it, such transfer is actionable as an act of infringement under section 501, and is fully subject to the remedies provided by sections 502 through 506 and 509, except that, pursuant to a written, nonprofit contract providing for the equitable sharing of the costs of such videotape and its transfer, a videotape nonsimultaneously transmitted by it, in accordance with clause (1), may be transferred by one cable system in Alaska to another system in Alaska, by one cable system in Hawaii permitted to make such nonsimultaneous transmissions to another such cable system in Hawaii, or by one cable system in Guam, the Northern Mariana Islands, or the Trust Territory of the Pacific Islands, to another cable system in any of those three territories, if—

(A) each such contract is available for public inspection in the offices of the cable systems involved, and a copy of such contract is filed, within thirty days after such contract is entered into, with the Copyright Office (which Office shall make each such contract available for public inspection); and

(B) the cable system to which the videotape is transferred complies with clause (1) (A), (B), (C) (i), (iii), and (iv), and (D) through (F); and

(C) such system provides a copy of the affidavit required to be made in accordance with clause (1) (D) to each cable system making a previous nonsimultaneous transmission of the same videotape.

(3) This subsection shall not be construed to supersede the exclusivity protection provisions of any existing agreement, or any such agreement hereafter entered into, between a cable system and a television broadcast station in the area in which the cable system is located, or a network with which such station is affiliated.

(4) As used in this subsection, the term "videotape", and each of its variant forms, means the reproduction of the images and sounds of a program or programs broadcast by a television broadcast station licensed by the Federal Communications Commission, regardless of the nature of the material objects, such as tapes or films, in which the reproduction is embodied.

(f) *Definitions*—As used in this section, the following terms and their variant forms mean the following:

A "primary transmission" is a transmission made to the public by the transmitting facility whose signals are being received and further transmitted by the secondary transmission service, regardless of where or when the performance or display was first transmitted.

A "secondary transmission" is the further transmitting of a primary transmission simultaneously with the primary transmission, or nonsimultaneously with the primary transmission if by a "cable system" not located in whole or in part within the boundary of the forty-eight contiguous States, Hawaii, or Puerto Rico: *Provided, however,* That a nonsimultaneous further transmission by a cable system located in Hawaii of a primary transmission shall be deemed to be a secondary transmission if the carriage of the television broadcast signal comprising such further transmission is permissible under the rules, regulations, or authorizations of the Federal Communications Commission.

A "cable system" is a facility, located in any State, Territory, Trust Territory, or Possession, that in whole or in part receives signals transmitted or programs broadcast by one or more television broadcast stations licensed by the Federal Communications Commission, and makes secondary transmissions of such signals or programs by wires, cables, or other communications channels to subscribing members of the public who pay for such service. For purposes of determining the royalty fee under subsection (d) (2), two or more cable systems in contiguous communities under common ownership or control or operating from one head-end shall be considered as one system.

The "local service area of a primary transmitter", in the case of a television broadcast station, comprises the area in which such station is entitled to insist upon its signal being retransmitted by a cable system pursuant to the rules, regulations, and authorizations of the Federal Communications Commission in effect on April 15, 1976, or in the case of a television broadcast station licensed by an appropriate governmental authority of Canada or Mexico, the area in which it would be entitled to insist upon its signal being retransmitted if it were a television broadcast station subject to such rules, regulations, and authorizations. The "local service area of a primary transmitter", in the case of a radio broadcast station, comprises the primary service area of such station, pursuant to the rules and regulations of the Federal Communications Commission.

A "distant signal equivalent" is the value assigned to the secondary transmission of any nonnetwork television programing carried by a cable system in whole or in part beyond the local service area of the primary transmitter of such programing. It is computed by assigning a value of one to each independent station and a value of one-quarter to each network station and noncommercial educational station for the nonnetwork programing so carried pursuant to the rules, regulations, and authorizations of the Federal Communications Commission. The foregoing values for independent, network, and noncommercial educational stations are subject, however, to the following exceptions and limitations. Where the rules and regulations of the Federal Communications Commission require a cable system to omit the further transmission of a particular program and such rules and regulations also permit the substitution of another program embodying a performance or display of a work in place of the omitted transmission, or where such rules and regulations in effect on the date of enactment of this Act permit a cable system, at its election, to effect such deletion and substitution of a nonlive program or to carry additional programs not transmitted by primary transmitters within whose local service area the cable system is located, no value shall be assigned for the substituted or additional program; where the rules, regulations, or authorizations of the Federal Communications Commission in ef-

138

fect on the date of enactment of this Act permit a cable system, at its election, to omit the further transmission of a particular program and such rules, regulations, or authorizations also permit the substitution of another program embodying a performance or display of a work in place of the omitted transmission, the value assigned for the substituted or additional program shall be, in the case of a live program, the value of one full distant signal equivalent multiplied by a fraction that has as its numerator the number of days in the year in which such substitution occurs and as its denominator the number of days in the year. In the case of a station carried pursuant to the late-night or specialty programing rules of the Federal Communications Commission, or a station carried on a part-time basis where full-time carriage is not possible because the cable system lacks the activated channel capacity to retransmit on a full-time basis all signals which it is authorized to carry, the values for independent, network, and noncommercial educational stations set forth above, as the case may be, shall be multiplied by a fraction which is equal to the ratio of the broadcast hours of such station carried by the cable system to the total broadcast hours of the station.

A "network station" is a television broadcast station that is owned or operated by, or affiliated with, one or more of the television networks in the United States providing nationwide transmissions, and that transmits a substantial part of the programing supplied by such networks for a substantial part of that station's typical broadcast day.

An "independent station" is a commerical television broadcast station other than a network station.

A "noncommercial educational station" is a television station that is a noncommercial educational broadcast station as defined in section 397 of title 47.

§ 112. Limitations on exclusive rights: Ephemeral recordings

(a) Notwithstanding the provisions of section 106, and except in the case of a motion picture or other audiovisual work, it is not an infringement of copyright for a transmitting organization entitled to transmit to the public a performance or display of a work, under a license or transfer of the copyright or under the limitations on exclusive rights in sound recordings specified by section 114 (a), to make no more than one copy or phonorecord of a particular transmission program embodying the performance or display, if—

(1) the copy or phonorecord is retained and used solely by the transmitting organization that made it, and no further copies or phonorecords are reproduced from it; and

(2) the copy or phonorecord is used solely for the transmitting organization's own transmissions within its local service area, or for purposes of archival preservation or security; and

(3) unless preserved exclusively for archival purposes, the copy or phonorecord is destroyed within six months from the date the transmission program was first transmitted to the public.

(b) Notwithstanding the provisions of section 106, it is not an infringement of copyright for a governmental body or other nonprofit organization entitled to transmit a performance or display of a work, under section 110(2) or under the limitations on exclusive rights in sound recordings specified by section 114(a), to make no more than thirty copies or phonorecords of a particular transmission program embodying the performance or display, if—

(1) no further copies or phonorecords are reproduced from the copies or phonorecords made under this clause; and

(2) except for one copy or phonorecord that may be preserved exclusively for archival purposes, the copies or phonorecords are destroyed within seven years from the date the transmission program was first transmitted to the public.

(c) Notwithstanding the provisions of section 106, it is not an infringement of copyright for a governmental body or other nonprofit organization to make for distribution no more than one copy or phonorecord, for each transmitting organization specified in clause (2) of this subsection, of a particular transmission program embodying a performance of a nondramatic musical work of a religious nature, or of a sound recording of such a musical work, if—

(1) there is no direct or indirect charge for making or distributing any such copies or phonorecords; and

(2) none of such copies or phonorecords is used for any performance other than a single transmission to the public by a transmitting organization entitled to transmit to the public a performance of the work under a license or transfer of the copyright; and

(3) except for one copy or phonorecord that may be preserved exclusively for archival purposes, the copies or phonorecords are all

destroyed within one year from the date the transmission program was first transmitted to the public.

(d) Notwithstanding the provisions of section 106, it is not an infringement of copyright for a governmental body or other nonprofit organization entitled to transmit a performance of a work under section 110(8) to make no more than ten copies or phonorecords embodying the performance, or to permit the use of any such copy or phonorecord by any governmental body or nonprofit organization entitled to transmit a performance of a work under section 110(8), if—

(1) any such copy or phonorecord is retained and used solely by the organization that made it, or by a governmental body or nonprofit organization entitled to transmit a performance of a work under section 110(8), and no further copies or phonorecords are reproduced from it; and

(2) any such copy or phonorecord is used solely for transmissions authorized under section 110(8), or for purposes of archival preservation or security; and

(3) the governmental body or nonprofit organization permitting any use of any such copy or phonorecord by any governmental body or nonprofit organization under this subsection does not make any charge for such use.

(e) The transmission program embodied in a copy or phonorecord made under this section is not subject to protection as a derivative work under this title except with the express consent of the owners of copyright in the preexisting works employed in the program.

§ 113. Scope of exclusive rights in pictorial, graphic, and sculptural works

(a) Subject to the provisions of subsections (b) and (c) of this section, the exclusive right to reproduce a copyrighted pictorial, graphic, or sculptural work in copies under section 106 includes the right to reproduce the work in or on any kind of article, whether useful or otherwise.

(b) This title does not afford, to the owner of copyright in a work that portrays a useful article as such, any greater or lesser rights with respect to the making, distribution, or display of the useful article so portrayed than those afforded to such works under the law, whether title 17 or the common law or statutes of a State, in effect on December 31, 1977, as held applicable and construed by a court in an action brought under this title.

(c) In the case of a work lawfully reproduced in useful articles that have been offered for sale or other distribution to the public, copyright does not include any right to prevent the making, distribution, or display of pictures or photographs of such articles in connection with advertisements or commentaries related to the distribution or display of such articles, or in connection with news reports.

§ 114.   Scope of exclusive rights in sound recordings

(a) The exclusive rights of the owner of copyright in a sound recording are limited to the rights specified by clauses (1), (2), and (3) of section 106, and do not include any right of performance under section 106(4).

(b) The exclusive right of the owner of copyright in a sound recording under clause (1) of section 106 is limited to the right to duplicate the sound recording in the form of phonorecords, or of copies of motion pictures and other audiovisual works, that directly or indirectly recapture the actual sounds fixed in the recording. The exclusive right of the owner of copyright in a sound recording under clause (2) of section 106 is limited to the right to prepare a derivative work in which the actual sounds fixed in the sound recording are rearranged, remixed, or otherwise altered in sequence or quality. The exclusive rights of the owner of copyright in a sound recording under clauses (1) and (2) of section 106 do not extend to the making or duplication of another sound recording that consists entirely of an independent fixation of other sounds, even though such sounds imitate or simulate those in the copyrighted sound recording. The exclusive rights of the owner of copyright in a sound recording under clauses (1), (2), and (3) of section 106 do not apply to sound recordings included in educational television and radio programs (as defined in section 397 of title 47) distributed or transmitted by or through public broadcasting entities (as defined by section 118(g)): *Provided,* That copies or phonorecords of said programs are not commercially distributed by or through public broadcasting entities to the general public.

(c) This section does not limit or impair the exclusive right to perform publicly, by means of a phonorecord, any of the works specified by section 106(4).

(d) On January 3, 1978, the Register of Copyrights, after consulting with representatives of owners of copyrighted materials, representatives of the broadcasting, recording, motion picture, entertainment industries, and arts organizations, representatives of organized labor and performers of copyrighted materials, shall submit to the Congress a report setting forth recommendations as to whether this section should be amended to provide for performers and copyright owners of copyrighted material any performance rights in such material. The report should describe the status of such rights in foreign countries, the views of major interested parties, and specific legislative or other recommendations, if any.

§ 115. Scope of exclusive rights in nondramatic musical works: Compulsory license for making and distributing phonorecords

In the case of nondramatic musical works, the exclusive rights provided by clauses (1) and (3) of section 106, to make and to distribute phonorecords of such works, are subject to compulsory licensing under the conditions specified by this section.

(a) *Availability and Scope of Compulsory License*—

(1) When phonorecords of a nondramatic musical work have been distributed to the public in the United States under the authority of the copyright owner, any other person may, be complying with the provisions of this section, obtain a compulsory license to make and distribute phonorecords of the work. A person may obtain a compulsory license only if his or her primary purpose in making phonorecords is to distribute them to the public for private use. A person may not obtain a compulsory license for use of the work in the making of phonorecords duplicating a sound recording fixed by another, unless: (i) such sound recording was fixed lawfully; and (ii) the making of the phonorecords was authorized by the owner of copyright in the sound recording or, if the sound recording was fixed before February 15, 1972, by any person who fixed the sound recording pursuant to an express license from the owner of the copyright in the musical work or pursuant to a valid compulsory license for use of such work in a sound recording.

(2) A compulsory license includes the privilege of making a musical arrangement of the work to the extent necessary to conform it to the style or manner of interpretation of the performance

involved, but the arrangement shall not change the basic melody or fundamental character of the work, and shall not be subject to protection as a derivative work under this title, except with the express consent of the copyright owner.

(b) *Notice of Intention to Obtain Compulsory License*—

(1) Any person who wishes to obtain a compulsory license under this section shall, before or within thirty days after making, and before distributing any phonorecords of the work, serve notice of intention to do so on the copyright owner. If the registration or other public records of the Copyright Office do not identify the copyright owner and include an address at which notice can be served, it shall be sufficient to file the notice of intention in the Copyright Office. The notice shall comply, in form, content, and manner of service, with requirements that the Register of Copyrights shall prescribe by regulation.

(2) Failure to serve or file the notice required by clause (1) forecloses the possibility of a compulsory license and, in the absence of a negotiated license, renders the making and distribution of phonorecords actionable as acts of infringement under section 501 and fully subject to the remedies provided by sections 502 through 506 and 509.

(c) *Royalty Payable Under Compulsory License*—

(1) To be entitled to receive royalties under a compulsory license, the copyright owner must be identified in the registration or other public records of the Copyright Office. The owner is entitled to royalties for phonorecords made and distributed after being so identified, but is not entitled to recover for any phonorecords previously made and distributed.

(2) Except as provided by clause (1), the royalty under a compulsory license shall be payable for every phonorecord made and distributed in accordance with the license. For this purpose, a phonorecord is considered "distributed" if the person exercising the compulsory license has voluntarily and permanently parted with its possession. With respect to each work embodied in the phonorecord, the royalty shall be either two and three-fourths cents, or one-half of one cent per minute of playing time or fraction thereof, whichever amount is larger.

(3) Royalty payments shall be made on or before the twentieth day of each month and shall include all royalties for the month next preceding. Each monthly payment shall be made under oath

and shall comply with requirements that the Register of Copyrights shall prescribe by regulation. The Register shall also prescribe regulations under which detailed cumulative annual statements of account, certified by a certified public accountant, shall be filed for every compulsory license under this section. The regulations covering both the monthly and the annual statements of account shall prescribe the form, content, and manner of certification with respect to the number of records made and the number of records distributed.

(4) If the copyright owner does not receive the monthly payment and the monthly and annual statements of account when due, the owner may give written notice to the licensee that, unless the default is remedied within thirty days from the date of the notice, the compulsory license will be automatically terminated. Such termination renders either the making or the distribution, or both, of all phonorecords for which the royalty has not been paid, actionable as acts of infringement under section 501 and fully subject to the remedies provided by sections 502 through 506 and 509.

§ 116. Scope of exclusive rights in nondramatic musical works: Public performances by means of coin-operated phonorecord players

(a) *Limitation on Exclusive Right*—In the case of a nondramatic musical work embodied in a phonorecord, the exclusive right under clause (4) of section 106 to perform the work publicly by means of a coin-operated phonorecord player is limited as follows:

(1) The proprietor of the establishment in which the public performance takes place is not liable for infringement with respect to such public performance unless—

(A) such proprietor is the operator of the phonorecord player; or

(B) such proprietor refuses or fails, within one month after receipt by registered or certified mail of a request, at a time during which the certificate required by clause (1)(C) of subsection (b) is not affixed to the phonorecord player, by the copyright owner, to make full disclosure, by registered or certified mail, of the identity of the operator of the phonorecord player.

(2) The operator of the coin-operated phonorecord player may obtain a compulsory license to perform the work publicly on that

phonorecord player by filing the application, affixing the certificate, and paying the royalties provided by subsection (b).

(b) *Recordation of Coin-Operated Phonorecord Player, Affixation of Certificate, and Royalty Payable Under Compulsory License*—

(1) Any operator who wishes to obtain a compulsory license for the public performance of works on a coin-operated phonorecord player shall fulfill the following requirements:

(A) Before or within one month after such performances are made available on a particular phonorecord player, and during the month of January in each succeeding year that such performances are made available on that particular phonorecord player, the operator shall file in the Copyright Office, in accordance with requirements that the Register of Copyrights, after consultation with the Copyright Royalty Tribunal (if and when the Tribunal has been constituted), shall prescribe by regulation, an application containing the name and address of the operator of the phonorecord player and the manufacturer and serial number or other explicit identification of the phonorecord player, and deposit with the Register of Copyrights a royalty fee for the current calendar year of $8 for that particular phonorecord player. If such performances are made available on a particular phonorecord player for the first time after July 1 of any year, the royalty fee to be deposited for the remainder of that year shall be $4.

(B) Within twenty days of receipt of an application and a royalty fee pursuant to subclause (A), the Register of Copyrights shall issue to the applicant a certificate for the phonorecord player.

(C) On or before March 1 of the year in which the certificate prescribed by subclause (B) of this clause is issued, or within ten days after the date of issue of the certificate, the operator shall affix to the particular phonorecord player, in a position where it can be readily examined by the public, the certificate, issued by the Register of Copyrights under subclause (B), of the latest application made by such operator under subclause (A) of this clause with respect to that phonorecord player.

(2) Failure to file the application, to affix the certificate, or to pay the royalty required by clause (1) of this subsection renders the public performance actionable as an act of infringement under sec-

tion 501 and fully subject to the remedies provided by sections 502 through 506 and 509.

(c) *Distribution of Royalties*—

(1) The Register of Copyrights shall receive all fees deposited under this section and, after deducting the reasonable costs incurred by the Copyright Office under this section, shall deposit the balance in the Treasury of the United States, in such manner as the Secretary of the Treasury directs. All funds held by the Secretary of the Treasury shall be invested in interest-bearing United States securities for later distribution with interest by the Copyright Royalty Tribunal as provided by this title. The Register shall submit to the Copyright Royalty Tribunal, on an annual basis, a detailed statement of account covering all fees received for the relevant period provided by subsection (b).

(2) During the month of January in each year, every person claiming to be entitled to compulsory license fees under this section for performances during the preceding twelve-month period shall file a claim with the Copyright Royalty Tribunal, in accordance with requirements that the Tribunal shall prescribe by regulation. Such claim shall include an agreement to accept as final, except as provided in section 810 of this title, the determination of the Copyright Royalty Tribunal in any controversy concerning the distribution of royalty fees deposited under subclause (A) of subsection (b) (1) of this section to which the claimant is a party. Notwithstanding any provisions of the antitrust laws, for purposes of this subsection any claimants may agree among themselves as to the proportionate division of compulsory licensing fees among them, may lump their claims together and file them jointly or as a single claim, or may designate a common agent to receive payment on their behalf.

(3) After the first day of October of each year, the Copyright Royalty Tribunal shall determine whether there exists a controversy concerning the distribution of royalty fees deposited under subclause (A) of subsection (b) (1). If the Tribunal determines that no such controversy exists, it shall, after deducting its reasonable administrative costs under this section, distribute such fees to the copyright owners entitled, or to their designated agents. If it finds that such a controversy exists, it shall, pursuant to chapter 8 of this title, conduct a proceeding to determine the distribution of royalty fees.

(4) The fees to be distributed shall be divided as follows:

(A) to every copyright owner not affiliated with a performing rights society, the pro rata share of the fees to be distributed to which such copyright owner proves entitlement.

(B) to the performing rights societies, the remainder of the fees to be distributed in such pro rata shares as they shall by agreement stipulate among themselves, or, if they fail to agree, the pro rata share to which such performing rights societies prove entitlement.

(C) during the pendency of any proceeding under this section, the Copyright Royalty Tribunal shall withhold from distribution an amount sufficient to satisfy all claims with respect to which a controversy exists, but shall have discretion to proceed to distribute any amounts that are not in controversy.

(5) The Copyright Royalty Tribunal shall promulgate regulations under which persons who can reasonably be expected to have claims may, during the year in which performances take place, without expense to or harassment of operators or proprietors of establishments in which phonorecord players are located, have such access to such establishments and to the phonorecord players located therein and such opportunity to obtain information with respect thereto as may be reasonably necessary to determine, by sampling procedures or otherwise, the proportion of contribution of the musical works of each such person to the earnings of the phonorecord players for which fees shall have been deposited. Any person who alleges that he or she has been denied the access permitted under the regulations prescribed by the Copyright Royalty Tribunal may bring an action in the United States District Court for the District of Columbia for the cancellation of the compulsory license of the phonorecord player to which such access has been denied, and the court shall have the power to declare the compulsory license thereof invalid from the date of issue thereof.

(d) *Criminal Penalties*— Any person who knowingly makes a false representation of a material fact in an application filed under clause (1) (A) of subsection (b), or who knowingly alters a certificate issued under clause (1) (B) of subsection (b) or knowingly affixes such a certificate to a phonorecord player other than the one it covers, shall be fined not more than $2,500.

(e) *Definitions*—As used in this section, the following terms and their variant forms mean the following:

(1) A "coin-operated phonorecord player" is a machine or device that—

(A) is employed solely for the performance of nondramatic musical works by means of phonorecords upon being activated by insertion of coins, currency, tokens, or other monetary units or their equivalent;

(B) is located in an establishment making no direct or indirect charge for admission;

(C) is accompanied by a list of the titles of all the musical works available for performance on it, which list is affixed to the phonorecord player or posted in the establishment in a prominent position where it can be readily examined by the public; and

(D) affords a choice of works available for performance and permits the choice to be made by the patrons of the establishment in which it is located.

(2) An "operator" is any person who, alone or jointly with others:

(A) owns a coin-operated phonorecord player; or

(B) has the power to make a coin-operated phonorecord player available for placement in an establishment for purposes of public performance; or

(C) has the power to exercise primary control over the selection of the musical works made available for public performance on a coin-operated phonorecord player.

(3) A "performing rights society" is an association or corporation that licenses the public performance of nondramatic musical works on behalf of the copyright owners, such as the American Society of Composers, Authors and Publishers, Broadcast Music, Inc., and SESAC, Inc.

§ 117. Limitations on exclusive rights: Computer programs

Notwithstanding the provisions of section 106, it is not an infringement for the owner of a copy of a computer program to make or authorize the making of another copy or adaptation of that computer program provided:

(1) that such a new copy or adaptation is created as an essential step in the utilization of the computer program in conjunction with a machine and that it is used in no other manner, or

(2) that such new copy or adaptation is for archival purposes only and that all archival copies are destroyed in the event that

continued possession of the computer program should cease to be rightful.

Any exact copies prepared in accordance with the provisions of this section may be leased, sold, or otherwise transferred, along with the copy from which such copies were prepared, only as part of the lease, sale, or other transfer of all rights in the program. Adaptations so prepared may be transferred only with the authorization of the copyright owner. (Amended December 12, 1980, Public Law 96–517, sec. 10(b), 94 Stat. 3028.)

§ 118. **Scope of exclusive rights: Use of certain works in connection with noncommercial broadcasting**

(a) The exclusive rights provided by section 106 shall, with respect to the works specified by subsection (b) and the activities specified by subsection (d), be subject to the conditions and limitations prescribed by this section.

(b) Not later than thirty days after the Copyright Royalty Tribunal has been constituted in accordance with section 802, the Chairman of the Tribunal shall cause notice to be published in the Federal Register of the initiation of proceedings for the purpose of determining reasonable terms and rates of royalty payments for the activities specified by subsection (d) with respect to published nondramatic musical works and published pictorial, graphic, and sculptural work during a period beginning as provided in clause (3) of this subsection and ending on December 31, 1982. Copyright owners and public broadcasting entities shall negotiate in good faith and cooperate fully with the Tribunal in an effort to reach reasonable and expeditious results. Notwithstanding any provision of the antitrust laws, any owners of copyright in works specified by this subsection and any public broadcasting entities, respectively, may negotiate and agree upon the terms and rates of royalty payments and the proportionate division of fees paid among various copyright owners, and may designate common agents to negotiate, agree to, pay, or receive payments.

(1) Any owner of copyright in a work specified in this subsection or any public broadcasting entity may, within one hundred and twenty days after publication of the notice specified in this subsection, submit to the Copyright Royalty Tribunal proposed licenses covering such activities with respect to such works. The Copyright Royalty Tribunal shall proceed on the basis of the proposals submitted to it as well as any other relevant information. The Copyright Royalty Tribunal shall permit any interested party to submit information relevant to such proceedings.

150

(2) License agreements voluntarily negotiated at any time between one or more copyright owners and one or more public broadcasting entities shall be given effect in lieu of any determination by the Tribunal: *Provided,* That copies of such agreements are filed in the Copyright Office within thirty days of execution in accordance with regulations that the Register of Copyrights shall prescribe.

(3) Within six months, but not earlier than one hundred and twenty days, from the date of publication of the notice specified in this subsection the Copyright Royalty Tribunal shall make a determination and publish in the Federal Register a schedule of rates and terms which, subject to clause (2) of this subsection, shall be binding on all owners of copyright in works specified by this subsection and public broadcasting entities, regardless of whether or not such copyright owners and public broadcasting entities have submitted proposals to the Tribunal. In establishing such rates and terms the Copyright Royalty Tribunal may consider the rates for comparable circumstances under voluntary license agreements negotiated as provided in clause (2) of this subsection. The Copyright Royalty Tribunal shall also establish requirements by which copyright owners may receive reasonable notice of the use of their works under this section, and under which records of such use shall be kept by public broadcasting entities.

(4) With respect to the period beginning on the effective date of this title and ending on the date of publication of such rates and terms, this title shall not afford to owners of copyright or public broadcasting entities any greater or lesser rights with respect to the activities specified in subsection (d) as applied to works specified in this subsection than those afforded under the law in effect on December 31, 1977, as held applicable and construed by a court in an action brought under this title.

(c) The initial procedure specified in subsection (b) shall be repeated and concluded between June 30 and December 31, 1982, and at five-year intervals thereafter, in accordance with regulations that the Copyright Royalty Tribunal shall prescribe.

(d) Subject to the transitional provisions of subsection (b) (4), and to the terms of any voluntary license agreements that have been negotiated as provided by subsection (b) (2), a public broadcasting entity may, upon compliance with the provisions of this section, including the rates and terms established by the Copyright Royalty Tribunal under subsection (b) (3), engage in the following activities with respect to published nondramatic musical works and published pictorial, graphic, and sculptural works:

(1) performance or display of a work by or in the course of a transmission made by a noncommercial educational broadcast station referred to in subsection (g); and

(2) production of a transmission program, reproduction of copies or phonorecords of such a transmission program, and distribution of such copies or phonorecords, where such production, reproduction, or distribution is made by a nonprofit institution or organization solely for the purpose of transmissions specified in clause (1); and

(3) the making of reproductions by a governmental body or a nonprofit institution of a transmission program simultaneously with its transmission as specified in clause (1), and the performance or display of the contents of such program under the conditions specified by clause (1) of section 110, but only if the reproductions are used for performances or displays for a period of no more than seven days from the date of the transmission specified in clause (1), and are destroyed before or at the end of such period. No person supplying, in accordance with clause (2), a reproduction of a transmission program to governmental bodies or nonprofit institutions under this clause shall have any liability as a result of failure of such body or institution to destroy such reproduction: *Provided,* That it shall have notified such body or institution of the requirement for such destruction pursuant to this clause: *And provided further,* That if such body or institution itself fails to destroy such reproduction it shall be deemed to have infringed.

(e) Except as expressly provided in this subsection, this section shall have no applicability to works other than those specified in subsection (b).

(1) Owners of copyright in nondramatic literary works and public broadcasting entities may, during the course of voluntary negotiations, agree among themselves, respectively, as to the terms and rates of royalty payments without liability under the antitrust laws. Any such terms and rates of royalty payments shall be effective upon filing in the Copyright Office, in accordance with regulations that the Register of Copyrights shall prescribe.

(2) On January 3, 1980, the Register of Copyrights, after consulting with authors and other owners of copyright in nondramatic

literary works and their representatives, and with public broadcasting entities and their representatives, shall submit to the Congress a report setting forth the extent to which voluntary licensing arrangements have been reached with respect to the use of nondramatic literary works by such broadcast stations. The report should also describe any problems that may have arisen, and present legislative or other recommendations, if warranted.

(f) Nothing in this section shall be construed to permit, beyond the limits of fair use as provided by section 107, the unauthorized dramatization of a nondramatic musical work, the production of a transmission program drawn to any substantial extent from a published compilation of pictorial, graphic, or sculptural works, or the unauthorized use of any portion of an audiovisual work.

(g) As used in this section, the term "public broadcasting entity" means a noncommercial educational broadcast station as defined in section 397 of title 47 and any nonprofit institution or organization engaged in the activities described in clause (2) of subsection (d).

Chapter 2—Copyright Ownership and Transfer

Sec.
201. Ownership of copyright.
202. Ownership of copyright as distinct from ownership of material object.
203. Termination of transfers and licenses granted by the author.
204. Execution of transfers of copyright ownership.
205. Recordation of transfers and other documents.

§ 201.   Ownership of copyright

(a) *Initial Ownership*—Copyright in a work protected under this title vests initially in the author or authors of the work. The authors of a joint work are coowners of copyright in the work.

(b) *Works Made for Hire*—In the case of a work made for hire, the employer or other person for whom the work was prepared is considered the author for purposes of this title, and, unless the parties have expressly agreed otherwise in a written instrument signed by them, owns all of the rights comprised in the copyright.

(c) *Contributions to Collective Works*—Copyright in each separate contribution to a collective work is distinct from copyright in the collective work as a whole, and vests initially in the author of the contribution. In the absence of an express transfer of the copyright or of any rights under it, the owner of copyright in the collective work is presumed to have acquired only the privilege of reproducing and distributing the contribution as part of that particular collective work, any revision of that collective work, and any later collective work in the same series.

(d) *Transfer of Ownership—*

(1) The ownership of a copyright may be transferred in whole or in part by any means of conveyance or by operation of law, and may be bequeathed by will or pass as personal property by the applicable laws of intestate succession.

(2) Any of the exclusive rights comprised in a copyright, including any subdivision of any of the rights specified by section 106, may be transferred as provided by clause (1) and owned separately. The owner of any particular exclusive right is entitled, to the extent of that right, to all of the protection and remedies accorded to the copyright owner by this title.

(e) *Involuntary Transfer—*When an individual author's ownership of a copyright, or of any of the exclusive rights under a copyright, has not previously been transferred voluntarily by that individual author, no action by any governmental body or other official or organization purporting to seize, expropriate, transfer, or exercise rights of ownership with respect to the copyright, or any of the exclusive rights under a copyright, shall be given effect under this title, except as provided under title 11. (Amended November 6, 1978, Public Law 95–598, sec. 313, 92 Stat. 2676.)

§ 202. **Ownership of copyright as distinct from ownership of material object**

Ownership of a copyright, or of any of the exclusive rights under a copyright, is distinct from ownership of any material object in which the work is embodied. Transfer of ownership of any material object, including the copy or phonorecord in which the work is first fixed, does not of itself convey any rights in the copyrighted work embodied in the object; nor, in the absence of an agreement, does transfer of ownership of a copyright or of any exclusive rights under a copyright convey property rights in any material object.

§ 203. **Termination of transfers and licenses granted by the author**

(a) *Conditions for Termination—*In the case of any work other than a work made for hire, the exclusive or nonexclusive grant of a transfer or license of copyright or of any right under a copyright, executed by the author on or after January 1, 1978, otherwise than by will, is subject to termination under the following conditions:

(1) In the case of a grant executed by one author, termination of the grant may be effected by that author or, if the author is dead, by the person or persons who, under clause (2) of this subsection, own and are entitled to exercise a total of more than one-half of that author's termination interest. In the case of a grant executed by two or more authors of a joint work, termination of the grant may be effected by a majority of the authors who executed it; if any of such authors is dead, the termination interest of any such author may be exercised as a unit by the person or persons who, under clause (2) of this subsection, own and are entitled to exercise a total of more than one-half of that author's interest.

(2) Where an author is dead, his or her termination interest is owned, and may be exercised, by his widow or her widower and his or her children or grandchildren as follows:

(A) the widow or widower owns the author's entire termination interest unless there are any surviving children or grandchildren of the author, in which case the widow or widower owns one-half of the author's interest;

(B) the author's surviving children, and the surviving children of any dead child of the author, own the author's entire termination interest unless there is a widow or widower, in which case the ownership of one-half of the author's interest is divided among them;

(C) the rights of the author's children and grandchildren are in all cases divided among them and exercised on a per stirpes basis according to the number of such author's children represented; the share of the children of a dead child in a termination interest can be exercised only by the action of a majority of them.

(3) Termination of the grant may be effected at any time during a period of five years beginning at the end of thirty-five years from the date of execution of the grant; or, if the grant covers the right of publication of the work, the period begins at the end of thirty-five years from the date of publication of the work under the grant or at the end of forty years from the date of execution of the grant, whichever term ends earlier.

(4) The termination shall be effected by serving an advance notice in writing, signed by the number and proportion of owners of termination interests required under clauses (1) and (2) of this

subsection, or by their duly authorized agents, upon the grantee or the grantee's successor in title.

(A) The notice shall state the effective date of the termination, which shall fall within the five-year period specified by clause (3) of this subsection, and the notice shall be served not less than two or more than ten years before that date. A copy of the notice shall be recorded in the Copyright Office before the effective date of termination, as a condition to its taking effect.

(B) The notice shall comply, in form, content, and manner of service, with requirements that the Register of Copyrights shall prescribe by regulation.

(5) Termination of the grant may be effected notwithstanding any agreement to the contrary, including an agreement to make a will or to make any future grant.

(b) *Effect of Termination*—Upon the effective date of termination, all rights under this title that were covered by the terminated grants revert to the author, authors, and other persons owning termination interests under clauses (1) and (2) of subsection (a), including those owners who did not join in signing the notice of termination under clause (4) of subsection (a), but with the following limitations:

(1) A derivative work prepared under authority of the grant before its termination may continue to be utilized under the terms of the grant after its termination, but this privilege does not extend to the preparation after the termination of other derivative works based upon the copyrighted work covered by the terminated grant.

(2) The future rights that will revert upon termination of the grant become vested on the date the notice of termination has been served as provided by clause (4) of subsection (a). The rights vest in the author, authors, and other persons named in, and in the proportionate shares provided by, clauses (1) and (2) of subsection (a).

(3) Subject to the provisions of clause (4) of this subsection, a further grant, or agreement to make a further grant, of any right covered by a terminated grant is valid only if it is signed by the same number and proportion of the owners, in whom the right has vested under clause (2) of this subsection, as are required to terminate the grant under clauses (1) and (2) of subsection (a). Such further grant or agreement is effective with respect to all of the persons in whom the right it covers has vested under clause (2) of this subsection, including those who did not join in signing it. If

156

any person dies after rights under a terminated grant have vested in him or her, that person's legal representatives, legatees, or heirs at law represent him or her for purposes of this clause.

(4) A further grant, or agreement to make a further grant, of any right covered by a terminated grant is valid only if it is made after the effective date of the termination. As an exception, however, an agreement for such a further grant may be made between the persons provided by clause (3) of this subsection and the original grantee or such grantee's successor in title, after the notice of termination has been served as provided by clause (4) of subsection (a).

(5) Termination of a grant under this section affects only those rights covered by the grants that arise under this title, and in no way affects rights arising under any other Federal, State, or foreign laws.

(6) Unless and until termination is effected under this section, the grant, if it does not provide otherwise, continues in effect for the term of copyright provided by this title.

§ 204. Execution of transfers of copyright ownership

(a) A transfer of copyright ownership, other than by operation of law, is not valid unless an instrument of conveyance, or a note or memorandum of the transfer, is in writing and signed by the owner of the rights conveyed or such owner's duly authorized agent.

(b) A certificate of acknowledgement is not required for the validity of a transfer, but is prima facie evidence of the execution of the transfer if—

(1) in the case of a transfer executed in the United States, the certificate is issued by a person authorized to administer oaths within the United States; or

(2) in the case of a transfer executed in a foreign country, the certificate is issued by a diplomatic or consular officer of the United States, or by a person authorized to administer oaths whose authority is proved by a certificate of such an officer.

§ 205. Recordation of transfers and other documents

(a) *Conditions for Recordation*—Any transfer of copyright ownership or other document pertaining to a copyright may be recorded in the Copyright Office if the document filed for recordation bears the actual signature of the person who executed it, or if it is accompanied by a sworn or official certification that it is a true copy of the original, signed document.

(b) *Certificate of Recordation*—The Register of Copyrights shall, upon receipt of a document as provided by subsection (a) and of the fee provided by section 708, record the document and return it with a certificate of recordation.

(c) *Recordation as Constructive Notice*—Recordation of a document in the Copyright Office gives all persons constructive notice of the facts stated in the recorded document, but only if—

(1) the document, or material attached to it, specifically identifies the work to which it pertains so that, after the document is indexed by the Register of Copyrights, it would be revealed by a reasonable search under the title or registration number of the work; and

(2) registration has been made for the work.

(d) *Recordation as Prerequisite to Infringement Suit*—No person claiming by virtue of a transfer to be the owner of copyright or of any exclusive right under a copyright is entitled to institute an infringement action under this title until the instrument of transfer under which such person claims has been recorded in the Copyright Office, but suit may be instituted after such recordation on a cause of action that arose before recordation.

(e) *Priority Between Conflicting Transfers*—As between two conflicting transfers, the one executed first prevails if it is recorded, in the manner required to give constructive notice under subsection (c), within one month after its execution in the United States or within two months after its execution outside the United States, or at any time before recordation in such manner of the later transfer. Otherwise the later transfer prevails if recorded first in such manner, and if taken in good faith, for valuable consideration or on the basis of a binding promise to pay royalties, and without notice of the earlier transfer.

(f) *Priority Between Conflicting Transfer of Ownership and Nonexclusive License*—A nonexclusive license, whether recorded or not, prevails over a conflicting transfer of copyright ownership if the license is evidenced by a written instrument signed by the owner of the rights licensed or such owner's duly authorized agent, and if—

(1) the license was taken before execution of the transfer; or

(2) the license was taken in good faith before recordation of the transfer and without notice of it.

CHAPTER 3—DURATION OF COPYRIGHT

SEC.
301. Preemption with respect to other laws.
302. Duration of copyright: Works created on or after January 1, 1978.
303. Duration of copyright: Works created but not published or copyrighted before January 1, 1978.
304. Duration of copyright: Subsisting copyrights.
305. Duration of copyright: Terminal date.

§ 301. Preemption with respect to other laws

(a) On and after January 1, 1978, all legal or equitable rights that are equivalent to any of the exclusive rights within the general scope of copyright as specified by section 106 in works of authorship that are fixed in a tangible medium of expression and come within the subject matter of copyright as specified by sections 102 and 103, whether created before or after that date and whether published or unpublished, are governed exclusively by this title. Thereafter, no person is entitled to any such right or equivalent right in any such work under the common law or statutes of any State.

(b) Nothing in this title annuls or limits any rights or remedies under the common law or statutes of any State with respect to—

(1) subject matter that does not come within the subject matter of copyright as specified by sections 102 and 103, including works of authorship not fixed in any tangible medium of expression; or

(2) any cause of action arising from undertakings commenced before January 1, 1978; or

(3) activities violating legal or equitable rights that are not equivalent to any of the exclusive rights within the general scope of copyright as specified by section 106.

(c) With respect to sound recordings fixed before February 15, 1972, any rights or remedies under the common law or statutes of any State shall not be annulled or limited by this title until February 15, 2047. The preemptive provisions of subsection (a) shall apply to any such rights and remedies pertaining to any cause of action arising from undertakings commenced on and after February 15, 2047. Notwithstanding the provisions of section 303, no sound recording fixed before February 15, 1972, shall be subject to copyright under this title before, on, or after February 15, 2047.

(d) Nothing in this title annuls or limits any rights or remedies under any other Federal statute.

§ 302. Duration of copyright: Works created on or after January 1, 1978

(a) *In General*—Copyright in a work created on or after January 1, 1978, subsists from its creation and, except as provided by the following subsections, endures for a term consisting of the life of the author and fifty years after the author's death.

(b) *Joint Works*—In the case of a joint work prepared by two or more authors who did not work for hire, the copyright endures for a term consisting of the life of the last surviving author and fifty years after such last surviving author's death.

(c) *Anonymous Works, Pseudonymous Works, and Works Made for Hire*—In the case of an anonymous work, a pseudonymous work, or a work made for hire, the copyright endures for a term of seventy-five years from the year of its first publication, or a term of one hundred years from the year of its creation, whichever expires first. If, before the end of such term, the identity of one or more of the authors of an anonymous or pseudonymous work is revealed in the records of a registration made for that work under subsections (a) or (d) of section 408, or in the records provided by this subsection, the copyright in the work endures for the term specified by subsection (a) or (b), based on the life of the author or authors whose identity has been revealed. Any person having an interest in the copyright in an anonymous or pseudonymous work may at any time record, in records to be maintained by the Copyright Office for that purpose, a statement identifying one or more authors of the work; the statement shall also identify the person filing it, the nature of that person's interest, the source of the information recorded, and the particular work affected, and shall comply in form and content with requirements that the Register of Copyrights shall prescribe by regulation.

(d) *Records Relating to Death of Authors*—Any person having an interest in a copyright may at any time record in the Copyright Office a statement of the date of death of the author of the copyrighted work, or a statement that the author is still living on a particular date. The statement shall identify the person filing it, the nature of that person's interest, and the source of the information recorded, and shall comply in form and content with requirements that the Register of Copyrights shall prescribe by regulation. The Register shall maintain current records of information relating to the death of authors of copyrighted works, based on such recorded statements and, to the extent the Register considers practicable, on data contained in any of the records of the Copyright Office or in other reference sources.

(e) *Presumption as to Author's Death*—After a period of seventy-five years from the year of first publication of a work, or a period of one hundred years from the year of its creation, whichever expires first, any person who obtains from the Copyright Office a certified report that the records provided by subsection (d) disclose nothing to indicate that the author of the work is living, or died less than fifty years before, is entitled to the benefit of a presumption that the author has been dead for at least fifty years. Reliance in good faith upon this presumption shall be a complete defense to any action for infringement under this title.

§ 303. Duration of copyright: Works created but not published or copyrighted before January 1, 1978

Copyright in a work created before January 1, 1978, but not theretofore in the public domain or copyrighted, subsists from January 1, 1978, and endures for the term provided by section 302. In no case, however, shall the term of copyright in such a work expire before December 31, 2002; and, if the work is published on or before December 31, 2002, the term of copyright shall not expire before December 31, 2027.

§ 304. Duration of copyright: Subsisting copyrights

(a) *Copyrights in Their First Term on January 1, 1978*—Any copyright, the first term of which is subsisting on January 1, 1978, shall endure for twenty-eight years from the date it was originally secured: *Provided,* That in the case of any posthumous work or of any periodical, cyclopedic, or other composite work upon which the copyright was originally secured by the proprietor thereof, or of any work copyrighted by a corporate body (otherwise than as assignee or licensee of the individual author) or by an employer for whom such work is made for hire, the proprietor of such copyright shall be entitled to a renewal and extension of the copyright in such work for the further term of forty-seven years when application for such renewal and extension shall have been made to the Copyright Office and duly registered therein within one year prior to the expiration of the original term of copyright: *And provided further,* That in the case of any other copyrighted work, including a contribution by an individual author to a periodical or to a cyclopedic or other composite work, the author of such work, if still living, or the widow, widower, or children of the author, if the author be not living, or if such author, widow, widower, or children be not living, then the author's executors, or in the absence of a will, his or her next of kin shall be entitled to a renewal and extension of the copyright in such work for a further term of forty-seven years when application for such renewal and extension shall have been made to the Copyright Office and duly registered therein within one year prior to the expiration of the original term of copyright: *And provided further,* That in default of the registration of such application for renewal and extension, the copyright in any work shall terminate at the expiration of twenty-eight years from the date copyright was originally secured.

(b) *Copyrights in Their Renewal Term or Registered for Renewal Before January 1, 1978*—The duration of any copyright, the renewal term of which is subsisting at any time between December 31, 1976, and December 31, 1977, inclusive, or for which renewal registration is made between December 31, 1976, and December 31, 1977, inclusive, is extended to endure for a term of seventy-five years from the date copyright was originally secured.

(c) *Termination of Transfers and Licenses Covering Extended Renewal Term*—In the case of any copyright subsisting in either its first or renewal term on January 1, 1978, other than a copyright in a work made for hire, the exclusive or nonexclusive grant of a transfer or license of the renewal copyright or any right under it, executed before January 1, 1978, by any of the persons designated by the second proviso of subsection (a) of this section, otherwise than by will, is subject to termination under the following conditions:

(1) In the case of a grant executed by a person or persons other than the author, termination of the grant may be effected by the surviving person or persons who executed it. In the case of a grant executed by one or more of the authors of the work, termination of the grant may be effected, to the extent of a particular author's share in the ownership of the renewal copyright, by the author who executed it or, if such author is dead, by the person or persons who, under clause (2) of this subsection, own and are entitled to exercise a total of more than one-half of that author's termination interest.

(2) Where an author is dead, his or her termination interest is owned, and may be exercised, by his widow or her widower and his or her children or grandchildren as follows:

162

(A) the widow or widower owns the author's entire termination interest unless there are any surviving children or grandchildren of the author, in which case the widow or widower owns one-half of the author's interest;

(B) the author's surviving children, and the surviving children of any dead child of the author, own the author's entire termination interest unless there is a widow or widower, in which case the ownership of one-half of the author's interest is divided among them;

(C) the rights of the author's children and grandchildren are in all cases divided among them and exercised on a per stirpes basis according to the number of such author's children represented; the share of the children of a dead child in a termination interest can be exercised only by the action of a majority of them.

(3) Termination of the grant may be effected at any time during a period of five years beginning at the end of fifty-six years from the date copyright was originally secured, or beginning on January 1, 1978, whichever is later.

(4) The termination shall be effected by serving an advance notice in writing upon the grantee or the grantee's successor in title. In the case of a grant executed by a person or persons other than the author, the notice shall be signed by all of those entitled to terminate the grant under clause (1) of this subsection, or by their duly authorized agents. In the case of a grant executed by one or more of the authors of the work, the notice as to any one author's share shall be signed by that author or his or her duly authorized agent or, if that author is dead, by the number and proportion of the owners of his or her termination interest required under clauses (1) and (2) of this subsection, or by their duly authorized agents.

(A) The notice shall state the effective date of the termination, which shall fall within the five-year period specified by clause (3) of this subsection, and the notice shall be served not less than two or more than ten years before that date. A copy of the notice shall be recorded in the Copyright Office before the effective date of termination, as a condition to its taking effect.

(B) The notice shall comply, in form, content, and manner of service, with requirements that the Register of Copyrights shall prescribe by regulation.

(5) Termination of the grant may be effected notwithstanding any agreement to the contrary, including an agreement to make a will or to make any future grant.

(6) In the case of a grant executed by a person or persons other than the author, all rights under this title that were covered by the terminated grant revert, upon the effective date of termination, to all of those entitled to terminate the grant under clause (1) of this subsection. In the case of a grant executed by one or more of the authors of the work, all of a particular author's rights under this title that were covered by the terminated grant revert, upon the effective date of termination, to that author or, if that author is dead, to the persons owning his or her termination interest under clause (2) of this subsection, including those owners who did not join in signing the notice of termination under clause (4) of this subsection. In all cases the reversion of rights is subject to the following limitations:

(A) A derivative work prepared under authority of the grant before its termination may continue to be utilized under the terms of the grant after its termination, but this privilege does not extend to the preparation after the termination of other derivative works based upon the copyrighted work covered by the terminated grant.

(B) The future rights that will revert upon termination of the grant become vested on the date the notice of termination has been served as provided by clause (4) of this subsection.

(C) Where the author's rights revert to two or more persons under clause (2) of this subsection, they shall vest in those persons in the proportionate shares provided by that clause. In such a case, and subject to the provisions of subclause (D) of this clause, a further grant, or agreement to make a further grant, of a particular author's share with respect to any right covered by a terminated grant is valid only if it is signed by the same number and proportion of the owners, in whom the right has vested under this clause, as are required to terminate the grant under clause (2) of this subsection. Such further grant or agreement is effective with respect to all of the persons in whom the right it covers has vested under this subclause, including those who did not join in signing it. If any person dies after rights under a terminated grant have vested in him or her, that person's legal

164

representatives, legatees, or heirs at law represent him or her for purposes of this subclause.

(D) A further grant, or agreement to make a further grant, of any right covered by a terminated grant is valid only if it is made after the effective date of the termination. As an exception, however, an agreement for such a further grant may be made between the author or any of the persons provided by the first sentence of clause (6) of this subsection, or between the persons provided by subclause (C) of this clause, and the original grantee or such grantee's successor in title, after the notice of termination has been served as provided by clause (4) of this subsection.

(E) Termination of a grant under this subsection affects only those rights covered by the grant that arise under this title, and in no way affects rights arising under any other Federal, State, or foreign laws.

(F) Unless and until termination is effected under this subsection, the grant, if it does not provide otherwise, continues in effect for the remainder of the extended renewal term.

§ 305. Duration of copyright: Terminal date

All terms of copyright provided by sections 302 through 304 run to the end of the calendar year in which they would otherwise expire.

CHAPTER 4—COPYRIGHT NOTICE, DEPOSIT, AND REGISTRATION

Sec.
401. Notice of copyright: Visually perceptible copies.
402. Notice of copyright: Phonorecords of sound recordings.
403. Notice of copyright: Publications incorporating United States Government works.
404. Notice of copyright: Contributions to collective works.
405. Notice of copyright: Omission of notice.
406. Notice of copyright: Error in name or date.
407. Deposit of copies or phonorecords for Library of Congress.
408. Copyright registration in general.
409. Application for copyright registration.
410. Registration of claim and issuance of certificate.
411. Registration as prerequisite to infringement suit.
412. Registration as prerequisite to certain remedies for infringement.

§ 401.   Notice of copyright: Visually perceptible copies

(a) *General Requirement*—Whenever a work protected under this title is published in the United States or elsewhere by authority of the copyright owner, a notice of copyright as provided by this section shall be placed on all publicly distributed copies from which the work can be visually perceived, either directly or with the aid of a machine or device.

(b) *Form of Notice*—The notice appearing on the copies shall consist of the following three elements:

(1) the symbol © (the letter C in a circle), or the word "Copyright", or the abbreviation "Copr."; and

(2) the year of first publication of the work; in the case of compilations or derivative works incorporating previously published material, the year date of first publication of the compilation or derivative work is sufficient. The year date may be omitted where a pictorial, graphic, or sculptural work, with accompanying text matter, if any, is reproduced in or on greeting cards, postcards, stationery, jewelry, dolls, toys, or any useful articles; and

(3) the name of the owner of copyright in the work, or an abbreviation by which the name can be recognized, or a generally known alternative designation of the owner.

(c) *Position of Notice*—The notice shall be affixed to the copies in such manner and location as to give reasonable notice of the claim of copyright. The Register of Copyrights shall prescribe by regulation, as examples, specific methods of affixation and positions of the notice on various types of works that will satisfy this requirement, but these specifications shall not be considered exhaustive.

§ 402.   Notice of copyright: Phonorecords of sound recordings

(a) *General Requirement*—Whenever a sound recording protected under this title is published in the United States or elsewhere by authority of the copyright owner, a notice of copyright as provided by this section shall be placed on all publicly distributed phonorecords of the sound recording.

(b) *Form of Notice*—The notice appearing on the phonorecords shall consist of the following three elements:

(1) the symbol ℗ (the letter P in a circle); and

(2) the year of first publication of the sound recording; and

(3) the name of the owner of copyright in the sound recording, or an abbreviation by which the name can be recognized, or a generally known alternative designation of the owner; if the producer of the sound recording is named on the phonorecord labels or containers, and if no other name appears in conjunction with the notice, the producer's name shall be considered a part of the notice.

(c) *Position of Notice*—The notice shall be placed on the surface of the phonorecord, or on the phonorecord label or container, in such manner and location as to give reasonable notice of the claim of copyright.

§ 403. Notice of copyright: Publications incorporating United States Government works

Whenever a work is published in copies or phonorecords consisting preponderantly of one or more works of the United States Government, the notice of copyright provided by sections 401 or 402 shall also include a statement identifying, either affirmatively or negatively, those portions of the copies or phonorecords embodying any work or works protected under this title.

§ 404. Notice of copyright: Contributions to collective works

(a) A separate contribution to a collective work may bear its own notice of copyright, as provided by sections 401 through 403. However, a single notice applicable to the collective work as a whole is sufficient to satisfy the requirements of sections 401 through 403 with respect to the separate contributions it contains (not including advertisements inserted on behalf of persons other than the owner of copyright in the collective work), regardless of the ownership of copyright in the contributions and whether or not they have been previously published.

(b) Where the person named in a single notice applicable to a collective work as a whole is not the owner of copyright in a separate contribution that does not bear its own notice, the case is governed by the provisions of section 406(a).

§ 405. Notice of copyright: Omission of notice

(a) *Effect of Omission on Copyright*—The omission of the copyright notice prescribed by sections 401 through 403 from copies or phonorecords publicly distributed by authority of the copyright owner does not invalidate the copyright in a work if—

(1) the notice has been omitted from no more than a relatively small number of copies or phonorecords distributed to the public; or

(2) registration for the work has been made before or is made within five years after the publication without notice, and a reasonable effort is made to add notice to all copies or phonorecords that are distributed to the public in the United States after the omission has been discovered; or

(3) the notice has been omitted in violation of an express requirement in writing that, as a condition of the copyright owner's authorization of the public distribution of copies or phonorecords, they bear the prescribed notice.

(b) *Effect of Omission on Innocent Infringers*—Any person who innocently infringes a copyright, in reliance upon an authorized copy or phonorecord from which the copyright notice has been omitted, incurs no liability for actual or statutory damages under section 504 for any infringing acts committed before receiving actual notice that registration for the work has been made under section 408, if such person proves that he or she was misled by the omission of notice. In a suit for infringement in such a case the court may allow or disallow recovery of any of the infringer's profits attributable to the infringement, and may enjoin the continuation of the infringing undertaking or may require, as a condition or permitting the continuation of the infringing undertaking, that the infringer pay the copyright owner a reasonable license fee in an amount and on terms fixed by the court.

(c) *Removal of Notice*—Protection under this title is not affected by the removal, destruction, or obliteration of the notice, without the authorization of the copyright owner, from any publicly distributed copies or phonorecords.

§ 406. Notice of copyright: Error in name or date

(a) *Error in Name*—Where the person named in the copyright notice on copies or phonorecords publicly distributed by authority of the copyright owner is not the owner of copyright, the validity and ownership of the copyright are not affected. In such a case, however, any person who innocently begins an undertaking that infringes the copyright has a complete defense to any action for such infringement if such person proves that he or she was misled by the notice and began the undertaking in good faith under a purported transfer or license from the person named therein, unless before the undertaking was begun—

(1) registration for the work had been made in the name of the owner of copyright; or

(2) a document executed by the person named in the notice and showing the ownership of the copyright had been recorded. The person named in the notice is liable to account to the copyright owner for all receipts from transfers or licenses purportedly made under the copyright by the person named in the notice.

(b) *Error in Date*—When the year date in the notice on copies or phonorecords distributed by authority of the copyright owner is earlier than the year in which publication first occurred, any period computed from the year of first publication under section 302 is to be computed from the year in the notice. Where the year date is more than one year later than the year in which publication first occurred, the work is considered to have been published without any notice and is governed by the provisions of section 405.

(c) *Omission of Name or Date*—Where copies or phonorecords publicly distributed by authority of the copyright owner contain no name or no date that could reasonably be considered a part of the notice, the work is considered to have been published without any notice and is governed by the provisions of section 405.

§ 407. Deposit of copies or phonorecords for Library of Congress

(a) Except as provided by subsection (c), and subject to the provisions of subsection (e), the owner of copyright or of the exclusive right of publication in a work published with notice of copyright in the United States shall deposit, within three months after the date of such publication—

(1) two complete copies of the best edition; or

(2) if the work is a sound recording, two complete phonorecords of the best edition, together with any printed or other visually perceptible material published with such phonorecords.

Neither the deposit requirements of this subsection nor the acquisition provisions of subsection (e) are conditions of copyright protection.

(b) The required copies or phonorecords shall be deposited in the Copyright Office for the use or disposition of the Library of Congress. The Register of Copyrights shall, when requested by the depositor and upon payment of the fee prescribed by section 708, issue a receipt for the deposit.

(c) The Register of Copyrights may by regulation exempt any categories of material from the deposit requirements of this section, or require deposit of only one copy or phonorecord with respect to any categories. Such regulations shall provide either for complete exemption from the deposit requirements of this section, or for alternative forms of deposit aimed at providing a satisfactory archival record of a work without imposing practical or financial hardships on the depositor, where the individual author is the owner of copyright in a pictorial, graphic, or sculptural work and (i) less than five copies of the work have been published, or (ii) the work has been published in a limited edition consisting of numbered copies, the monetary value of which would make the mandatory deposit of two copies of the best edition of the work burdensome, unfair, or unreasonable.

(d) At any time after publication of a work as provided by subsection (a), the Register of Copyrights may make written demand for the required deposit on any of the persons obligated to make the deposit under subsection (a). Unless deposit is made within three months after the demand is received, the person or persons on whom the demand was made are liable—

(1) to a fine of not more than $250 for each work; and

(2) to pay into a specially designated fund in the Library of Congress the total retail price of the copies or phonorecords demanded, or, if no retail price has been fixed, the reasonable cost of the Library of Congress of acquiring them; and

(3) to pay a fine of $2,500, in addition to any fine or liability imposed under clauses (1) and (2), if such person willfully or repeatedly fails or refuses to comply with such a demand.

(e) With respect to transmission programs that have been fixed and transmitted to the public in the United States but have not been published, the Register of Copyrights shall, after consulting with the Librarian of Congress and other interested organizations and officials, establish regulations governing the acquisition, through deposit or otherwise, of copies or phonorecords of such programs for the collections of the Library of Congress.

(1) The Librarian of Congress shall be permitted, under the standards and conditions set forth in such regulations, to make a fixation of a transmission program directly from a transmission to

170

the public, and to reproduce one copy or phonorecord from such fixation for archival purposes.

(2) Such regulations shall also provide standards and procedures by which the Register of Copyrights may make written demand, upon the owner of the right of transmission in the United States, for the deposit of a copy or phonorecord of a specific transmission program. Such deposit may, at the option of the owner of the right of transmission in the United States, be accomplished by gift, by loan for purposes of reproduction, or by sale at a price not to exceed the cost of reproducing and supplying the copy or phono-record. The regulations established under this clause shall provide reasonable periods of not less than three months for compliance with a demand, and shall allow for extensions of such periods and adjustments in the scope of the demand or the methods for fulfilling it, as reasonably warranted by the circumstances. Willful failure or refusal to comply with the conditions prescribed by such regulations shall subject the owner of the right of transmission in the United States to liability for an amount, not to exceed the cost of reproducing and supplying the copy or phonorecord in question, to be paid into a specially designated fund in the Library of Congress.

(3) Nothing in this subsection shall be construed to require the making or retention, for purposes of deposit, of any copy or phonorecord of an unpublished transmission program, the transmission of which occurs before the receipt of a specific written demand as provided by clause (2).

(4) No activity undertaken in compliance with regulations prescribed under clauses (1) or (2) of this subsection shall result in liability if intended solely to assist in the acquisition of copies or phonorecords under this subsection.

§ 408.   Copyright registration in general

(a) *Registration Permissive*—At any time during the subsistence of copyright in any published or unpublished work, the owner of copyright or of any exclusive right in the work may obtain registration of the copyright claim by delivering to the Copyright Office the deposit specified by this section, together with the application and fee specified by sections 409 and 708. Subject to the provisions of section 405(a), such registration is not a condition of copyright protection.

(b) *Deposit for Copyright Registration*—Except as provided by subsection (c), the material deposited for registration shall include—

(1) in the case of an unpublished work, one complete copy or phonorecord;

(2) in the case of a published work, two complete copies or phonorecords of the best edition;

(3) in the case of a work first published outside the United States, one complete copy or phonorecord as so published;

(4) in the case of a contribution to a collective work, one complete copy or phonorecord of the best edition of the collective work.

Copies or phonorecords deposited for the Library of Congress under section 407 may be used to satisfy the deposit provisions of this section, if they are accompanied by the prescribed application and fee, and by any additional identifying material that the Register may, by regulation, require. The Register shall also prescribe regulations establishing requirements under which copies or phonorecords acquired for the Library of Congress under subsection (e) of section 407, otherwise than by deposit, may be used to satisfy the deposit provisions of this section.

(c) *Administrative Classification and Optional Deposit*—

(1) The Register of Copyrights is authorized to specify by regulation the administrative classes into which works are to be placed for purposes of deposit and registration, and the nature of the copies or phonorecords to be deposited in the various classes specified. The regulations may require or permit, for particular classes, the deposit of identifying material instead of copies or phonorecords, the deposit of only one copy or phonorecord where two would normally be required, or a single registration for a group of related works. This administrative classification of works has no significance with respect to the subject matter of copyright or the exclusive rights provided by this title.

(2) Without prejudice to the general authority provided under clause (1), the Register of Copyrights shall establish regulations specifically permitting a single registration for a group of works by the same individual author, all first published as contributions to periodicals, including newspapers, within a twelve-month period, on the basis of a single deposit application, and registration fee, under all of the following conditions—

172

(A) if each of the works as first published bore a separate copyright notice, and the name of the owner of copyright in the work, or an abbreviation by which the name can be recognized, or a generally known alternative designation of the owner was the same in each notice; and

(B) if the deposit consists of one copy of the entire issue of the periodical, or of the entire section in the case of a newspaper, in which each contribution was first published; and

(C) if the application identifies each work separately, including the periodical containing it and its date of first publication.

(3) As an alternative to separate renewal registrations under subsection (a) of section 304, a single renewal registration may be made for a group of works by the same individual author, all first published as contributions to periodicals, including newspapers, upon the filing of a single application and fee, under all of the following conditions:

(A) the renewal claimant or claimants, and the basis of claim or claims under section 304(a), is the same for each of the works; and

(B) the works were all copyrighted upon their first publication, either through separate copyright notice and registration or by virtue of a general copyright notice in the periodical issue as a whole; and

(C) the renewal application and fee are received not more than twenty-eight or less than twenty-seven years after the thirty-first day of December of the calendar year in which all of the works were first published; and

(D) the renewal application identifies each work separately, including the periodical containing it and its date of first publication.

(d) *Corrections and Amplifications*—The Register may also establish, by regulation, formal procedures for the filing of an application for supplementary registration, to correct an error in a copyright registration or to amplify the information given in a registration. Such application shall be accompanied by the fee provided by section 708, and shall clearly identify the registration to be corrected or amplified. The information contained in a supplementary registration augments but does not supersede that contained in the earlier registration.

173

(e) *Published Edition of Previously Registered Work*—Registration for the first published edition of a work previously registered in unpublished form may be made even though the work as published is substantially the same as the unpublished version.

§ 409. Application for copyright registration

The application for copyright registration shall be made on a form prescribed by the Register of Copyrights and shall include—

(1) the name and address of the copyright claimant;

(2) in the case of a work other than an anonymous or pseudonymous work, the name and nationality or domicile of the author or authors, and, if one or more of the authors is dead, the dates of their deaths;

(3) if the work is anonymous or pseudonymous, the nationality or domicile of the author or authors;

(4) in the case of a work made for hire, a statement to this effect;

(5) if the copyright claimant is not the author, a brief statement of how the claimant obtained ownership of the copyright;

(6) the title of the work, together with any previous or alternative titles under which the work can be identified;

(7) the year in which creation of the work was completed;

(8) if the work has been published, the date and nation of its first publication;

(9) in the case of a compilation or derivative work, an identification of any preexisting work or works that it is based on or incorporates, and a brief, general statement of the additional material covered by the copyright claim being registered;

(10) in the case of a published work containing material of which copies are required by section 601 to be manufactured in the United States, the names of the persons or organizations who performed the processes specified by subsection (c) of section 601 with respect to that material, and the places where those processes were performed; and

(11) any other information regarded by the Register of Copyrights as bearing upon the preparation or identification of the work or the existence, ownership, or duration of the copyright.

§ 410.   Registration of claim and issuance of certificate

(a) When, after examination, the Register of Copyrights determines that, in accordance with the provisions of this title, the material deposited constitutes copyrightable subject matter and that the other legal and formal requirements of this title have been met, the Register shall register the claim and issue to the applicant a certificate of registration under the seal of the Copyright Office. The certificate shall contain the information given in the application, together with the number and effective date of the registration.

(b) In any case in which the Register of Copyrights determines that, in accordance with the provisions of this title, the material deposited does not constitute copyrightable subject matter or that the claim is invalid for any other reason, the Register shall refuse registration and shall notify the applicant in writing of the reasons for such refusal.

(c) In any judicial proceedings the certificate of a registration made before or within five years after first publication of the work shall constitute prima facie evidence of the validity of the copyright and of the facts stated in the certificate. The evidentiary weight to be accorded the certificate of a registration made thereafter shall be within the discretion of the court.

(d) The effective date of a copyright registration is the day on which an application, deposit, and fee, which are later determined by the Register of Copyrights or by a court of competent jurisdiction to be acceptable for registration, have all been received in the Copyright Office.

§ 411.   Registration as prerequisite to infringement suit

(a) Subject to the provisions of subsection (b), no action for infringement of the copyright in any work shall be instituted until registration of the copyright claim has been made in accordance with this title. In any case, however, where the deposit, application, and fee required for registration have been delivered to the Copyright Office in proper form and registration has been refused, the applicant is entitled to institute an action for infringement if notice thereof, with a copy of the complaint, is served on the Register of Copyrights. The Register may, at his or her option, become a party to the action with respect to the issue of registrability of the copyright claim by entering an appearance within sixty days after such service, but the

Register's failure to become a party shall not deprive the court of jurisdiction to determine that issue.

(b) In the case of a work consisting of sounds, images, or both, the first fixation of which is made simultaneously with its transmission, the copyright owner may, either before or after such fixation takes place, institute an action for infringement under section 501, fully subject to the remedies provided by sections 502 through 506 and sections 509 and 510, if, in accordance with requirements that the Register of Copyrights shall prescribe by regulation, the copyright owner—

(1) serves notice upon the infringer, not less than ten or more than thirty days before such fixation, identifying the work and the specific time and source of its first transmission, and declaring an intention to secure copyright in the work; and

(2) makes registration for the work within three months after its first transmission.

§ 412.   **Registration as prerequisite to certain remedies for infringement**

In any action under this title, other than an action instituted under section 411(b), no award of statutory damages or of attorney's fees, as provided by sections 504 and 505, shall be made for—

(1) any infringement of copyright in an unpublished work commenced before the effective date of its registration; or

(2) any infringement of copyright commenced after first publication of the work and before the effective date of its registration, unless such registration is made within three months after the first publication of the work.

CHAPTER 5—COPYRIGHT INFRINGEMENT AND REMEDIES

SEC.
501. Infringement of copyright.
502. Remedies for infringement: Injunctions.
503. Remedies for infringement: Impounding and disposition of infringing articles.
504. Remedies for infringement: Damage and profits.
505. Remedies for infringement: Costs and attorney's fees.
506. Criminal offenses.
507. Limitations on actions.
508. Notification of filing and determination of actions.
509. Seizure and forfeiture.
510. Remedies for alteration of programing by cable systems.

§ 501. Infringement of copyright

(a) Anyone who violates any of the exclusive rights of the copyright owner as provided by sections 106 through 118, or who imports copies or phonorecords into the United States in violation of section 602, is an infringer of the copyright.

(b) The legal or beneficial owner of an exclusive right under a copyright is entitled, subject to the requirements of sections 205(d) and 411, to institute an action for any infringement of that particular right committed while he or she is the owner of it. The court may require such owner to serve written notice of the action with a copy of the complaint upon any person shown, by the records of the Copyright Office or otherwise, to have or claim an interest in the copyright, and shall require that such notice be served upon any person whose interest is likely to be affected by a decision in the case. The court may require the joinder, and shall permit the intervention, of any person having or claiming an interest in the copyright.

(c) For any secondary transmission by a cable system that embodies a performance or a display of a work which is actionable as an act of infringement under subsection (c) of section 111, a television broadcast station holding a copyright or other license to transmit or perform the same version of that work shall, for purposes of subsection (b) of this section, be treated as a legal or beneficial owner if such secondary transmission occurs within the local service area of that television station.

(d) For any secondary transmission by a cable system that is actionable as an act of infringement pursuant to section 111(c) (3), the following shall also have standing to sue: (i) the primary transmitter whose transmission has been altered by the cable system; and (ii) any broadcast station within whose local service area the secondary transmission occurs.

§ 502. Remedies for infringement: Injunctions

(a) Any court having jurisdiction of a civil action arising under this title may, subject to the provisions of section 1498 of title 28, grant temporary and final injunctions on such terms as it may deem reasonable to prevent or restrain infringement of a copyright.

(b) Any such injunction may be served anywhere in the United States on the person enjoined; it shall be operative throughout the United States and shall be enforceable, by proceedings in contempt or otherwise, by any United States court having jurisdiction of that person. The clerk of the court granting the injunction shall, when requested by any other court in which enforcement of the injunction is sought, transmit promptly to the other court a certified copy of all the papers in the case on file in such clerk's office.

§ 503. Remedies for infringement: Impounding and disposition of infringing articles

(a) At any time while an action under this title is pending, the court may order the impounding, on such terms as it may deem reasonable, of all copies or phonorecords claimed to have been made or used in violation of the copyright owner's exclusive rights, and of all plates, molds, matrices, masters, tapes, film negatives, or other articles by means of which such copies or phonorecords may be reproduced.

(b) As part of a final judgment or decree, the court may order the destruction or other reasonable disposition of all copies or phonorecords found to have been made or used in violation of the copyright owner's exclusive rights, and of all plates, molds, matrices, masters, tapes, film negatives, or other articles by means of which such copies or phonorecords may be reproduced.

§ 504. Remedies for infringement: Damages and profits

(a) *In General*—Except as otherwise provided by this title, an infringer of copyright is liable for either—

(1) the copyright owner's actual damages and any additional profits of the infringer, as provided by subsection (b); or

(2) statutory damages, as provided by subsection (c).

(b) *Actual Damages and Profits*—The copyright owner is entitled to recover the actual damages suffered by him or her as a result of the infringement, and any profits of the infringer that are attributable to the infringement and are not taken into account in computing the actual damages. In establishing the infringer's profits, the copyright owner is required to present proof only of the infringer's gross revenue, and the infringer is required to prove his or her deductible expenses and the elements of profit attributable to factors other than the copyrighted work.

(c) *Statutory Damages*—

(1) Except as provided by clause (2) of this subsection, the copyright owner may elect, at any time before final judgment is rendered, to recover, instead of actual damages and profits, an

award of statutory damages for all infringements involved in the action, with respect to any one work, for which any one infringer is liable individually, or for which any two or more infringers are liable jointly and severally, in a sum of not less than $250 or more than $10,000 as the court considers just. For the purposes of this subsection, all the parts of a compilation or derivative work constitute one work.

(2) In a case where the copyright owner sustains the burden of proving, and the court finds, that infringement was committed willfully, the court in its discretion may increase the award of statutory damages to a sum of not more than $50,000. In a case where the infringer sustains the burden of proving, and the court finds, that such infringer was not aware and had no reason to believe that his or her acts constituted an infringement of copyright, the court at its discretion may reduce the award of statutory damages to a sum of not less than $100. The court shall remit statutory damages in any case where an infringer believed and had reasonable grounds for believing that his or her use of the copyrighted work was a fair use under section 107, if the infringer was: (i) an employee or agent of a nonprofit educational institution, library, or archives acting within the scope of his or her employment who, or such institution, library, or archives itself, which infringed by reproducing the work in copies or phonorecords; or (ii) a public broadcasting entity which or a person who, as a regular part of the nonprofit activities of a public broadcasting entity (as defined in subsection (g) of section 118) infringed by performing a published nondramatic literary work or by reproducing a transmission program embodying a performance of such a work.

§ 505.   Remedies for infringement: Costs and attorney's fees

In any civil action under this title, the court in its discretion may allow the recovery of full costs by or against any party other than the United States or an officer thereof. Except as otherwise provided by this title, the court may also award a reasonable attorney's fee to the prevailing party as part of the costs.

§ 506.   Criminal offenses

(a) *Criminal infringement*—Any person who infringes a copyright willfully and for purposes of commercial advantage or private finan-

179

cial gain shall be punished as provided in section 2319 of title 18. (Amended May 24, 1982, Public Law 97–180 sec. 5, 96 Stat. 93.)

(b) *Forfeiture and Destruction*—When any person is convicted of any violation of subsection (a), the court in its judgment of conviction shall, in addition to the penalty therein prescribed, order the forfeiture and destruction or other disposition of all infringing copies or phonorecords and all implements, devices, or equipment used in the manufacture of such infringing copies or phonorecords.

(c) *Fraudulent Copyright Notice*—Any person who, with fraudulent intent, places on any article a notice of copyright or words of the same purport that such person knows to be false, or who, with fraudulent intent, publicly distributes or imports for public distribution any article bearing such notice or words that such person knows to be false, shall be fined not more than $2,500.

(d) *Fraudulent Removal of Copyright Notice*—Any person who, with fraudulent intent, removes or alters any notice of copyright appearing on a copy of a copyrighted work shall be fined not more than $2,500.

(e) *False Representation*—Any person who knowingly makes a false representation of a material fact in the application for copyright registration provided for by section 409, or in any written statement filed in connection with the application, shall be fined not more than $2,500.

§ 507. Limitations on actions

(a) *Criminal Proceedings*—No criminal proceeding shall be maintained under the provisions of this title unless it is commenced within three years after the cause of action arose.

(b) *Civil Actions*—No civil action shall be maintained under the provisions of this title unless it is commenced within three years after the claim accrued.

§ 508. Notification of filing and determination of actions

(a) Within one month after the filing of any action under this title, the clerks of the courts of the United States shall send written notification to the Register of Copyrights setting forth, as far as is shown by the papers filed in the court, the names and addresses of the parties and the title, author, and registration number of each work involved in the action. If any other copyrighted work is later included in the action by amendment, answer, or other pleading, the clerk shall also send a notification concerning it to the Register within one month after the pleading is filed.

(b) Within one month after any final order or judgment is issued in the case, the clerk of the court shall notify the Register of it, sending with the notification a copy of the order or judgment together with the written opinion, if any, of the court.

(c) Upon receiving the notifications specified in this section, the Register shall make them a part of the public records of the Copyright Office.

§ 509.   Seizure and forfeiture

(a) All copies or phonorecords manufactured, reproduced, distributed, sold, or otherwise used, intended for use, or possessed with intent to use in violation of section 506(a), and all plates, molds, matrices, masters, tapes, film negatives, or other articles by means of which such copies or phonorecords may be reproduced, and all electronic, mechanical, or other devices for manufacturing, reproducing, or assembling such copies or phonorecords may be seized and forfeited to the United States.

(b) The applicable procedures relating to (i) the seizure, summary and judicial forfeiture, and condemnation of vessels, vehicles, merchandise, and baggage for violations of the customs laws contained in title 19, (ii) the disposition of such vessels, vehicles, merchandise, and baggage or the proceeds from the sale thereof, (iii) the remission or mitigation of such forfeiture, (iv) the compromise of claims, and (v) the award of compensation to informers in respect of such forfeitures, shall apply to seizures and forfeitures incurred, or alleged to have been incurred, under the provisions of this section, insofar as applicable and not inconsistent with the provisions of this section; except that such duties as are imposed upon any officer or employee of the Treasury Department or any other person with respect to the seizure and forfeiture of vessels, vehicles, merchandise; and baggage under the provisions of the customs laws contained in title 19 shall be performed with respect to seizure and forfeiture of all articles described in subsection (a) by such officers, agents, or other persons as may be authorized or designated for that purpose by the Attorney General.

§ 510. Remedies for alteration of programing by cable systems

(a) In any action filed pursuant to section 111(c)(3), the following remedies shall be available:

(1) Where an action is brought by a party identified in subsections (b) or (c) of section 501, the remedies provided by sections 502 through 505, and the remedy provided by subsection (b) of this section; and

(2) When an action is brought by a party identified in subsection (d) of section 501, the remedies provided by sections 502 and 505, together with any actual damages suffered by such party as a result of the infringement, and the remedy provided by subsection (b) of this section.

(b) In any action filed pursuant to section 111(c)(3), the court may decree that, for a period not to exceed thirty days, the cable system shall be deprived of the benefit of a compulsory license for one or more distant signals carried by such cable system.

Chapter 6—Manufacturing Requirements and Importation

Sec.
601. Manufacture, importation, and public distribution of certain copies.
602. Infringing importation of copies or phonorecords.
603. Importation prohibitions: Enforcement and disposition of excluded articles.

§ 601. Manufacture, importation, and public distribution of certain copies

(a) Prior to July 1, 1986, and except as provided by subsection (b), the importation into or public distribution in the United States of copies of a work consisting preponderantly of nondramatic literary material that is in the English language and is protected under this title is prohibited unless the portions consisting of such material have been manufactured in the United States or Canada. (Amended July 13, 1982, Public Law 97–215, 96 Stat. 178.)

(b) The provisions of subsection (a) do not apply—

(1) where, on the date when importation is sought or public distribution in the United States is made, the author of any substantial part of such material is neither a national nor a domiciliary of the United States or, if such author is a national of the United States, he or she has been domiciled outside the United States for a

continuous period of at least one year immediately preceding that date; in the case of a work made for hire, the exemption provided by this clause does not apply unless a substantial part of the work was prepared for an employer or other person who is not a national or domiciliary of the United States or a domestic corporation or enterprise;

(2) where the United States Customs Service is presented with an import statement issued under the seal of the Copyright Office, in which case a total of no more than two thousand copies of any one such work shall be allowed entry; the import statement shall be issued upon request to the copyright owner or to a person designated by such owner at the time of registration for the work under section 408 or at any time thereafter;

(3) where importation is sought under the authority or for the use, other than in schools, of the Government of the United States or of any State or political subdivision of a State;

(4) where importation, for use and not for sale, is sought—

(A) by any person with respect to no more than one copy of any work at any one time;

(B) by any person arriving from outside the United States, with respect to copies forming part of such person's personal baggage; or

(C) by an organization operated for scholarly, educational, or religious purposes and not for private gain, with respect to copies intended to form a part of its library;

(5) where the copies are reproduced in raised characters for the use of the blind; or

(6) where, in addition to copies imported under clauses (3) and (4) of this subsection, no more than two thousand copies of any one such work, which have not been manufactured in the United States or Canada, are publicly distributed in the United States; or

(7) where, on the date when importation is sought or public distribution in the United States is made—

(A) the author of any substantial part of such material is an individual and receives compensation for the transfer or license of the right to distribute the work in the United States; and

(B) the first publication of the work has previously taken place outside the United States under a transfer or license granted by such author to a transferee or licensee who was not a national or domiciliary of the United States or a domestic corporation or enterprise; and

(C) there has been no publication of an authorized edition of the work of which the copies were manufactured in the United States; and

(D) the copies were reproduced under a transfer or license granted by such author or by the transferee or licensee of the right of first publication as mentioned in subclause (B), and the transferee or the licensee of the right of reproduction was not a national or domiciliary of the United States or a domestic corporation or enterprise.

(c) The requirement of this section that copies be manufactured in the United States or Canada is satisfied if—

(1) in the case where the copies are printed directly from type that has been set, or directly from plates made from such type, the setting of the type and the making of the plates have been performed in the United States or Canada; or

(2) in the case where the making of plates by a lithographic or photoengraving process is a final or intermediate step preceding the printing of the copies, the making of the plates has been performed in the United States or Canada; and

(3) in any case, the printing or other final process of producing multiple copies and any binding of the copies have been performed in the United States or Canada.

(d) Importation or public distribution of copies in violation of this section does not invalidate protection for a work under this title. However, in any civil action or criminal proceeding for infringement of the exclusive rights to reproduce and distribute copies of the work, the infringer has a complete defense with respect to all of the nondramatic literary material comprised in the work and any other parts of the work in which the exclusive rights to reproduce and distribute copies are owned by the same person who owns such exclusive rights in the nondramatic literary material, if the infringer proves—

(1) that copies of the work have been imported into or publicly distributed in the United States in violation of this section by or with the authority of the owner of such exclusive rights; and

(2) that the infringing copies were manufactured in the United States or Canada in accordance with the provisions of subsection (c); and

(3) that the infringement was commenced before the effective date of registration for an authorized edition of the work, the copies of which have been manufactured in the United States or Canada in accordance with the provisions of subsection (c).

(e) In any action for infringement of the exclusive rights to reproduce and distribute copies of a work containing material required by this section to be manufactured in the United States or Canada, the copyright owner shall set forth in the complaint the names of the persons or organizations who performed the processes specified by subsection (c) with respect to that material, and the places where those processes were performed.

§ 602. Infringing importation of copies or phonorecords

(a) Importation into the United States, without the authority of the owner of copyright under this title, of copies or phonorecords of a work that have been acquired outside the United States is an infringement of the exclusive right to distribute copies or phonorecords under section 106, actionable under section 501. This subsection does not apply to—

(1) importation of copies or phonorecords under the authority or for the use of the Government of the United States or of any State or political subdivision of a State, but not including copies or phonorecords for use in schools, or copies of any audiovisual work imported for purposes other than archival use;

(2) importation, for the private use of the importer and not for distribution, by any person with respect to no more than one copy or phonorecord of any one work at any one time, or by any person arriving from outside the United States with respect to copies or phonorecords forming part of such person's personal baggage; or

(3) importation by or for an organization operated for scholarly, educational, or religious purposes and not for private gain, with respect to no more than one copy of an audiovisual work solely for its archival purposes, and no more than five copies or phonorecords of any other work for its library lending or archival purposes, unless the importation of such copies or phonorecords is part of an activity consisting of systematic reproduction or distribution, engaged in by such organization in violation of the provisions of section 108(g) (2).

(b) In a case where the making of the copies or phonorecords would have constituted an infringement of copyright if this title had

185

been applicable, their importation is prohibited. In a case where the copies or phonorecords were lawfully made, the United States Customs Service has no authority to prevent their importation unless the provisions of section 601 are applicable. In either case, the Secretary of the Treasury is authorized to prescribe, by regulation, a procedure under which any person claiming an interest in the copyright in a particular work may, upon payment of a specified fee, be entitled to notification by the Customs Service of the importation of articles that appear to be copies or phonorecords of the work.

§ 603. Importation prohibitions: Enforcement and disposition of excluded articles

(a) The Secretary of the Treasury and the United States Postal Service shall separately or jointly make regulations for the enforcement of the provisions of this title prohibiting importation.

(b) These regulations may require, as a condition for the exclusion of articles under section 602—

(1) that the person seeking exclusion obtain a court order enjoining importation of the articles; or

(2) that the person seeking exclusion furnish proof, of a specified nature and in accordance with prescribed procedures, that the copyright in which such person claims an interest is valid and that the importation would violate the prohibition in section 602; the person seeking exclusion may also be required to post a surety bond for any injury that may result if the detention or exclusion of the articles proves to be unjustified.

(c) Articles imported in violation of the importation prohibitions of this title are subject to seizure and forfeiture in the same manner as property imported in violation of the customs revenue laws. Forfeited articles shall be destroyed as directed by the Secretary of the Treasury or the court, as the case may be; however, the articles may be returned to the country of export whenever it is shown to the satisfaction of the Secretary of the Treasury that the importer had no reasonable grounds for believing that his or her acts constituted a violation of law.

CHAPTER 7—COPYRIGHT OFFICE

SEC.
701. The Copyright Office: General responsibilities and organization.
702. Copyright Office regulations.

703. Effective date of actions in Copyright Office.
704. Retention and disposition of articles deposited in Copyright Office.
705. Copyright Office records: Preparation, maintenance, public inspection, and searching.
706. Copies of Copyright Office records.
707. Copyright Office forms and publications.
708. Copyright Office fees.
709. Delay in delivery caused by disruption of postal or other services.
710. Reproductions for use of the blind and physically handicapped: Voluntary licensing forms and procedures.

§ 701. The Copyright Office: General responsibilities and organization

(a) All administrative functions and duties under this title, except as otherwise specified, are the responsibility of the Register of Copyrights as director of the Copyright Office of the Library of Congress. The Register of Copyrights, together with the subordinate officers and employees of the Copyright Office, shall be appointed by the Librarian of Congress, and shall act under the Librarian's general direction and supervision.

(b) The Register of Copyrights shall adopt a seal to be used on and after January 1, 1978, to authenticate all certified documents issued by the Copyright Office.

(c) The Register of Copyrights shall make an annual report to the Librarian of Congress of the work and accomplishments of the Copyright Office during the previous fiscal year. The annual report of the Register of Copyrights shall be published separately and as a part of the annual report of the Librarian of Congress.

(d) Except as provided by section 706(b) and the regulations issued thereunder, all actions taken by the Register of Copyrights under this title are subject to the provisions of the Administrative Procedure Act of June 11, 1946, as amended (c. 324, 60 Stat. 237, title 5, United States Code, Chapter 5, Subchapter II and Chapter 7).

§ 702. Copyright Office regulations

The Register of Copyrights is authorized to establish regulations not inconsistent with law for the administration of the functions and duties made the responsibility of the Register under this title. All regulations established by the Register under this title are subject to the approval of the Librarian of Congress.

§ 703. Effective date of actions in Copyright Office

In any case in which time limits are prescribed under this title for the performance of an action in the Copyright Office, and in which the last day of the prescribed period falls on a Saturday, Sunday, holiday, or other nonbusiness day within the District of Columbia or the Federal Government, the action may be taken on the next succeeding business day, and is effective as of the date when the period expired.

§ 704. Retention and disposition of articles deposited in Copyright Office

(a) Upon their deposit in the Copyright Office under sections 407 and 408, all copies, phonorecords, and identifying material, including those deposited in connection with claims that have been refused registration, are the property of the United States Government.

(b) In the case of published works, all copies, phonorecords, and identifying material deposited are available to the Library of Congress for its collections, or for exchange or transfer to any other library. In the case of unpublished works, the Library is entitled, under regulations that the Register of Copyrights shall prescribe, to select any deposits for its collections or for transfer to the National Archives of the United States or to a Federal records center, as defined in section 2901 of title 44.

(c) The Register of Copyrights is authorized, for specific or general categories of works, to make a facsimile reproduction of all or any part of the material deposited under section 408, and to make such reproduction a part of the Copyright Office records of the registration, before transferring such material to the Library of Congress as provided by subsection (b), or before destroying or otherwise disposing of such material as provided by subsection (d).

(d) Deposits not selected by the Library under subsection (b), or identifying portions or reproductions of them, shall be retained under the control of the Copyright Office, including retention in Government storage facilities, for the longest period considered practicable and desirable by the Register of Copyrights and the Librarian of Congress. After that period it is within the joint discretion of the Register and the Librarian to order their destruction or other disposition; but, in the case of unpublished works, no deposit shall be knowingly or intentionally destroyed or otherwise disposed of during its term of copyright unless a facsimile reproduction of the entire deposit has been made a part of the Copyright Office records as provided by subsection (c).

(e) The depositor of copies, phonorecords, or identifying material under section 408, or the copyright owner of record, may request retention, under the control of the Copyright Office, of one or more of such articles for the full term of copyright in the work. The Register of Copyrights shall prescribe, by regulation, the conditions under which such requests are to be made and granted, and shall fix the fee to be charged under section 708(a) (11) if the request is granted.

§ 705. Copyright Office records: Preparation, maintenance, public inspection, and searching

(a) The Register of Copyrights shall provide and keep in the Copyright Office records of all deposits, registrations, recordations, and other actions taken under this title, and shall prepare indexes of all such records.

(b) Such records and indexes, as well as the articles deposited in connection with completed copyright registrations and retained under the control of the Copyright Office, shall be open to public inspection.

(c) Upon request and payment of the fee specified by section 708, the Copyright Office shall make a search of its public records, indexes, and deposits, and shall furnish a report of the information they disclose with respect to any particular deposits, registrations, or recorded documents.

§ 706. Copies of Copyright Office records

(a) Copies may be made of any public records or indexes of the Copyright Office; additional certificates of copyright registration and copies of any public records or indexes may be furnished upon request and payment of the fees specified by section 708.

(b) Copies or reproductions of deposited articles retained under the control of the Copyright Office shall be authorized or furnished only under the conditions specified by the Copyright Office regulations.

§ 707. Copyright Office forms and publications

(a) *Catalog of Copyright Entries*—The Register of Copyrights shall compile and publish at periodic intervals catalogs of all copyright registrations. These catalogs shall be divided into parts in accordance with the various classes of works, and the Register has discretion to determine, on the basis of practicability and usefulness, the form and frequency of publication of each particular part.

(b) *Other Publications*—The Register shall furnish, free of charge upon request, application forms for copyright registration and general informational material in connection with the functions of the Copyright Office. The Register also has the authority to publish compilations of information, bibliographies, and other material he or she considers to be of value to the public.

(c) *Distribution of Publications*—All publications of the Copyright Office shall be furnished to depository libraries as specified under section 1905 of title 44, and, aside from those furnished free of charge, shall be offered for sale to the public at prices based on the cost of reproduction and distribution.

§ 708. Copyright Office fees

(a) The following fees shall be paid to the Register of Copyrights:

(1) on filing each application for registration of a copyright claim or a supplementary registration under section 408, including the issuance of a certificate of registration if registration is made, $10;

(2) on filing each application for registration of a claim to renewal of a subsisting copyright in its first term under section 304(a), including the issuance of a certificate of registration if registration is made, $6; and

(3) for the issuance of a receipt for a deposit under section 407, $2;

(4) for the recordation, as provided by section 205, of a transfer of copyright ownership or other document of six pages or less, covering no more than one title, $10; for each page over six and each title over one, 50 cents additional;

(5) for the filing, under section 115(b), of a notice of intention to make phonorecords, $6;

(6) for the recordation, under section 302(c), of a statement revealing the identity of an author of an anonymous or pseudonymous work, or for the recordation, under section 302(d), of a statement relating to the death of an author, $10 for a document of six pages or less, covering no more than one title; for each page over six and for each title over one, $1 additional;

(7) for the issuance, under section 601, of an import statement, $3;

(8) for the issuance, under section 706, of an additional certificate of registration, $4;

(9) for the issuance of any other certification, $4; the Register of Copyrights has discretion, on the basis of their cost, to fix the fees for preparing copies of Copyright Office records, whether they are to be certified or not;

(10) for the making and reporting of a search as provided by section 705, and for any related services, $10 for each hour or fraction of an hour consumed;

(11) for any other special services requiring a substantial amount of time or expense, such fees as the Register of Copyrights may fix on the basis of the cost of providing the service.

(b) The fees prescribed by or under this section are applicable to the United States Government and any of its agencies, employees, or officers, but the Register of Copyrights has discretion to waive the requirement of this subsection in occasional or isolated cases involving relatively small amounts.

(c) All fees received under this section shall be deposited by the Register of Copyrights in the Treasury of the United States and shall be credited to the appropriation for necessary expenses of the Copyright Office. The Register may, in accordance with regulations that he or she shall prescribe, refund any sum paid by mistake or in excess of the fee required by this section. (Amended August 5, 1977, Public Law 95–94, sec. 406(b), 91 Stat. 682; October 25, 1982, Public Law 97–366, sec. 1, 96 Stat. 1759.)

§ 709. **Delay in delivery caused by disruption of postal or other services**

In any case in which the Register of Copyrights determines, on the basis of such evidence as the Register may by regulation require, that a deposit, application, fee, or any other material to be delivered to the Copyright Office by a particular date, would have been received in the Copyright Office in due time except for a general disruption or suspension of postal or other transportation or communications services, the actual receipt of such material in the Copyright Office within one month after the date on which the Register determines that the disruption or suspension of such services has terminated, shall be considered timely.

§ 710. Reproduction for use of the blind and physically handicapped: Voluntary licensing forms and procedures

The Register of Copyrights shall, after consultation with the Chief of the Division for the Blind and Physically Handicapped and other appropriate officials of the Library of Congress, establish by regulation standardized forms and procedures by which, at the time applications covering certain specified categories of nondramatic literary works are submitted for registration under section 408 of this title, the copyright owner may voluntarily grant to the Library of Congress a license to reproduce the copyrighted work by means of Braille or similar tactile symbols, or by fixation of a reading of the work in a phonorecord, or both, and to distribute the resulting copies or phonorecords solely for the use of the blind and physically handicapped and under limited conditions to be specified in the standardized forms.

CHAPTER 8—COPYRIGHT ROYALTY TRIBUNAL

SEC.
801. Copyright Royalty Tribunal: Establishment and purpose.
802. Membership of the Tribunal.
803. Procedures of the Tribunal.
804. Institution and conclusion of proceedings.
805. Staff of the Tribunal.
806. Administrative support of the Tribunal.
807. Deduction of costs of proceedings.
808. Reports.
809. Effective date of final determinations.
810. Judicial review.

§ 801. Copyright Royalty Tribunal: Establishment and purpose

(a) There is hereby created an independent Copyright Royalty Tribunal in the legislative branch.

(b) Subject to the provisions of this chapter, the purposes of the Tribunal shall be—

(1) to make determinations concerning the adjustment of reasonable copyright royalty rates as provided in sections 115 and 116, and to make determinations as to reasonable terms and rates of royalty payments as provided in section 118. The rates applicable under sections 115 and 116 shall be calculated to achieve the following objectives:

192

(A) To maximize the availability of creative works to the public;

(B) To afford the copyright owner a fair return for his creative work and the copyright user a fair income under existing economic conditions;

(C) To reflect the relative roles of the copyright owner and the copyright user in the product made available to the public with respect to relative creative contribution, technological contribution, capital investment, cost, risk, and contribution to the opening of new markets for creative expression and media for their communication;

(D) To minimize any disruptive impact on the structure of the industries involved and on generally prevailing industry practices.

(2) to make determinations concerning the adjustment of the copyright royalty rates in section 111 solely in accordance with the following provisions:

(A) The rates established by section 111(d) (2) (B) may be adjusted to reflect (i) national monetary inflation or deflation or (ii) changes in the average rates charged cable subscribers for the basic service of providing secondary transmissions to maintain the real constant dollar level of the royalty fee per subscriber which existed as of the date of enactment of this Act: *Provided,* That if the average rates charged cable system subscribers for the basic service of providing secondary transmissions are changed so that the average rates exceed national monetary inflation, no change in the rates established by section 111(d) (2) (B) shall be permitted: *And provided further,* That no increase in the royalty fee shall be permitted based on any reduction in the average number of distant signal equivalents per subscriber. The Commission may consider all factors relating to the maintenance of such level of payments including, as an extenuating factor, whether the cable industry has been restrained by subscriber rate regulating authorities from increasing the rates for the basic service of providing secondary transmissions.

(B) In the event that the rules and regulations of the Federal Communications Commission are amended at any time after April 15, 1976, to permit the carriage by cable systems of additional television broadcast signals beyond the local service area of the primary transmitters of such signals, the royalty rates established by section 111(d) (2) (B) may be adjusted to insure that the rates for the additional distant signal equivalents resulting from such carriage are reasonable in the light of the changes effected by the amendment to such rules and regulations. In determining the reasonableness of rates proposed following an amendment of Federal Communications Commission rules and regulations, the Copyright Royalty Tribunal shall consider, among other factors, the economic impact on copyright owners and users: *Provided*, That no adjustment in royalty rates shall be made under this subclause with respect to any distant signal equivalent or fraction thereof represented by (i) carriage of any signal permitted under the rules and regulations of the Federal Communications Commission in effect on April 15, 1976, or the carriage of a signal of the same type (that is, independent, network, or noncommercial educational) substituted for such permitted signal, or (ii) a television broadcast signal first carried after April 15, 1976, pursuant to an individual waiver of the rules and regulations of the Federal Communications Commission, as such rules and regulations were in effect on April 15, 1976.

(C) In the event of any change in the rules and regulations of the Federal Communications Commission with respect to syndicated and sports program exclusivity after April 15, 1976, the rates established by section 111(d) (2) (B) may be adjusted to assure that such rates are reasonable in light of the changes to such rules and regulations, but any such adjustment shall apply only to the affected television broadcast signals carried on those systems affected by the change.

(D) The gross receipts limitations established by section 111(d) (2) (C) and (D) shall be adjusted to reflect national monetary inflation or deflation or changes in the average rates charged cable system subscribers for the basic service of providing secondary transmissions to maintain the real constant dollar value of the exemption provided by such section; and the royalty rate specified therein shall not be subject to adjustment; and

(3) to distribute royalty fees deposited with the Register of Copyrights under sections 111 and 116, and to determine, in cases where controversy exists, the distribution of such fees.

(c) As soon as possible after the date of enactment of this Act, and no later than six months following such date, the President shall

194

publish a notice announcing the initial appointments provided in section 802, and shall designate an order of seniority among the initially-appointed commissioners for purposes of section 802(b).

§ 802. Membership of the Tribunal

(a) The Tribunal shall be composed of five commissioners appointed by the President with the advice and consent of the Senate for a term of seven years each; of the first five members appointed, three shall be designated to serve for seven years from the date of the notice specified in section 801(c), and two shall be designated to serve for five years from such date, respectively. Commissioners shall be compensated at the highest rate now or hereafter prescribe for grade 18 of the General Schedule pay rates (5 U.S.C. 5332).

(b) Upon convening the commissioners shall elect a chairman from among the commissioners appointed for a full seven-year term. Such chairman shall serve for a term of one year. Thereafter, the most senior commissioner who has not previously served as chairman shall serve as chairman for a period of one year, except that, if all commissioners have served a full term as chairman, the most senior commissioner who has served the least number of terms as chairman shall be designated as chairman.

(c) Any vacancy in the Tribunal shall not affect its powers and shall be filled, for the unexpired term of the appointment, in the same manner as the original appointment was made.

§ 803. Procedures of the Tribunal

(a) The Tribunal shall adopt regulations, not inconsistent with law, governing its procedure and methods of operation. Except as otherwise provided in this chapter, the Tribunal shall be subject to the provisions of the Administrative Procedure Act of June 11, 1946, as amended (c. 324, 60 Stat. 237, title 5, United States Code, chapter 5, subchapter II and chapter 7).

(b) Every final determination of the Tribunal shall be published in the Federal Register. It shall state in detail the criteria that the Tribunal determined to be applicable to the particular proceeding, the various facts that it found relevant to its determination in that proceeding, and the specific reasons for its determination.

§ 804. Institution and conclusion of proceedings

(a) With respect to proceedings under section 801(b) (1) concerning the adjustment of royalty rates as provided in sections 115 and 116, and with respect to proceedings under section 801(b) (2) (A) and (D)—

(1) on January 1, 1980, the Chairman of the Tribunal shall cause to be published in the Federal Register notice of commencement of proceedings under this chapter; and

(2) during the calendar years specified in the following schedule, any owner or user of a copyrighted work whose royalty rates are specified by this title, or by a rate established by the Tribunal, may file a petition with the Tribunal declaring that the petitioner requests an adjustment of the rate. The Tribunal shall make a determination as to whether the applicant has a significant interest in the royalty rate in which an adjustment is requested. If the Tribunal determines that the petitioner has a significant interest, the Chairman shall cause notice of this determination, with the reasons therefor, to be published in the Federal Register, together with notice of commencement of proceedings under this chapter.

(A) In proceedings under section 801(b) (2) (A) and (D), such petition may be filed during 1985 and in each subsequent fifth calendar year.

(B) In proceedings under section 801(b) (1) concerning the adjustment of royalty rates as provided in section 115, such petition may be filed in 1987 and in each subsequent tenth calendar year.

(C) In proceedings under section 801(b) (1) concerning the adjustment of royalty rates under section 116, such petition may be filed in 1990 and in each subsequent tenth calendar year.

(b) With respect to proceedings under subclause (B) or (C) of section 801(b) (2), following an event described in either of those subsections, any owner or user of a copyrighted work whose royalty rates are specified by section 111, or by a rate established by the Tribunal, may, within twelve months, file a petition with the Tribunal declaring that the petitioner requests an adjustment of the rate. In this event the Tribunal shall proceed as in subsection (a) (2), above. Any change in royalty rates made by the Tribunal pursuant to this subsection may be reconsidered in 1980, 1985, and each fifth

196

calendar year thereafter, in accordance with the provisions in section 801(b) (2) (B) or (C), as the case may be.

(c) With respect to proceedings under section 801(b) (1), concerning the determination of reasonable terms and rates of royalty payments as provided in section 118, the Tribunal shall proceed when and as provided by that section.

(d) With respect to proceedings under section 801(b) (3), concerning the distribution of royalty fees in certain circumstances under sections 111 or 116, the Chairman of the Tribunal shall, upon determination by the Tribunal that a controversy exists concerning such distribution, cause to be published in the Federal Register notice of commencement of proceedings under this chapter.

(e) All proceedings under this chapter shall be initiated without delay following publication of the notice specified in this section, and the Tribunal shall render its final decision in any such proceeding within one year from the date of such publication.

§ 805. Staff of the Tribunal

(a) The Tribunal is authorized to appoint and fix the compensation of such employees as may be necessary to carry out the provisions of this chapter, and to prescribe their functions and duties.

(b) The Tribunal may procure temporary and intermittent services to the same extent as is authorized by section 3109 of title 5.

§ 806. Administrative support of the Tribunal

(a) The Library of Congress shall provide the Tribunal with necessary administrative services, including those related to budgeting, accounting, financial reporting, travel, personnel, and procurement. The Tribunal shall pay the Library for such services, either in advance or by reimbursement from the funds of the Tribunal, at amounts to be agreed upon between the Librarian and the Tribunal.

(b) The Library of Congress is authorized to disburse funds for the Tribunal, under regulations prescribed jointly by the Librarian of Congress and the Tribunal and approved by the Comptroller General. Such regulations shall establish requirements and procedures under which every voucher certified for payment by the Library of Congress under this chapter shall be supported with a certification by a duly authorized officer or employee of the Tribunal, and shall prescribe the responsibilities and accountability of said officers and employees of the Tribunal with respect to such certifications.

§ 807. Deduction of costs of proceedings

Before any funds are distributed pursuant to a final decision in a proceeding involving distribution of royalty fees, the Tribunal shall assess the reasonable costs of such proceeding.

§ 808. Reports

In addition to its publication of the reports of all final determinations as provided in section 803(b), the Tribunal shall make an annual report to the President and the Congress concerning the Tribunal's work during the preceding fiscal year, including a detailed fiscal statement of account.

§ 809. Effective date of final determinations

Any final determination by the Tribunal under this chapter shall become effective thirty days following its publication in the Federal Register as provided in section 803(b), unless prior to that time an appeal has been filed pursuant to section 810, to vacate, modify, or correct such determination, and notice of such appeal has been served on all parties who appeared before the Tribunal in the proceeding in question. Where the proceeding involves the distribution of royalty fees under sections 111 or 116, the Tribunal shall, upon the expiration of such thirty-day period, distribute any royalty fees not subject to an appeal filed pursuant to section 810.

§ 810. Judicial review

Any final decision of the Tribunal in a proceeding under section 801(b) may be appealed to the United States Court of Appeals, within thirty days after its publication in the Federal Register by an aggrieved party. The judicial review of the decision shall be had, in accordance with chapter 7 of title 5, on the basis of the record before the Tribunal. No court shall have jurisdiction to review a final decision of the Tribunal except as provided in this section.

NOTES OF OTHER STATUTES

Note.—Some sections, or portions of sections, of other titles of the United States Code, of the District of Columbia Code, and of the Canal Zone Code, relating to patents, trademarks, copyrights, or to the Patent and Trademark Office, are reprinted or noted here for convenience. This collection does not purport to be complete.

PAGE

I. Remedies for Infringement of Patents and Trademarks and Other Actions—
    A. Federal District Courts 200
    B. Courts of Appeal 202
    C. Restrictions on importation: Unfair practices 209
    D. Documentary evidence in patent cases 209
II. The Patent and Trademark Office—
    A. Establishment, officers and employees 211
    B. Restrictions on employees; bribery 212
    C. Accounts 220
III. Proceedings in the Patent and Trademark Office—
    Holidays 220
IV. Practice Before the Patent and Trademark Office—
    A. Regulations for agents and attorneys 223
    B. Advertising, restrictions 228
    C. Small-business concerns 228
V. Patent Fees 229
VI. Examination of Applications—
    Information on patents for drugs 229
VII. Plants—
    Plant Variety Protection Act (Note) 230
VIII. Secrecy—
    Respect of security classification by
    Secretary of Commerce 230
IX. Government Interests in Patents—
    A. Department of Energy/Nuclear Regulatory Commission—
        1. Inventions relating to atomic weapons 231
        2. General provisions 240
        3. Rights to inventions arising from
           sponsored R&D 243
    B. National Aeronautics and Space Administration 250
    C. Department of Health and Human Services 255
    D. Department of the Interior 255
    E. Department of Defense 257
    F. Consumer Product Safety Commission 258
    G. Department of Commerce 259
    H. Department of State 259
    I. Department of Transportation 260
    J. Department of the Treasury 260

K. Environmental Protection Agency 260
L. National Science Foundation 262
M. Tennessee Valley Authority 262
X. Treatment of Patents under the Federal Income Tax 263
XI. Miscellaneous—International 267
XII. Copyright and Criminal Law—
    A. National Stolen Property Act 268
    B. Piracy and Counterfeiting Amendments of 1982 269

I. REMEDIES FOR INFRINGEMENT OF PATENTS AND TRADEMARKS AND OTHER ACTIONS

A. FEDERAL DISTRICT COURTS—JURISDICTION, VENUE AND SERVICE OF PROCESS

28 U.S.C. 1338. Patents, plant variety protection, copyrights, trademarks, and unfair competition

(a) The district courts shall have original jurisdiction of any civil action arising under any Act of Congress relating to patents, plant variety protection, copyrights and trademarks. Such jurisdiction shall be exclusive of the courts of the states in patent, plant variety protection and copyright cases.

(b) The district courts shall have original jurisdiction of any civil action asserting a claim of unfair competition when joined with a substantial and related claim under the copyright, patent, plant variety protection or trademark laws. (June 25, 1948, ch. 646, 62 Stat. 931; amended Public Law 91–577, December 24, 1970, 84 Stat. 1559.)

28 U.S.C. 1391. Venue generally

(a) A civil action wherein jurisdiction is founded only on diversity of citizenship may, except as otherwise provided by law, be brought only in the judicial district where all plaintiffs or all defendants reside, or in which the claim arose.

(b) A civil action wherein jurisdiction is not founded solely on diversity of citizenship may be brought only in the judicial district where all defendants reside, or in which the claim arose, except as otherwise provided by law.

(c) A corporation may be sued in any judicial district in which it is incorporated or licensed to do business or is doing business, and such judicial district shall be regarded as the residence of such corporation for venue purposes.

28 U.S.C. 1400.   Patents and copyrights

(a) Civil actions, suits, or proceedings arising under any Act of Congress relating to copyrights may be instituted in the district in which the defendant or his agent resides or may be found.

(b) Any civil action for patent infringement may be brought in the judicial district where the defendant resides, or where the defendant has committed acts of infringement and has a regular and established place of business (June 25, 1948, ch. 646, 62 Stat. 936.)

28 U.S.C. 1498.   Patent and copyright cases

(a) Whenever an invention described in and covered by a patent of the United States is used or manufactured by or for the United States without license of the owner thereof or lawful right to use or manufacture the same, the owner's remedy shall be by action against the United States in the United States Claims Court for the recovery of his reasonable and entire compensation for such use and manufacture.

For the purposes of this section, the use or manufacture of an invention described in and covered by a patent of the United States by a contractor, a subcontractor, or any person, firm, or corporation for the Government and with the authorization or consent of the Government, shall be construed as use or manufacture for the United States.

The court shall not award compensation under this section if the claim is based on the use or manufacture by or for the United States of any article owned, leased, used by, or in the possession of the United States prior to July 1, 1918.

A Government employee shall have the right to bring suit against the Government under this section except where he was in a position to order, influence, or induce use of the invention by the Government. This section shall not confer a right of action on any patentee or any assignee of such patentee with respect to any invention discovered or invented by a person while in the employment or service of the United States, where the invention was related to the official functions of the employee, in cases in which such functions included research and development, or in the making of which Government time, materials or facilities were used.

* * *

(c) The provisions of this section shall not apply to any claim arising in a foreign country. * * * (June 25, 1958, ch. 646, 62 Stat. 941; amended May 24, 1949, ch. 139, 81st Cong., 63 Stat.

201

102; amended Public Law 248, 82d Cong., October 31, 1951, 65 Stat. 727; amended Public Law 582, 82d Cong., July 17, 1952, 66 Stat. 757.)

28 U.S.C. 1694.   Patent infringement action

In a patent infringement action commenced in a district where the defendant is not a resident but has a regular and established place of business, service of process, summons or subpoena upon such defendant may be made upon his agent or agents conducting such business. (June 25, 1948, ch. 646, 62 Stat. 945.)

28 U.S.C. 1928.   Patent infringement action; disclaimer not filed

Whenever a judgment is rendered for the plaintiff in any patent infringement action involving a part of a patent and it appears that the patentee, in his specifications, claimed to be, but was not, the original and first inventor or discoverer of any material or substantial part of the thing patented, no costs shall be included in such judgment, unless the proper disclaimer has been filed in the Patent Office prior to the commencement of the action. (June 25, 1948, ch. 646, 62 Stat. 957.)

B. COURTS OF APPEAL—JURISDICTION—U.S. COURT OF APPEALS FOR THE FEDERAL CIRCUIT

28 U.S.C. 44.   Appointment, tenure, residence and salary of circuit judges

(a) The President shall appoint, by and with the advice and consent of the Senate, circuit judges for the several circuits as follows:

Circuits	Number of judges
District of Columbia	11
First	4
Second	11
Third	10
Fourth	10
Fifth	14
Sixth	11
Seventh	9
Eighth	9
Ninth	23
Tenth	8
Eleventh	12
Federal	12

(Amended April 2, 1982, Public Law 97–164, sec. 102(a), 96 Stat. 25.)

Note.—Sections 165, 166, and 168 of Public Law 97–164 contain miscellaneous provisions regarding the membership of the United States Court of Appeals for the Federal Circuit, as follows.

§ 165. Continued service of current judges

The judges of the United States Court of Claims and of the United States Court of Customs and Patent Appeals in regular active service on the effective date of this Act shall continue in office as judges of the United States Court of Appeals for the Federal Circuit. Senior judges of the United States Court of Claims and of the United States Court of Customs and Patent Appeals on the effective date of this Act shall continue in office as senior judges of the United States Court of Appeals for the Federal Circuit.

§ 166. Appointment of chief judge of Court of Appeals for the Federal Circuit

Notwithstanding the provisions of section 45(a) of title 28, United States Code, the first chief judge of the United States Court of Appeals for the Federal Circuit shall be the Chief Judge of the United States Court of Claims or the Chief Judge of the United States Court of Customs and Patent Appeals, whoever has served longer as chief judge of his court. Notwithstanding section 45 of title 28, United States Code, whichever of the two chief judges does not become the first chief judge of the United States Court of Appeals for the Federal Circuit under the preceding sentence shall, while in active service, have precedence and be deemed senior in commission over all the circuit judges of the United States Court of Appeals for the Federal Circuit (other than the first chief judge of that circuit). When the person who first serves as chief judge of the United States Court of Appeals for the Federal Circuit vacates that position, the position shall be filled in accordance with section 45(a) of title 28, United States Code, as modified by the preceding sentence of this section.

§ 168. Appointment of judges by the President

The Congress—

(1) takes notice of the fact that the quality of the Federal judiciary is determined by the competence and experience of its judges; and

(2) suggests that the President, in nominating individuals to judgeships on the United States Court of Appeals for the Federal Circuit and the United States Claims Court, select from a broad range of qualified individuals.

28 U.S.C. 46.   Assignment of judges; divisions; hearings; quorum

(a) Circuit judges shall sit on the court and its panels in such order and at such times as the court directs, at least a majority of whom shall be judges of that court, unless such judges cannot sit because recused or disqualified, or unless the chief judge of that court certifies that there is an emergency including, but not limited to, the unavailability of a judge of the court because of illness.

The United States Court of Appeals for the Federal Circuit shall determine by rule a procedure for the rotation of judges from panel to panel to ensure that all of the judges sit on a representative cross section of the cases heard and, notwithstanding the first sentence of this subsection, may determine by rule the number of judges, not less than three, who constitute a panel.

(b) In each circuit the court may authorize the hearing and determination of cases and controversies by separate panels, each consisting of three judges. Such panels shall sit at the times and places and hear the cases and controversies assigned as the court directs.

(c) Cases and controversies shall be heard and determined by a court or division of not more than three judges (except that the United States Court of Appeals for the Federal Circuit may sit in panels of more than three judges if its rules so provide), unless a hearing or rehearing before the court in banc is ordered by a majority of the circuit judges of the circuit who are in regular active service. A court in banc shall consist of all circuit judges in regular active service. A circuit judge of the circuit who has retired from regular active service shall also be competent to sit as a judge of the court in banc in the rehearing of a case or controversy if he sat in the court or division at the original hearing thereof.

(d) A majority of the number of judges authorized to constitute a court or panel thereof, as provided in paragraph (c), shall constitute a quorum. (June 25, 1948, c. 646, sec. 1, 62 Stat. 871; November 13, 1963, Public Law 88–176, sec. 1(b), 77 Stat. 331; April 2, 1982, Public Law 97–164, sec. 103, 96 Stat. 25.)

28 U.S.C. 1291.   Final decisions of district courts

The courts of appeals (other than the United States Court of Appeals for the Federal Circuit) shall have jurisdiction of appeals from all final decisions of the district courts of the United States, the United States District Court for the District of the Canal Zone, the District Court of Guam, and the District Court of the Virgin Islands, except where a direct review may be had in the Supreme Court. The jurisdiction of the United States Court of Appeals for the Federal Circuit shall be limited to the jurisdiction described in section 1292(c) and (d) of this title. (June 25, 1948, c. 646, sec. 1, 62 Stat. 929; October 31, 1951, c. 655, sec. 48, 65 Stat. 726; July 7, 1958, Public Law 85–508, sec. 12(e), 72 Stat. 348; 6 April 2, 1982, Public Law 97–164, sec. 124, 96 Stat. 36.)

§ 28 U.S.C. 1292. Interlocutory decisions

(a) Except as provided in subsections (c) and (d) of this section, the courts of appeals shall have jurisdiction of appeals from:

(1) Interlocutory orders of the district courts of the United States, the United States District Court for the District of the Canal Zone, the District Court of Guam, and the District Court of the Virgin Islands, or of the judges thereof, granting, continuing, modifying, refusing or dissolving injunctions, or refusing to dissolve or modify injunctions, except where a direct review may be had in the Supreme Court;

(2) Interlocutory orders appointing receivers, or refusing orders to wind up receiverships or to take steps to accomplish the purposes thereof, such as directing sales or other disposals of property;

(3) Interlocutory decrees of such district courts or the judges thereof determining the rights and liabilities of the parties to admiralty cases in which appeals from final decrees are allowed.

(b) When a district judge, in making in a civil action an order not otherwise appealable under this section, shall be of the opinion that such order involves a controlling question of law as to which there is substantial ground for difference of opinion and that an immediate appeal from the order may materially advance the ultimate termination of the litigation, he shall so state in writing in such order. The Court of Appeals may thereupon, in its discretion, permit an appeal to be taken from such order, if application is made to it within ten days after the entry of the order: *Provided,* however, That application for an appeal hereunder shall not stay proceedings in the district court unless the district judge or the Court of Appeals or a judge thereof shall so order.

(c) The United States Court of Appeals for the Federal Circuit shall have exclusive jurisdiction—

(1) of an appeal from an interlocutory order or decree described in subsection (a) of this section in any case over which the court would have jurisdiction of an appeal under section 1295 of this title; and

(2) of an appeal from a judgment in a civil action for patent infringement which would otherwise be appealable to the United States Court of Appeals for the Federal Circuit and is final except for an accounting.

(d)(1) When the chief judge of the Court of International Trade issues an order under the provisions of section 256(b) of this title, or when any judge of the Court of International Trade, in issuing any other interlocutory order, includes in the order a statement that a controlling question of law is involved with respect to which there is a substantial ground for difference of opinion and that an immediate appeal from that order may materially advance the ultimate termination of the litigation, the United States Court of Appeals for the Federal Circuit may, in its discretion, permit an appeal to be taken from such order, if application is made to that Court within ten days after the entry of such order.

(2) When any judge of the United States Claims Court, in issuing an interlocutory order, includes in the order a statement that a controlling question of law is involved with respect to which there is a substantial ground for difference of opinion and that an immediate appeal from that order may materially advance the ultimate termination of the litigation, the United States Court of Appeals for the Federal Circuit may, in its discretion, permit an appeal to be taken from such order, if application is made to that Court within ten days after the entry of such order.

(3) Neither the application for nor the granting of an appeal under this subsection shall stay proceedings in the Court of International Trade or in the Claims Court, as the case may be, unless a stay is ordered by a judge of the Court of International Trade or of the Claims Court or by the United States Court of Appeals for the Federal Circuit or a judge of that court. (June 25, 1948, c. 646, sec. 1, 62 Stat. 929; October 31, 1951, c. 655, sec. 49, 65 Stat. 726; July 7, 1958, Public Law 85–508, sec. 12(e), 72 Stat. 348; September 2, 1958, Public Law 85–919, 72 Stat. 1770; April 2, 1982, Public Law 97–164, sec. 125(b), 96 Stat. 36.

§ 28 U.S.C. 1295. Jurisdiction of the United States Court of Appeals for the Federal Circuit

(a) The United States Court of Appeals for the Federal Circuit shall have exclusive jurisdiction—

(1) of an appeal from a final decision of a district court of the United States, the United States District Court for the District of the Canal Zone, the District Court of Guam, the District Court of the Virgin Islands, or the District Court for the Northern Mariana Islands, if the jurisdiction of that court was based, in whole or in part, on section 1338 of this title, except that a case involving a claim arising under any Act of Congress relating to copyrights or trademarks and no other claims under section 1338(a) shall be governed by sections 1291, 1292, and 1294 of this title;

(2) of an appeal from a final decision of a district court of the United States, the United States District Court for the District of the Canal Zone, the District Court of Guam, the District Court of the Virgin Islands, or the District Court for the Northern Mariana Islands, if the jurisdiction of that court was based, in whole or in part, on section 1346 of this title, except that jurisdiction of an appeal in a case brought in a district court under section 1346(a)(1), 1346(b), 1346(e), or 1346(f) of this title or under section 1346(a)(2) when the claim is founded upon an Act of Congress or a regulation of an executive department providing for internal revenue shall be governed by sections 1291, 1292, and 1294 of this title;

(3) of an appeal from a final decision of the United States Claims Court;

(4) of an appeal from a decision of—

(A) the Board of Appeals or the Board of Patent Interferences of the Patent and Trademark Office with respect to patent applications and interferences, at the instance of an applicant for a patent or any party to a patent interference, and any such appeal shall waive the right of such applicant or party to proceed under section 145 or 146 of title 35;

(B) the Commissioner of Patents and Trademarks or the Trademark Trial and Appeal Board with respect to applications for registration of marks and other proceedings as provided in section 21 of the Trademark Act of 1946 (15 U.S.C. 1071); or

(C) a district court to which a case was directed pursuant to section 145 or 146 of title 35;

207

(5) of an appeal from a final decision of the United States Court of International Trade;

(6) to review the final determinations of the United States International Trade Commission relating to unfair practices in import trade, made under section 337 of the Tariff Act of 1930 (19 U.S.C. 1337);

(7) to review, by appeal on questions of law only, findings of the Secretary of Commerce under headnote 6 to schedule 8, part 4, of the Tariff Schedules of the United States (relating to importation of instruments or apparatus);

(8) of an appeal under section 71 of the Plant Variety Protection Act (7 U.S.C. 2461);

(9) of an appeal from a final order or final decision of the Merit Systems Protection Board, pursuant to sections 7703(b)(1) and 7703(d) of title 5; and

(10) of an appeal from a final decision of an agency board of contract appeals pursuant to section 8(g)(1) of the Contract Disputes Act of 1978 (41 U.S.C. 607(g)(1)).

(b) The head of any executive department or agency may, with the approval of the Attorney General, refer to the Court of Appeals for the Federal Circuit for judicial review any final decision rendered by a board of contract appeals pursuant to the terms of any contract with the United States awarded by that department or agency which the head of such department or agency has concluded is not entitled to finality pursuant to the review standards specified in section 10(b) of the Contract Disputes Act of 1978 (41 U.S.C. 609(b)). The head of each executive department or agency shall make any referral under this section within one hundred and twenty days after the receipt of a copy of the final appeal decision.

(c) The Court of Appeals for the Federal Circuit shall review the matter referred in accordance with the standards specified in section 10(b) of the Contract Disputes Act of 1978. The court shall proceed with judicial review on the administrative record made before the board of contract appeals on matters so referred as in other cases pending in such court, shall determine the issue of finality of the appeal decision, and shall, if appropriate, render judgment thereon, or remand the matter to any administrative or executive body or official with such direction as it may deem proper and just. (April 2, 1982, Public Law 97–164, sec. 127, 96 Stat. 37.)

C. Restrictions on Importation: Unfair Practices

19 U.S.C. 1337.   Unfair practices in import trade

(a) *Unfair methods of competition declared unlawful.* Unfair methods of competition and unfair acts in the importation of articles into the United States, or in their sale by the owner, importer, consignee, or agent of either, the effect or tendency of which is to destroy or substantially injure an industry, efficiently and economically operated, in the United States, or to prevent the establishment of such an industry, or to restrain or monopolize trade and commerce in the United States, are declared unlawful, and when found by the (United States International Trade) Commission to exist shall be dealt with, in addition to any other provisions of law, as provided in this section.
* * *

(i) *Importation by or for United States.* Any exclusion from entry or order under subsection (d), (e), or (f) of this section, in cases based on claims of United States letters patent, shall not apply to any articles imported by and for the use of the United States or imported for, and to be used for, the United States with the authorization or consent of the Government. Whenever any article would have been excluded from entry or would not have been entered pursuant to the provisions of such subsections but for the operation of this subsection, a patent owner adversely affected shall be entitled to reasonable and entire compensation in an action before the Court of Claims pursuant to the procedures of section 1498 of Title 28. (June 17, 1930, ch. 497, 46 Stat. 703; Amended Public Law 93–618, January 3, 1975, 88 Stat. 2053.)

19 U.S.C. 1337a.   Importation of products made, etc. under process covered by United States patent

The importation for use, sale, or exchange of a product made, produced, processed, or mined under or by means of a process covered by the claims of any unexpired valid United States letters patent, shall have the same status for the purposes of section 1337 of this title (Title 19.—Customs Duties) as the importation of any product or article covered by the claims of any unexpired valid United States letters patent. (July 2, 1940, ch. 515, 54 Stat. 724.)

D. Documentary Evidence in Patent Cases

28 U.S.C. 1733.   Government records and papers; copies

(a) Books or records of account or minutes of proceedings of any department or agency of the United States shall be admissible to prove the act, transaction or occurrence as a memorandum of which the same were made or kept.

(b) Properly authenticated copies or transcripts of any books, records, papers or documents of any department or agency of the United States shall be admitted in evidence equally with the originals thereof.

(c) This section does not apply to cases, actions, and proceedings to which the Federal Rules of Evidence apply. (June 25, 1948, ch. 646, 62 Stat. 946; amended Public Law 93–595, January 2, 1975, 88 Stat. 1949.)

28 U.S.C. 1741. Foreign official documents

An official record or document of a foreign country may be evidenced by a copy, summary, or excerpt authenticated as provided in the Federal Rules of Civil Procedure. (As amended, Public Law 88–619, October 3, 1964, 78 Stat. 996.)

28 U.S.C. 1744. Copies of Patent Office documents, generally

Copies of letters patent or of any records, books, papers, or drawings belonging to the Patent Office and relating to patents, authenticated under the seal of the Patent Office and certified by the Commissioner of Patents, or by another officer of the Patent Office authorized to do so by the Commissioner, shall be admissible in evidence with the same effect as the originals.

Any person making application and paying the required fee may obtain such certified copies. (June 25, 1948, ch. 646, 62 Stat. 948; amended May 24, 1949, 63 Stat. 103.)

28 U.S.C. 1745. Copies of foreign patent documents

Copies of specifications and drawings of foreign letters patent, or applications for foreign letters patent, and copies of excerpts of the official journals and other official publications of foreign patent offices belonging to the United States Patent Office, certified in the manner provided by section 1744 of this title are prima facie evidence of their contents and of the dates indicated on their face. (As amended, Public Law 88–619, October 3, 1964, 78 Stat. 996.)

28 U.S.C. 1781. Transmittal of letter rogatory or request

(a) The Department of State has power, directly, or through suitable channels—

(1) to receive a letter rogatory issued, or request made, by a foreign or international tribunal, to transmit it to the tribunal, officer, or agency in the United States to whom it is addressed, and to receive and return it after execution; and

(2) to receive a letter rogatory issued, or request made, by a tribunal in the United States, to transmit it to the foreign or international tribunal, officer, or agency to whom it is addressed, and to receive and return it after execution.

(b) This section does not preclude—

(1) the transmittal of a letter rogatory or request directly from a foreign or international tribunal to the tribunal, officer, or agency in the United States to whom it is addressed and its return in the same manner; or

(2) the transmittal of a letter rogatory or request directly from a tribunal in the United States to the foreign or international tribunal, officer, or agency to whom it is addressed and its return in the same manner. (As amended Public Law 88–619, October 3, 1964, 78 Stat. 996.)

II. THE PATENT AND TRADEMARK OFFICE

A. Establishment, Officers and Employees

15 U.S.C. 1511. Bureaus in Department

The following named bureaus, administrations, services, offices, and programs of the public service, and all that pertains thereto, shall be under the jurisdiction and subject to the control of the Secretary of Commerce:

* * *

(e) Patent and Trademark Office; * * * (As amended, Public Law 93–498, October 29, 1974, 88 Stat. 1549; Public Law 93–596, January 2, 1975, 88 Stat. 1949.)

Note.—By executive order, the Department of Commerce also has special responsibility in respect of patent protection abroad of inventions resulting from research financed by the government. (Executive Order No. 9865, June 16, 1947, 12 Federal Register 3907; U.S. Code Congressional Service, 80th Cong., 1st sess., p. 2028.)

5 U.S.C. 3104. Employment of specially qualified scientific and professional personnel

(a) The head of an agency named below may establish scientific or professional positions to carry out the research and development functions of his agency which require the services of specially qualified personnel within the following limits: * * *

(4) Department of Commerce—not more than 30, of which at least 5 are for the United States Patent Office in its examining and related activities. * * * (Public Law 89–554. September 6, 1966, 80 Stat. 415.)

5 U.S.C. 3325. Appointments to scientific and professional positions

(a) Positions established under section 3104 of this title are in the competitive service. However, appointments to the positions are made without competitive examination on approval of the qualifications of the proposed appointee by the Civil Service Commission or its designee for this purpose. * * * (Public Law 89–554, September 6, 1966, 80 Stat. 423.)

5 U.S.C. 5102. Definitions; application * * *

(c) This chapter (ch 51—Classification) does not apply to * * *

(23) examiners-in-chief and designated examiners-in-chief in the Patent Office, Department of Commerce; * * * (Public Law 89–554, September 6, 1966, 80 Stat. 444.)

5 U.S.C. 5316. Positions at level V

Level V of the Executive Schedule applies to the following positions * * * : * * *

(48) Commissioner of Patents, Department of Commerce. * * * (Public Law 89–554, September 6, 1966, 80 Stat. 463.)

*   *   *   *   *   *   *

B. RESTRICTIONS ON EMPLOYEES; BRIBERY * * *

18 U.S.C. 201. Bribery of public officials and witnesses

(a) For the purpose of this section:

"public official" means Member of Congress, the Delegate from the District of Columbia, or Resident Commissioner, either before or after he has qualified, or an officer or employee or person acting for or on behalf of the United States, or any department, agency or branch of Government thereof, including the District of Columbia, in any official function, under or by authority of any such department, agency, or branch of Government or a juror; and

"person who has been selected to be a public official" means any person who has been nominated or appointed to be a public official, or has been officially informed that he will be so nominated or appointed; and

"official act" means any decision or action on any question, matter, cause, suit, proceeding or controversy, which may at any time be pending, or which may by law be brought before any public official, in his official capacity, or in his place of trust or profit.

(b) Whoever, directly or indirectly, corruptly gives, offers or promises anything of value to any public official or person who has been selected to be a public official, or offers or promises any public official or any person who has been selected to be a public official to give anything of value to any other person or entity, with intent

(1) to influence any official act; or

(2) to influence such public official or person who has been selected to be a public official to commit or aid in committing, or collude in or allow, any fraud, or make opportunity for the commission of any fraud, on the United States; or

(3) to induce such public official or such person who has been selected to be a public official to do or omit to do any act in violation of his lawful duty, or

(c) Whoever, being a public official or person selected to be a public official, directly or indirectly, corruptly asks, demands, exacts, solicits, seeks, accepts, receives, or agrees to receive anything of value for himself or for any other person or entity, in return for:

(1) being influenced in his performance of any official act; or

(2) being influenced to commit or aid in committing, or to collude in, or allow, any fraud, or make opportunity for the commission of any fraud, on the United States; or

(3) being induced to do or omit to do any act in violation of his official duty; or

(d) Whoever, directly or indirectly, corruptly gives, offers, or promises anything of value to any person, or offers or promises such person to give anything of value to any other person or entity, with intent to influence the testimony under oath or affirmation of such first-mentioned person as a witness upon a trial, hearing, or other proceeding, before any court, any committee of either House or both Houses of Congress, or any agency, commission, or officer authorized by the laws of the United States to hear evidence or take testimony, or with intent to influence such person to absent himself therefrom; or

(e) Whoever, directly or indirectly, corruptly asks, demands, exacts, solicits, seeks, accepts, receives, or agrees to receive anything of value for himself or for any other person or entity in return for being influenced in his testimony under oath or affirmation as a witness upon any such trial, hearing or other proceeding, or in return for absenting himself therefrom—

Shall be fined not more than $20,000 or three times the monetary equivalent of the thing of value, whichever is greater, or imprisoned for not more than fifteen years, or both, and may be disqualified from holding any office of honor, trust, or profit under the United States.

(f) Whoever, otherwise than as provided by law for the proper discharge of official duty, directly or indirectly gives, offers, or promises anything of value to any public official, former public official, or person selected to be a public official, for or because of any official act performed or to be performed by such public official, former public official, or person selected to be a public official; or

(g) Whoever, being a public official, former public official, or person selected to be a public official, otherwise than as provided by law for the proper discharge of official duty, directly or indirectly asks, demands, exacts, solicits, seeks, accepts, receives, or agrees to receive anything of value for himself for or because of any official act performed or to be performed by him; or

(h) Whoever, directly or indirectly, gives, offers, or promises anything of value to any person, for or because of the testimony under oath or affirmation given or to be given by such person as a witness upon a trial, hearing, or other proceeding before any court, any committee of either House or both Houses of Congress, or any agency, commission, or officer authorized by the laws of the United States to hear evidence or take testimony, or for or because of his absence therefrom; or

(i) Whoever, directly or indirectly, asks, demands, exacts, solicits, seeks, accepts, receives, or agrees to receive anything of value for himself for or because of the testimony under oath or affirmation given or to be given by him as a witness upon any such trial, hearing, or other proceeding, or for or because of his absence therefrom—

Shall be fined not more than $10,000 or imprisoned for not more than two years, or both.

(j) Subsections (d), (e), (h), and (i) shall not be construed to prohibit the payment or receipt of witness fees provided by law, or the payment, by the party upon whose behalf a witness is called and receipt by a witness, of the reasonable cost of travel and subsistence incurred and the reasonable value of time lost in attendance at any such trial, hearing, or proceeding, or in the case of expert witnesses, involving a technical or professional opinion, a reasonable fee for times spent in the preparation of such opinion, and in appearing and testifying.

(k) The offenses and penalties prescribed in this section are separate from and in addition to those prescribed in sections 1503, 1504, and 1505 of this title. (Added Public Law 87–849, October 23, 1962, 76 Stat. 1119; amended Public Law 91–405, September 22, 1970, 84 Stat. 853.)

Note.—See also Executive Order No. 11222, "Standards of Ethical Conduct for Government Officers and Employees," published May 8, 1965, 30 Federal Register 6469; Executive Order No. 11590, published April 23, 1971, 36 Federal Register 7831; Executive Order No. 12107, published December 28, 1978, 44 Federal Register 1055.

18 U.S.C. 203. Compensation to Members of Congress, officers, and others in matters affecting the Government

(a) Whoever, otherwise than as provided by law for the proper discharge of official duties, directly or indirectly receives or agrees to receive, or asks, demands, solicits, or seeks, any compensation for any services rendered or to be rendered either by himself or another—

(1) at a time when he is a Member of Congress, Member of Congress Elect, Delegate from the District of Columbia, Delegate Elect from the District of Columbia, Resident Commissioner, or Resident Commissioner Elect; or

(2) at a time when he is an officer or employee of the United States in the executive, legislative, or judicial branch of the Government, or in any agency of the United States, including the District of Columbia,

in relation to any proceeding, application, request for a ruling or other determination, contract, claim, controversy, charge, accusation, arrest, or other particular matter in which the United States is a party or has a direct and substantial interest, before any department, agency, court-martial, officer, or any civil, military, or naval commission, or

(b) Whoever, knowingly, otherwise than as provided by law for the proper discharge of official duties, directly or indirectly gives, promises, or offers any compensation for any such services rendered or to be rendered at a time when the person to whom the compensation is given, promised, or offered, is or was such a Member, Delegate, Commissioner, officer, or employee—

Shall be fined not more than $10,000 or imprisoned for not more than two years, or both; and shall be incapable of holding any office of honor, trust, or profit under the United States.

(c) A special Government employee shall be subject to subsection (a) only in relation to a particular matter involving a specific party or parties (1) in which he has at any time participated personally and substantially as a Government employee or as a special Government employee through decision, approval, disapproval, recommendation, the rendering of advice, investigation or otherwise, or (2) which is pending in the department or agency of the Government in which he is serving: *Provided,* That clause (2) shall not apply in the case of a special Government employee who has served in such department or agency no more than sixty days during the immediately preceding period of three hundred and sixty-five consecutive days. (Added Public Law 87–849, October 23, 1962, 76 Stat. 1121; amended Public Law 91–405, September 22, 1970, 84 Stat. 853.)

18 U.S.C. 205. Activities of officers and employees in claims against and other matters affecting the Government

Whoever, being an officer or employee of the United States in the executive, legislative, or judicial branch of the Government or in any agency of the United States, including the District of Columbia, otherwise than in the proper discharge of his official duties—

(1) acts as agent or attorney for prosecuting any claim against the United States, or receives any gratuity, or any share of or interest in any such claim in consideration of assistance in the prosecution of such claim, or

(2) acts as agent or attorney for anyone before any department, agency, court, court-martial, officer, or any civil, military, or naval commission in connection with any proceeding, application, request for a ruling or other determination, contract, claim, controversy, charge, accusation, arrest, or other particular matter in which the United States is a party or has a direct and substantial interest—

Shall be fined not more than $10,000 or imprisoned for not more than two years, or both.

A special Government employee shall be subject to the preceding paragraphs only in relation to a particular matter involving a specific party or parties (1) in which he has at any time participated personally and substantially as a Government employee or as a special Government employee through decision, approval, disapproval, recommendation, the rendering of advice, investigation or otherwise, or (2) which is pending in the department or agency of the Government in which he is serving: *Provided,* That clause (2) shall not apply in the case of a special Government employee who has served in such department or agency no more than sixty days during the immediately preceding period of three hundred and sixty-five consecutive days.

Nothing herein prevents an officer or employee, if not inconsistent with the faithful performance of his duties, from acting without compensation as agent or attorney for any person who is the subject of disciplinary, loyalty, or other personnel administration proceedings in connection with those proceedings.

Nothing herein or in section 203 prevents an officer or employee, including a special Government employee, from acting, with or without compensation, as agent or attorney for his parents, spouse, child, or any person for whom, or for any estate for which, he is serving as guardian, executor, administrator, trustee, or other personal fiduciary except in those matters in which he has participated personally and substantially as a Government employee, through decision, approval, disapproval, recommendation, the rendering of advice, investigation, or otherwise, or which are the subject of his official responsibility, provided that the Government official responsible for appointment to his position approves.

Nothing herein or in section 203 prevents a special Government employee from acting as agent or attorney for another person in the performance of work under a grant by, or a contract with or for the benefit of, the United States provided that the head of the department or agency concerned with the grant or contract shall certify in writing that the national interest so requires.

Such certification shall be published in the Federal Register.

Nothing herein prevents an officer or employee from giving testimony under oath or from making statements required to be made under penalty for perjury or contempt. (Added Public Law 87–849, October 23, 1962, 76 Stat. 1122.)

18 U.S.C. 206. Exemption of retired officers of the uniformed services

Sections 203 and 205 of this title shall not apply to a retired officer of the uniformed services of the United States while not on active duty and not otherwise an officer or employee of the United States, or to any person specially excepted by Act of Congress. (Added Public Law 87–849, October 23, 1962, 76 Stat. 1123.)

18 U.S.C. 208. Acts affecting a personal financial interest

(a) Except as permitted by subsection (b) hereof, whoever, being an officer or employee of the executive branch of the United States Government, of any independent agency of the United States, a Federal Reserve bank director, officer or employee, or of the District of Columbia, including a special Government employee, participates personally and substantially as a Government officer or employee, through decision, approval, disapproval, recommendation, the rendering of advice, investigation, or otherwise, in a judicial or other proceeding, application, request for a ruling or other determination, contract, claim, controversy, charge, accusation, arrest, or other particular matter in which, to his knowledge, he, his spouse, minor child, partner, organization in which he is serving as officer, director, trustee, partner or employee, or any person or organization with whom he is negotiating or has any arrangement concerning prospective employment, has a financial interest—

Shall be fined not more than $10,000, or imprisoned not more than two years, or both.

(b) Subsection (a) hereof shall not apply (1) if the officer or employee first advises the Government official responsible for appointment to his position of the nature and circumstances of the judicial or other proceeding, application, request for a ruling or other determination, contract, claim, controversy, charge, accusation, arrest, or other particular matter and makes full disclosure of the financial interest and receives in advance a written determination made by such official that the interest is not so substantial as to be deemed likely to affect the integrity of the services which the Government may expect from such officer or employee, or (2) if, by general rule or regulation published in the Federal Register, the financial interest has been exempted from the requirements of clause (1) hereof as being too remote or too inconsequential to affect the integrity of Government officers' or employees' services. In the case of class A and

B directors of Federal Reserve banks, the Board of Governors of the Federal Reserve System shall be the Government official responsible for appointment. (Added Public Law 87–849, October 23, 1962, 76 Stat. 1124; Amended Public Law 95–188, November 16, 1977, 91 Stat. 1388.)

18 U.S.C. 209.   Salary of Government officials and employees payable only by United States

(a) Whoever receives any salary, or any contribution to or supplementation of salary, as compensation for his services as an officer or employee of the executive branch of the United States Government, of any independent agency of the United States, or of the District of Columbia, from any source other than the Government of the United States, except as may be contributed out of the treasury of any State, county, or municipality; or

Whoever, whether an individual, partnership, association, corporation, or other organization pays, or makes any contribution to, or in any way supplements the salary of, any such officer or employee under circumstances which would make its receipt a violation of this subsection—

Shall be fined not more than $5,000 or imprisoned not more than one year, or both.

(b) Nothing herein prevents an officer or employee of the executive branch of the United States Government, or of any independent agency of the United States, or of the District of Columbia, from continuing to participate in a bona fide pension, retirement, group life, health or accident insurance, profit-sharing stock bonus, or other employee welfare or benefit plan maintained by a former employer.

(c) This section does not apply to a special Government employee or to an officer or employee of the Government serving without compensation, whether or not he is a special Government employee, or to any person paying, contributing to, or supplementing his salary as such.

(d) This section does not prohibit payment or acceptance of contributions, awards, or other expenses under the terms of the Government Employees Training Act. (Public Law 85–507, 72 Stat. 327; 5 U.S.C. 2301–2319, July 7, 1958.) (Added Public Law 87–849, October 23, 1962, 76 Stat. 1125.)

(e) This section does not prohibit the payment of actual relocation expenses incident to participation, or the acceptance of same by a participant in an executive exchange or fellowship program in an executive agency: *Provided,* That such program has been established by statute or Executive order of the President, offers appointments not to exceed three hundred and sixty-five days, and permits no extensions in excess of ninety additional days. (As amended December 29, 1979, Public Law 96–174, sec. 1, 93 Stat. 1288.)

* * * * * * *

C. ACCOUNTS

31 U.S.C. 72. Same; settlement of accounts
* * *

Sixth. Said (General Accounting) office shall receive and examine all accounts of salaries and incidental expenses of the office of the Secretary of Commerce, and of all bureaus and offices under his direction, all accounts relating to * * * Patents * * * and certify the balances arising thereon to the Secretary of Commerce. * * * (As amended, Public Law 91–375, August 12, 1970, 84 Stat. 782.)

31 U.S.C. 725e. Permanent Appropriations Repeal Act; appropriations repealed

(a) * * * (R)eceipts theretofore authorized to be credited to the appropriation accounts appearing on the books of the Government and listed in subsection (b) of this section shall be deposited into the Treasury of the United States as miscellaneous receipts, and there are authorized to be appropriated from the general fund of the Treasury such amounts as may be necessary for the Patent Office * * *

(b)(1) Salaries and expenses, Patent Office (6s 289). (June 26, 1934, ch. 756, 73d Cong., 48 Stat. 1228.)

* * * * * * *

III. PROCEEDINGS IN THE PATENT AND TRADEMARK OFFICE

A. HOLIDAYS

5 U.S.C. 6103. Holidays

(a) The following are legal public holidays:

New Year's Day, January 1.

Washington's Birthday, the third Monday in February.

Memorial Day, the last Monday in May.

Independence Day, July 4.

Labor Day, the first Monday in September.

Columbus Day, the second Monday in October.

Veterans Day, November 11.

Thanksgiving Day, the fourth Thursday in November.

Christmas Day, December 25.

(b) For the purpose of statutes relating to pay and leave of employees, with respect to a legal public holiday and any other day declared to be a holiday by Federal statute or Executive order, the following rules apply:

(1) Instead of a holiday that occurs on a Saturday, the Friday immediately before is a legal public holiday for—

(A) Employees whose basic workweek is Monday through Friday; and

(B) the purpose of section 6309 (*Leave of Absence, etc.*) of this title.

(2) Instead of a holiday that occurs on a regular weekly non-workday of an employee whose basic workweek is other than Monday through Friday, except the regular weekly nonworkday administratively scheduled for the employee instead of Sunday, the workday immediately before that regular weekly nonworkday is a legal public holiday for the employee.

This subsection, except subparagraph (B) of paragraph (1), does not apply to an employee whose basic workweek is Monday through Saturday.

(c) January 20 of each fourth year after 1965, Inauguration Day, is a legal public holiday for the purpose of statutes relating to pay and leave of employees as defined by section 2105 of this title and individuals employed by the government of the District of Columbia employed in the District of Columbia, Montgomery and Prince Georges Counties in Maryland, Arlington and Fairfax Counties in Virginia, and the cities of Alexandria and Falls Church in Virginia. When January 20 of any fourth year after 1965 falls on Sunday, the next succeeding day selected for the public observance of the inauguration of the President is a legal holiday for the purpose of this

221

subsection. (Public Law 89–554, September 6, 1966, 80 Stat. 515; amended Public Law 90–363, June 28, 1968, 82 Stat. 250; Public Law 94–97, September 18, 1975, 89 Stat. 479.)

D.C. Code Sec. 28–2701. Holidays designated—Time for performing acts intended

The following days in each year, namely the first day of January, commonly called New Year's Day; the fifteenth day of January, commonly called Dr. King's Birthday; the twenty-second day of February known as Washington's Birthday; the Fourth of July; the thirtieth day of May, commonly called Decoration Day; the first Monday in September, known as Labor Day; the twenty-fifth day of December, commonly called Christmas Day; every Saturday, after twelve o'clock noon; any day appointed or recommended by the President of the United States as a day of public feasting or thanksgiving, and the day of the inauguration of the President, in every fourth year are holidays in the District for all purposes. When a day set apart as a legal holiday falls on Sunday the next succeeding day is a holiday. In such cases, and when a Sunday and a holiday fall on successive days, all commercial paper falling due on any of those days shall, for all purposes of presenting for payment or acceptance, be deemed to mature and be presentable for payment or acceptance on the next secular business day succeeding. Every Saturday is a holiday in the District for (1) every bank institution having an office or banking house located within the District, (2) every Federal savings and loan association whose main office is in the District, and (3) every building association, building and loan association, or savings and loan association, incorporated or unincorporated, organized and operating under the laws of and having an office located within the District. An act which would otherwise be required, authorized, or permitted to be performed on Saturday in the District at the office or banking house of, or by, any such bank or bank institution, Federal savings and loan association, building association, building and loan association, or savings and loan association, if Saturday were not a holiday, shall or may be so performed on the next succeeding business day, and liability or loss of rights of any kind may not result from such delay. (Public Law 88–509, August 30, 1964, 78 Stat. 671; amended D.C. Law 1–11, August 1, 1975.)

* * * * * * *

IV. PRACTICE BEFORE THE PATENT AND TRADEMARK OFFICE

A. REGULATIONS FOR AGENTS AND ATTORNEYS

5 U.S.C. 500. Administrative practice; general provisions
* * *

(b) An individual who is a member in good standing of the bar of the highest court of a State may represent a person before an agency on filing with the agency a written declaration that he is currently qualified as provided by this subsection and is authorized to represent the particular person in whose behalf he acts. * * *

(e) Subsections (b)–(d) of this section do not apply to practice before the Patent Office with respect to patent matters that continue to be covered by chapter 3 (sections 31–33) of title 35. * * * (Added Public Law 90–83, September 11, 1967, 81 Stat. 195.)

18 U.S.C. 207. Disqualification of former officers and employees; disqualification of partners of current officers and employees

(a) Whoever, having been an officer or employee of the executive branch of the United States Government, of any independent agency of the United States, or of the District of Columbia, including a special Government employee, after his employment has ceased, knowingly acts as agent or attorney for, or otherwise represents, any other person (except the United States), in any formal or informal appearance before, or, with the intent to influence, makes any oral or written communication on behalf of any other person (except the United States) to—

(1) any department, agency, court, court-martial, or any civil, military, or naval commission of the United States or the District of Columbia, or any officer or employee thereof, and

(2) in connection with any judicial or other proceeding, application, request for a ruling or other determination, contract, claim, controversy, investigation, charge, accusation, arrest, or other particular matter involving a specific party or parties in which the United States or the District of Columbia is a party or has a direct and substantial interest, and

(3) in which he participated personally and substantially as an officer or employee through decision, approval, disapproval, recommendation, the rendering of advice, investigation or otherwise, while so employed; or

(b) Whoever, (i) having been so employed, within two years after his employment has ceased, knowingly acts as agent or attorney for, or otherwise represents, any other person (except the United States), in any formal or informal appearance before, or, with the intent to influence, makes any oral or written communication on behalf of any other person (except the United States) to, or (ii) having been so employed and as specified in subsection (d) of this section, within two years after his employment has ceased, knowingly represents or aids, counsels, advises, consults, or assists in representing any other person (except the United States) by personal presence at any formal or informal appearance before—

(1) any department, agency, court, court-martial, or any civil, military or naval commission of the United States or the District of Columbia, or any officer or employee thereof, and

(2) in connection with any judicial or other proceeding, application, request for a ruling or other determination, contract, claim, controversy, investigation, charge, accusation, arrest or other particular matter involving a specific party or parties in which the United States or the District of Columbia is a party or has a direct and substantial interest, and

(3), as to (i), which was actually pending under his official responsibility as an officer or employee within a period of one year prior to the termination of such responsibility, or, as to (ii), in which he participated personally and substantially as an officer or employee; or

(c) Whoever, other than a special Government employee who serves for less than sixty days in a given calendar year, having been so employed as specified in subsection (d) of this section, within one year after such employment has ceased, knowingly acts as agent or attorney for, or otherwise represents, anyone other than the United States in any formal or informal appearance before, or, with the intent to influence, makes any oral or written communication on behalf of anyone other than the United States, to—

(1) the department or agency in which he served as an officer or employee, or any officer or employee thereof, and

(2) in connection with any judicial, rulemaking, or other pro-

ceeding, application, request for a ruling or other determination, contract, claim, controversy, investigation, charge, accusation, arrest, or other particular matter, and

(3) which is pending before such department or agency or in which such department or agency has a direct and substantial interest—

shall be fined not more than $10,000 or imprisoned for not more than two years, or both.

(d)(1) Subsection (c) of this section shall apply to a person employed—

(A) at a rate of pay specified in or fixed according to subchapter II of chapter 53 of title 5, United States Code [5 USCS §§ 5301 et seq.], or a comparable or greater rate of pay under other authority;

(B) on active duty as a commissioned officer of a uniformed service assigned to pay grade of O-9 or above as described in section 201 of title 37, United States Code [37 USCS § 201]; or

(C) in a position which involves significant decision-making or supervisory responsibility, as designated under this subparagraph by the Director of the Office of Government Ethics, in consultation with the department or agency concerned. Only positions which are not covered by subparagraphs (A) and (B) above, and for which the basic rate of pay is equal to or greater than the basic rate of pay for GS-17 of the General Schedule prescribed by section 5332 of title 5, United States Code [5 USCS § 5332], or positions which are established within the Senior Executive Service pursuant to the Civil Service Reform Act of 1978 [5 USCS §§ 1101 et seq.], or positions of active duty commissioned officers of the uniformed services assigned to pay O-7 or O-8, as described in section 201 of title 37, United States Code [37 USCS § 201], may be designated. As to persons in positions designated under this subparagraph, the Director may limit the restrictions of subsection (c) to permit a former officer or employee, who served in a separate agency or bureau within a department or agency, to make appearances before or communications to persons in an unrelated agency or bureau, within the same department or agency, having separate and distinct subject matter jurisdiction, upon a determination by the Director that there exists no potential for use of undue influence or unfair advantage based on past government service.

On an annual basis, the Director of the Office of Government Ethics shall review the designations and determinations made under this subparagraph and, in consultation with the department or agency concerned, make such additions and deletions as are necessary. Departments and agencies shall cooperate to the fullest extent with the Director of the Office of Government Ethics in the exercise of his responsibilities under this paragraph.

(2) The prohibition of subsection (c) shall not apply to appearances, communications, or representation by a former officer or employee, who is—

    (A) an elected official of a State or local government, or

    (B) whose principal occupation or employment is with (i) an agency or instrumentality of a State or local government, (ii) an accredited, degree-granting institution of higher education, as defined in section 1201(a) of the Higher Education Act of 1965 [20 USCS § 1141(a)], or (iii) a hospital or medical research organization, exempted and defined under section 501(c)(3) of the Internal Revenue Code of 1954 [26 USCS § 501(c)(3)], and the appearance, communication, or representation is on behalf of such government, institution, hospital, or organization.

(e) For the purposes of subsection (c), whenever the Director of the Office of Government Ethics determines that a separate statutory agency or bureau within a department or agency exercises functions which are distinct and separate from the remaining functions of the department or agency, the Director shall by rule designate such agency or bureau as a separate department or agency; except that such designation shall not apply to former heads of designated bureaus or agencies, or former officers and employees of the department or agency whose official responsibilities included supervision of said agency or bureau.

(f) The prohibitions of subsections (a), (b), and (c) shall not apply with respect to the making of communications solely for the purpose of furnishing scientific or technological information under procedures acceptable to the department or agency concerned, or if the head of the department or agency concerned with the particular matter, in consultation with the Director of the Office of Government Ethics, makes a certification, published in the Federal Register, that the former officer or employee has outstanding qualifications in a scientific, technological, or other technical discipline, and is acting with respect to a particular matter which requires such qualifications, and that the national interest would be served by the participation of the former officer or employee.

(g) Whoever, being a partner of an officer or employee of the executive branch of the United States Government, of any independent agency of the United States, or of the District of Columbia, including a special Government employee, acts as agent or attorney for anyone other than the United States before any department, agency, court, court-martial, or any civil, military, or naval commission of the United States or the District of Columbia, or any officer or employee thereof, in connection with any judicial or other proceeding, application, request for a ruling or other determination, contract, claim, controversy, investigation, charge, accusation, arrest, or other particular matter in which the United States or the District of Columbia is a party or has a direct and substantial interest and in which such officer or employee or special Government employee participates or has participated personally and substantially as an officer or employee through decision, approval, disapproval, recommendation, the rendering of advice, investigation, or otherwise, or which is the subject of his official responsibility, shall be fined not more than $5,000, or imprisoned for not more than one year, or both.

(h) Nothing in this section shall prevent a former officer or employee from giving testimony under oath, or from making statements required to be made under penalty of perjury.

(i) The prohibition contained in subsection (c) shall not apply to appearances or communications by a former officer or employee concerning matters of a personal and individual nature, such as personal income taxes or pension benefits; nor shall the prohibition of that subsection prevent a former officer or employee from making or providing a statement, which is based on the former officer's or employee's own special knowledge in the particular area that is the subject of the statement, provided that no compensation is thereby received, other than that regularly provided for by law or regulation for witnesses.

(j) If the head of the department or agency in which the former officer or employee served finds, after notice and opportunity for a hearing, that such former officer or employee violated subsection (a), (b), or (c) of this section, such department or agency head may prohibit that person from making, on behalf of any other person (except the United States), any informal or formal appearance before, or, with the intent to influence, any oral or written communication to, such department or agency on a pending matter of business for a period not to exceed five years, or may take other appropriate disciplinary action. Such disciplinary action shall be subject to review in an appropriate United States district court. No later than six months after the effective date of this Act [effective July 1, 1979], departments and agencies shall, in consultation with the Director of the Office of Government Ethics, establish procedures to carry out this subsection. (As amended October 26, 1978, Public Law 95–521, Title V, sec. 501(a), 92 Stat. 1864; June 22, 1979, Public Law 96–28, 93 Stat. 76.)

* * * * * * *

B. ADVERTISING, RESTRICTIONS

5 U.S.C. 501.   Advertising practice; restrictions

An individual, firm, or corporation practicing before an agency of the United States may not use the name of a Member of either House of Congress or of an individual in the service of the United States in advertising the business. (Public Law 89–554, September 6, 1966, 80 Stat. 381.)

* * * * * * *

C. SMALL-BUSINESS CONCERNS

15 U.S.C. 638.   Research and development—Declaration of policy
* * *

(d)(1) The Administrator (Small Business Administration) is authorized to consult with representatives of small-business concerns with a view to assisting and encouraging such firms to undertake joint programs for research and development. * * * Such joint programs may, among other things, include the following purposes: * * *

(E) to prosecute applications for patents and render patent services for participating members; and

(F) to negotiate and grant licenses under patents held under the joint program, and to establish corporations designed to exploit particular patents obtained by it. * * * (As amended, Public Law 85–536, July 18, 1958, 72 Stat. 392.)

* * * * * * *

V. Patent Fees

31 U.S.C. 725r.   Fees deposited into Treasury

Effective July 1, 1935, moneys received as Patent Office [Patent and Trademark Office] fees; unearned moneys, lands (Interior Department); reentry permit fees (Labor [Justice] Department); naturalization fees (Labor [Justice] Department); and registry fees (Labor [Justice] Department); and held in the official checking accounts of disbursing officers, shall be deposited in the Treasury of the United States to appropriately designated trust-fund receipt accounts and shall be available for refunds, and for transfer of the earned portions thereof into appropriate receipt fund titles on the books of the Government: Provided, That donations, quasi-public and unearned moneys carried in official checking accounts of disbursing officers and of others required to account to the Comptroller General (excluding clerks and marshals of the United States District Courts), administered by officers of the United States by virtue of their official capacity, shall be deposited similarly into the Treasury as trust funds and are hereby appropriated and made available for disbursement under the terms of the trust. (June 26, 1934, ch 756, sec. 19, 48 Stat. 1232; December 21, 1944, ch 631, sec. 2, 58 Stat. 845.)

* * * * * * *

VI. EXAMINATION OF APPLICATIONS

Information on Patents for Drugs

21 U.S.C. 372.   Examinations and Investigations
* * *

(d) The Secretary (of Health, Education, and Welfare) is authorized and directed, upon request from the Commissioner of Patents, to furnish full and complete information with respect to such questions relating to drugs as the Commissioner may submit concerning any patent application. The Secretary is further authorized, upon receipt of any such request, to conduct or cause to be conducted, such research as may be required. * * * (Public Law 87–782, October 10, 1962, 76 Stat. 796.)

* * * * * * *

VII. PLANTS

Plant Variety Protection Act

Note.—The "Plant Variety Protection Act," protecting novel varieties of sexually reproduced plants, comprises Chapter 57 of title 7; sections 1545 and 2353 of title 28; amendments to 7 U.S.C. 1551, 1562 (The Federal Seed Act) and sections 1338 and 1498 of title 28; and enacting provisions. (Public Law 91–577, December 24, 1970, 84 Stat. 1542.)

The text of the Act and the Regulations and Rules of Practice of the Plant Variety Protection Office are available in pamphlet form from that Office, Room 301 National Agricultural Library, AMS, USDA, Beltsville, Md. 20705.

* * * * * * *

VIII. SECRECY

Respect of Security Classification by Secretary of Commerce

15 U.S.C. 1155.   General standards and limitations; preservation of security classification

Notwithstanding any other provision of this chapter (ch. 23—Dissemination of Technical, Scientific and Engineering Information), the Secretary (of Commerce) shall respect and preserve the security classification of any scientific or technical information, data, patents, inventions, or discoveries in, or coming into, the possession or control of the Department of Commerce, the classified status of which the President or his designee or designees certify as being essential in the interest of national defense, and nothing in this chapter shall be construed as modifying or limiting any other statute relating to the classification of information for reasons of national defense or security. (September 9, 1950, ch. 936, 64 Stat. 824.)

* * * * * * *

IX. GOVERNMENT INTERESTS IN PATENTS

A. DEPARTMENT OF ENERGY/NUCLEAR REGULATORY COMMISSION

1. INVENTIONS RELATING TO ATOMIC WEAPONS

Note.—References to the "Commission" in sections 42 U.S.C. 2014 and 2181–2190 incl., no longer mean the Atomic Energy Commission, which has been abolished. See sections 42 U.S.C. 5811, 5814, 5841, and 7151 *infra,* pp. 87, 88 under which its functions have been transferred to the Department of Energy and the Nuclear Regulatory Commission. Under the transitional provisions (42 U.S.C. 5871) a reference to "Commission" in any existing statute may mean either of these new agencies.

42 U.S.C. 2014.   Definitions

The intent of the Congress in the definitions as given in this section should be construed from the words or phrases used in the definitions. As used in this chapter (ch. 23—Development and Control of Atomic Energy):
* * *

(c) The term "atomic energy" means all forms of energy released in the course of nuclear fission or nuclear transformation.

(d) The term "atomic weapon" means any device utilizing atomic energy, exclusive of the means for transporting or propelling the device (where such means is a separable and divisible part of the device), the principal purpose of which is for use as, for development of, a weapon, a weapon prototype, or a weapon test device.
* * *

(u) The term "produce," when used in relation to special nuclear material, means (1) to manufacture, make, produce, or refine special nuclear material; (2) to separate special nuclear material from other substances in which such material may be contained; or (3) to make or to produce new special nuclear material.
* * *

(z) The term "source material" means (1) uranium, thorium, or any other material which is determined by the Commission pursuant to the provisions of section 2091 of this title to be source material; or (2) ores containing one or more of the foregoing materials, in such concentration as the Commission may by regulation determine from time to time.

(aa) The term "special nuclear material" means (1) plutonium, uranium enriched in the isotope 233 or in the isotope 235, and any other material which the Commission, pursuant to the provisions of section 2071 of this title, determines to be special nuclear material, but does not include source material; or (2) any material artificially enriched by any of the foregoing, but does not include source material. * * * (Public Law 703, 83d Cong., August 30, 1954, 68 Stat. 922; amended Public Law 87–206, September 6, 1961, 75 Stat. 476; Public Law 89–645, October 13, 1966, 80 Stat. 891.)

42 U.S.C. 2181. Inventions Relating to Atomic Weapons, and Filing of Reports

(a) No patent shall hereafter be granted for any invention or discovery which is useful solely in the utilization of special nuclear material or atomic energy in an atomic weapon. Any patent granted for any such invention or discovery is revoked, and just compensation shall be made therefor.

(b) No patent hereafter granted shall confer any rights with respect to any invention or discovery to the extent that such invention or discovery is used in the utilization of special nuclear material or atomic energy in atomic weapons. Any rights conferred by any patent heretofore granted for any invention or discovery are revoked to the extent that such invention or discovery is so used, and just compensation shall be made therefore.

(c) *Report of invention to Commission.* Any person who has made or hereafter makes any invention or discovery useful in the production or utilization of special nuclear material or atomic energy, shall file with the Commission a report containing a complete description thereof unless such invention or discovery is described in an application for a patent filed with the Commissioner of Patents by such person within the time required for the filing of such report. The report covering any such invention or discovery shall be filed on or before the one hundred and eightieth day after such person first discovers or first has reason to believe that such invention or discovery is useful in such production or utilization.

(d) The Commissioner of Patents shall notify the Commission of all applications for patents heretofore or hereafter filed which, in his opinion, disclose inventions or discoveries required to be reported under subsection (c) of this section, and shall provide the Commission access to all such applications.

(e) Reports filed pursuant to subsection (c) of this section, and applications to which access is provided under subsection (d) of this section, shall be kept in confidence by the Commission, and no information concerning the same given without authority of the inventor or owner unless necessary to carry out the provisions of any Act of Congress or in such special circumstances as may be determined by the Commission. (Public Law 703, 83d Cong., August 30, 1954, 68 Stat. 943; amended Public Law 87–206, September 6, 1961, 75 Stat. 477.)

42 U.S.C. 2182. Inventions conceived during Commission contracts

Any invention or discovery, useful in the production or utilization of special nuclear material or atomic energy, made or conceived in the course of or under any contract, subcontract, or arrangement entered into with or for the benefit of the Commission, regardless of whether the contract, subcontract, or arrangement involved the expenditure of funds by the Commission, shall be vested in, and be the property of, the Commission, except that the Commission may waive its claim to any such invention or discovery under such circumstances as the Commission may deem appropriate, consistent with the policy of this section. No patent for any invention or discovery, useful in the production or utilization of special nuclear material or atomic energy, shall be issued unless the applicant files with the application, or within thirty days after request therefor by the Commissioner of Patents (unless the Commission advises the Commissioner of Patents that its rights have been determined and that accordingly no statement is necessary) a statement under oath setting forth the full facts surrounding the making or conception of the invention or discovery described in the application and whether the invention or discovery was made or conceived in the course of or under any contract, subcontract, or arrangement entered into with or for the benefit of the Commission, regardless of whether the contract, subcontract, or arrangement involved the expenditure of funds by the Commission. The Commissioner of Patents shall as soon as the application is otherwise in condition for allowance forward copies of the application and the statement to the Commission.

The Commissioner of Patents may proceed with the application and issue the patent to the applicant (if the invention or discovery is otherwise patentable) unless the Commission, within 90 days after receipt of copies of the application and statement, directs the Commissioner of Patents to issue the patent to the Commission (if the invention or discovery is otherwise patentable) to be held by the Commission as the agent of and on behalf of the United States.

If the Commission files such a direction with the Commissioner of Patents, and if the applicant's statement claims, and the applicant still believes, that the invention or discovery was not made or conceived in the course of or under any contract, subcontract or arrangement entered into with or for the benefit of the Commission entitling the Commission to the title to the application or the patent the applicant may, within 30 days after notification of the filing of such a direction, request a hearing before a Board of Patent Interferences. The Board shall have the power to hear and determine whether the Commission was entitled to the direction filed with the Commissioner of Patents. The Board shall follow the rules and procedures established for interference cases and an appeal may be taken by either the applicant or the Commission from the final order of the Board to the United States Court of Appeals for the Federal Circuit in accordance with the procedures governing the appeals from the Board of Patent Interferences.

If the statement filed by the applicant should thereafter be found to contain false material statements any notification by the Commission that it has no objections to the issuance of a patent to the applicant shall not be deemed in any respect to constitute a waiver of the provisions of this section or of any applicable civil or criminal statute, and the Commission may have the title to the patent transferred to the Commission on the records of the Commissioner of Patents in accordance with the provisions of this section. A determination of rights by the Commissioner pursuant to a contractual provision or other arrangement prior to the request of the Commissioner of Patents for the statement, shall be final in the absence of false material statements or nondisclosure of material facts by the applicant. (As amended Public Law 87–206, September 6, 1961, 75 Stat. 477; amended Public Law 87–615, August 29, 1962, 76 Stat. 411; Public Law 97–164, April 2, 1982, 96 Stat. 49.)

42 U.S.C. 2183. Nonmilitary utilization

(a) The Commission may, after giving the patent owner an opportunity for a hearing, declare any patent to be affected with the public interest if (1) the invention or discovery covered by the patent is of primary importance in the production or utilization of special nuclear material or atomic energy; and (2) the licensing of such invention or discovery under this section is of primary importance to effectuate the policies and purposes of this chapter (Ch. 23—Development and Control of Atomic Energy).

(b) Whenever any patent has been declared affected with the public interest, pursuant to subsection (a) of this section—

(1) the Commission is hereby licensed to use the invention or discovery covered by such patent in performing any of its powers under this chapter; and

(2) any person may apply to the Commission for a nonexclusive patent license to use the invention or discovery covered by such patent, and the Commission shall grant such patent license to the extent that it finds that the use of the invention or discovery is of primary importance to the conduct of an activity by such person authorized under this chapter.

(c) Any person—

(1) who has made application to the Commission for a license under sections 2073, 2092, 2093, 2111, 2133 or 2134 of this title, or a permit or lease under section 2097 of this title;

(2) to whom such license, permit, or lease has been issued by the Commission;

(3) who is authorized to conduct such activities as such applicant is conducting or proposes to conduct under a general license issued by the Commission under sections 2092 or 2111 of this title; or

(4) whose activities or proposed activities are authorized under section 2051 of this title,

may at any time make application to the Commission for a patent license for the use of an invention or discovery useful in the production or utilization of special nuclear material or atomic energy covered by a patent. Each such application shall set forth the nature and purpose of the use which the applicant intends to make of the patent license, the steps taken by the applicant to obtain a patent license from the owner of the patent, and a statement of the effects, as estimated by the applicant, on the authorized activities which will result from failure to obtain such patent license and which will result from the granting of such patent license.

(d) Whenever any person has made an application to the Commission for a patent license pursuant to subsection (c) of this section—

(1) the Commission, within 30 days after the filing of such application, shall make available to the owner of the patent all of the information contained in such application, and shall notify the owner of the patent of the time and place at which a hearing will be held by the Commission;

(2) the Commission shall hold a hearing within 60 days after the filing of such application at a time and place designated by the Commission; and

(3) in the event an applicant applies for two or more patent licenses, the Commission may, in its discretion, order the consolidation of such applications, and if the patents are owned by more than one owner, such owners may be made parties to one hearing.

(e) If, after any hearing conducted pursuant to subsection (d) of this section, the Commission finds that—

(1) the invention or discovery covered by the patent is of primary importance in the production or utilization of special nuclear material or atomic energy;

(2) the licensing of such invention or discovery is of primary importance to the conduct of the activities of the applicant;

(3) the activities to which the patent license are proposed to be applied by such applicant are of primary importance to the furtherance of policies and purposes of this chapter; and

(4) such applicant cannot otherwise obtain a patent license from the owner of the patent on terms which the Commission deems to be reasonable for the intended use of the patent to be made by such applicant,

the Commission shall license the applicant to use the invention or discovery covered by the patent for the purposes stated in such application on terms deemed equitable by the Commission and generally not less fair than those granted by the patentee or by the Commission to similar licensees for comparable use.

(f) The Commission shall not grant any patent license pursuant to subsection (e) of this section for any other purpose than that stated in the application. Nor shall the Commission grant any patent license to any other applicant for a patent license on the same patent without an application being made by such applicant pursuant to subsection (c) of this section, and without separate notification and hearing as provided in subsection (d) of this section, and without a separate finding as provided in subsection (e) of this section.

(g) The owner of the patent affected by a declaration or a finding made by the Commission pursuant to subsection (b) or (e) of this section shall be entitled to a reasonable royalty fee from the licensee for any use of an invention or discovery licensed by this section. Such royalty fee may be agreed upon by such owner and the patent licensee, or in the absence of such agreement shall be determined for each patent license by the Commission pursuant to section 2187(c) of this title.

(h) The provisions of this section shall apply to any patent the application for which shall have been filed before September 1, 1979. (Public Law 703, 83d Cong., August 30, 1954, 68 Stat. 945; amended variously as to date in (h) the latest being Public Law 93–377, August 17, 1974, 88 Stat. 475.)

42 U.S.C. 2184.   Injunctions

No court shall have jurisdiction or power to stay, restrain, or otherwise enjoin the use of any invention or discovery by a patent licensee, to the extent that such use is licensed by section 2183(b) or 2183(e) of this title. If, in any action against such patent licensee, the court shall determine that the defendant is exercising such license, the measure of damages shall be the royalty fee determined pursuant to section 2187(c) of this title, together with such costs, interest, and reasonable attorney's fees as may be fixed by the court. If no royalty fee has been determined, the court shall stay the proceeding until the royalty fee is determined pursuant to section 2187(c) of this title. If any such patent licensee shall fail to pay such royalty fee, the patentee may bring an action in any court of competent jurisdiction for such royalty fee, together with such costs, interest, and reasonable attorney's fees as may be fixed by the court. (Public Law 703, 83d Cong., August 30, 1954, 68 Stat. 946.)

42 U.S.C. 2185.   Prior Art

In connection with applications for patents covered by this subchapter, the fact that the invention or discovery was known or used before shall be a bar to the patenting of such invention or discovery even though such prior knowledge or use was under secrecy within the atomic energy program of the United States. (Public Law 703, 83d Cong., August 30, 1954, 68 Stat. 947.)

42 U.S.C. 2186.   Commission patent licenses

The Commission shall establish standard specifications upon which it may grant a patent license to use any patent declared to be affected with the public interest pursuant to section 2183(a) of this title. Such a patent license shall not waive any of the other provisions of this chapter. (Public Law 703, 83d Cong., August 30, 1954, 68 Stat. 947; Public Law 96–517, December 12, 1980, 94 Stat. 3027.)

42 U.S.C. 2187.   Compensation, awards, and royalties

(a) *Patent Compensation Board.*—The Commission shall designate a Patent Compensation Board to consider applications under this section. The members of the Board shall receive a per diem compensation for each day spent in meetings or conferences, and all members shall receive their necessary traveling or other expenses while engaged in the work of the Board. The members of the Board may serve as such without regard to the provisions of sections 281, 283, or 284 of Title 18, except insofar as such sections may prohibit any such member from receiving compensation in respect of any particular matter which directly involves the Commission or in which the Commission is directly interested.

(b) *Eligibility.*—

(1) Any owner of a patent licensed under section 2188 or 2183(b) or 2183(e) of this title, or any patent licensee thereunder may make application to the Commission for the determination of a reasonable royalty fee in accordance with such procedures as the Commission by regulation may establish.

(2) Any person seeking to obtain the just compensation provided in section 2181 of this title shall make application therefor to the Commission in accordance with such procedures as the Commission may by regulation establish.

(3) Any person making any invention or discovery useful in the production or utilization of special nuclear material or atomic energy, who is not entitled to compensation or a royalty therefor under this chapter and who has complied with the provisions of section 2181(c) of this title may make application to the Commission for, and the Commission may grant, an award. The Commission may also, after consultation with the General Advisory Committee, and with the approval of the President, grant an award for

any especially meritorious contribution to the development, use, or control of atomic energy.

(c) *Standards.*—

(1) In determining a reasonable royalty fee as provided for in section 2183(b) or 2183(c) of this title, the Commission shall take into consideration (A) the advice of the Patent Compensation Board; (B) any defense, general or special, that might be pleaded by a defendant in an action for infringement; (C) the extent to which, if any, such patent was developed through federally financed research; and (D) the degree of utility, novelty, and importance of the invention or discovery, and may consider the cost to the owner of the patent of developing such invention or discovery or acquiring such patent.

(2) In determining what constitutes just compensation as provided for in section 2181 of this title, or in determining the amount of any award under subsection (b)(3) of this section, the Commission shall take into account the considerations set forth in paragraph (1) of this subsection and the actual use of such invention or discovery. Such compensation may be paid by the Commission in periodic payments or in a lump sum.

(d) *Limitations.*—Every application under this section shall be barred unless filed within six years after the date on which first accrues the right to such reasonable royalty fee, just compensation, or award for which such application is filed. (Public Law 703, 83d Cong., August 30, 1954, 68 Stat. 947; amended Public Law 87–206, September 6, 1961, 75 Stat. 478; Public Law 93–276, May 10, 1974, 88 Stat. 119.)

Note.—The Patent Compensation Board and the General Advisory Committee, referred to above, have been transferred to the Department of Energy. (See 42 U.S.C. 5814(d) and 7151, *infra,* pp. 152, 153.)

42 U.S.C. 2188.   Monopolistic use of patents

Whenever the owner of any patent hereafter granted for any invention or discovery of primary use in the utilization or production of special nuclear material or atomic energy is found by a court of competent jurisdiction to have intentionally used such patent in a manner so as to violate any of the antitrust laws specified in section 2135(a) of this title, there may be included in the judgments of the court, in its discretion and in addition to any other lawful sanctions, a requirement that such owner license such patent to any other licensee of the

Commission who demonstrates a need therefore. If the court, at its discretion, deems that such licensee shall pay a reasonable royalty to the owner of the patent, the reasonable royalty shall be determined in accordance with section 2187 of this title. (As amended, Public Law 87–206, September 6, 1961, 75 Stat. 478.)

42 U.S.C. 2189.   Federally financed research

Nothing in this chapter (ch. 23—Development and Control of Atomic Energy) shall affect the right of the Commission to require that patents granted on inventions, made or conceived during the course of federally financed research or operations, be assigned to the United States. (Public Law 703, 83d Cong., August 30, 1954, 68 Stat. 948.)

42 U.S.C. 2190.   Saving clause

Any patent application on which a patent was denied by the United States Patent Office under sections 11(a)(1), 11(a)(2), or 11(b) of the Atomic Energy Act of 1946, and which is not prohibited by section 2181 or 2185 of this title may be reinstated upon application to the Commissioner of Patents within one year after August 30, 1954, and shall then be deemed to have been continuously pending since its original filing date: *Provided, however,* That no patent issued upon any patent application so reinstated shall in any way furnish a basis of claim against the Government of the United States. (Public Law 703, 83d Cong., August 30, 1954, 68 Stat. 948.)

*   *   *   *   *   *   *

2. GENERAL PROVISIONS

42 U.S.C. 2201.   General Provisions

In the performance of its functions the Commission is authorized to
* * *

(g) acquire, purchase, lease, and hold real and personal property, including patents, as agent of and on behalf of the United States, subject to the provisions of section 2224 of this title, and to sell, lease, grant and dispose of such real and personal property as provided in this chapter; * * * (Public Law 703, 83d Cong., August 30, 1954, 68 Stat. 948.)

42 U.S.C. 5811. Establishment of Energy Research and Development Administration

There is hereby established an independent executive agency to be known as the Energy Research and Development Administration (hereinafter in this chapter referred to as the "Administration"). (Public Law 93–438, October 11, 1974, 88 Stat. 1234.)

Note.—The functions of the Energy Research and Development Administration have been transferred to the Department of Energy. See 42 U.S.C. 7151, *infra* p. 153.

42 U.S.C. 5814. Abolition and transfers

(a) The Atomic Energy Commission is hereby abolished.

(b) All other functions of the Commission, the Chairman and members of the Commission, and the officers and components of the Commission are hereby transferred or allowed to lapse pursuant to the provisions of this chapter.

(c) There are hereby transferred to and vested in the Administrator all functions of the Atomic Energy Commission, the Chairman and members of the Commission, and the officers and components of the Commission, except as otherwise provided in this chapter.

(d) The General Advisory Committee established pursuant to section 2036 of this title, the Patent Compensation Board established pursuant to section 2187 of this title * * * are transferred to the Energy Research and Development Administration and the functions of the Commission with respect thereto * * * are transferred to the Administration. * * * (Public Law 93–438, October 11, 1974, 88 Stat. 1239.)

Note.—The functions of the Energy Research and Development Administration have been transferred to the Department of Energy. See 42 U.S.C. 7151.

42 U.S.C. 5817. Powers of the Administrator (now Secretary of Energy)

(a) *Research and development.* * * * Such functions of the Administrator under this chapter as are applicable to the nuclear activities transferred pursuant to this subchapter shall be subject to the provisions of the Atomic Energy Act of 1954, as amended, and to other authority applicable to such nuclear activities.
* * *

(d) *Acquisition of copyrights and patents.* The administrator is authorized to acquire any of the following described rights if the property acquired thereby is for the use in, or is useful to, the performance of functions vested in him:

(1) Copyrights, patents, and applications for patents, designs, processes, specifications, and data.

(2) Licenses under copyrights, patents, and applications for patents.

(3) Releases, before suit is brought, for past infringement of patents or copyrights. * * * (Public Law 93–438, October 11, 1974, 88 Stat. 1240.)

Note.—The functions of the Administrator referred to in this section have been transferred to the Secretary of Energy. See 42 U.S.C. 7151 and 7261, below.

42 U.S.C. 5841. Establishment and transfers—Composition * * * (etc.)

(a)(1) There is established an independent regulatory Commission to be known as the Nuclear Regulatory Commission which shall be composed of five members * * *

(f) There are hereby transferred to the Commission all the licensing and related regulatory functions of the Atomic Energy Commission * * * which functions * * * are excepted from the transfer to the Administrator by section 5814(c) of this title. * * * (Public Law 93–438, October 11, 1974, 88 Stat. 1242; Public Law 94–79, August 9, 1975, 89 Stat. 413.)

42 U.S.C. 5845. Office of Nuclear Regulatory Research * * *

(b) Subject to the provisions of this chapter, the Director of Nuclear Regulatory Research shall perform such functions as the Commission shall delegate, including:
* * *

(2) Engaging in or contracting for research which the Commission deems necessary for the performance of its licensing and related regulatory functions. * * * (Public Law 93–438, October 11, 1974, 88 Stat. 1246.)

42 U.S.C. 7151. General transfers

(a) Except as otherwise provided in this Act, there are hereby transferred to, and vested in, the Secretary (of Energy) all of the functions vested by law in * * * the Administrator of the Energy Research and Development Administration or the Energy Research and Development Administration * * * (Public Law 95–91, August 4, 1977, 91 Stat. 577.)

42 U.S.C. 7261.   Acquisition of copyrights, patents etc.

The Secretary is authorized to acquire any of the following described rights if the property acquired thereby is for use by or for, or useful to, the Department:

(1) copyrights, patents, and applications for patents, designs, processes, and manufacturing data;

(2) licenses under copyrights, patents, and applications for patents; and

(3) releases, before suit is brought, for past infringement of patents or copyrights. (Public Law 95–91, August 4, 1977, 91 Stat. 601.)

* * * * * * *

3. Rights To Inventions Arising From Sponsored R&D

42 U.S.C. 5908.   Patents and inventions

(a) *Vesting of title to inventions and issuance of patents to United States, prerequisites.* Whenever any invention is made or conceived in the course of or under any contract of the Administration, (now Department of Energy) other than nuclear energy research, development, and demonstration pursuant to the Atomic Energy Act of 1954 and the Administrator (now Secretary of Energy) determines that—

(1) the person who made the invention was employed or assigned to perform research, development, or demonstration work and the invention is related to the work he was employed or assigned to perform, or that it was within the scope of his employment duties, whether or not it was made during working hours, or with a contribution by the Government or the use of Government facilities, equipment, materials, allocated funds, information proprietary to the Government, or services of Government employees during working hours; or

(2) the person who made the invention was not employed or assigned to perform research, development, or demonstration

work, but the invention is nevertheless related to the contract or to the work or duties he was employed or assigned to perform, and was made during working hours, or with a contribution from the Government of the sort referred to in clause (1), title to such invention shall vest in the United States, and if patents on such invention are issued they shall be issued to the United States, unless in particular circumstances the Administrator waives all or any part of the rights of the United States to such invention in conformity with the provisions of this section.

(b) *Contract as requiring report to Administration of inventions, etc., made in course of contract.* Each contract entered into by the Administration with any person shall contain effective provisions under which such person shall furnish promptly to the Administration a written report containing full and complete technical information concerning any invention, discovery, improvement, or innovation which may be made in the course of or under such contract.

(c) *Waiver by Administrator of rights of United States: regulations prescribing procedures; record of waiver determinations; objectives.* Under such regulations in conformity with the provisions of this section as the Administrator shall prescribe, the Administrator may waive all or any part of the rights of the United States under this section with respect to any invention or class of inventions made or which may be made by any person or class of persons in the course of or under any contract of the Administration if he determines that the interests of the United States and the general public will best be served by such waiver. The Administration shall maintain a publicly available, periodically updated record of waiver determinations. In making such determinations, the Administrator shall have the following objectives:

(1) Making the benefits of the energy research, development, and demonstration program widely available to the public in the shortest practicable time.

(2) Promoting the commercial utilization of such inventions.

(3) Encouraging participation by private persons in the Administration's energy research, development, and demonstration program.

(4) Fostering competition and preventing undue market concentration or the creation or maintenance of other situations inconsistent with the antitrust laws.

(d) *Considerations applicable at time of contracting for waiver determination by Administrator.* In determining whether a waiver to the contractor at the time of contracting will best serve the interests of the United States and the general public, the Administrator shall specifically include as considerations—

(1) the extent to which the participation of the contractor will expedite the attainment of the purposes of the program;

(2) the extent to which a waiver of all or any part of such rights in any or all fields of technology is needed to secure the participation of the particular contractor;

(3) the extent to which the contractor's commercial position may expedite utilization of the research, development, and demonstration program results;

(4) the extent to which the Government has contributed to the field of technology to be funded under the contract;

(5) the purpose and nature of the contract, including the intended use of the results developed thereunder;

(6) the extent to which the contractor has made or will make substantial investment of financial resources or technology developed at the contractor's private expense which will directly benefit the work to be performed under the contract;

(7) the extent to which the field of technology to be funded under the contract has been developed at the contractor's private expense;

(8) the extent to which the Government intends to further develop to the point of commercial utilization the results of the contract effort;

(9) the extent to which the contract objectives are concerned with the public health, public safety, or public welfare;

(10) the likely effect of the waiver on competition and market concentration; and

(11) in the case of a nonprofit educational institution, the extent to which such institution has a technology transfer capability and program, approved by the Administrator as being consistent with the applicable policies of this section.

(e) *Considerations applicable to identified invention for waiver determination by Administrator.* In determining whether a waiver to the contractor or inventor of rights to an identified invention will best serve the interests of the United States and the general public, the Administrator shall specifically include as considerations paragraphs (4) through (11) of subsection (d) of this section as applied to the invention and—

(1) the extent to which such waiver is a reasonable and necessary incentive to call forth private risk capital for the development and commercialization of the invention; and

(2) the extent to which the plans, intentions, and ability of the contractor or inventor will obtain expeditious commercialization of such invention.

(f) *Rights subject to reservation where title to invention vested in United States.* Whenever title to an invention is vested in the United States, there may be reserved to the contractor or inventor—

(1) a revocable or irrevocable nonexclusive, paid-up license for the practice of the invention throughout the world; and

(2) the rights to such invention in any foreign country where the United States has elected not to secure patent rights and the contractor elects to do so, subject to the rights set forth in paragraphs (2), (3), (6), and (7) of subsection (h) of this section: *Provided,* That when specifically requested by the Administration and three years after issuance of such a patent, the contractor shall submit the report specified in subsection (h)(1) of this section.

(g)(1) Subject to paragraph (2) of this subsection, the Administrator shall determine and promulgate regulations specifying the terms and conditions upon which licenses may be granted in any invention to which title is vested in the United States.

(2) Pursuant to paragraph (1) of this subsection, the Administrator may grant exclusive or partially exclusive licenses in any invention only if, after notice and opportunity for hearing, it is determined that—

(A) the interests of the United States and the general public will best be served by the proposed license, in view of the applicant's intentions, plans, and ability to bring the invention to the point of practical or commercial applications;

(B) the desired practical or commercial applications have not been achieved, or are not likely expeditiously to be achieved, under any nonexclusive license which has been granted, or which may be granted, on the invention;

(C) exclusive or partially exclusive licensing is a reasonable and necessary incentive to call forth risk capital and expenses to bring the invention to the point of practical or commercial applications; and

(D) the proposed terms and scope of exclusivity are not substantially greater than necessary to provide the incentive for bringing the invention to the point of practical or commercial applications and to permit the licensee to recoup its cost and a reasonable profit thereon:

Provided, That, the Administrator shall not grant such exclusive or partially exclusive license if he determines that the grant of such license will tend substantially to lessen competition or result in undue concentration in any section of the country in any line of commerce to which the technology to be licensed relates. The Administration shall maintain a publicly available, periodically updated record of determinations to grant such licenses.

(h) Each waiver of rights or grant of an exclusive or partially exclusive license shall contain such terms and conditions as the Administrator may determine to be appropriate for the protection of the interests of the United States and the general public, including provisions for the following:

(1) Periodic written reports at reasonable intervals, and when specifically requested by the Administration, on the commercial use that is being made or is intended to be made of the invention.

(2) At least an irrevocable, nonexclusive, paid-up license to make, use, and sell the invention throughout the world by or on behalf of the United States (including any Government agency) and States and domestic municipal governments, unless the Administrator determines that it would not be in the public interest to acquire the license for the States and domestic municipal governments.

(3) The right in the United States to sublicense any foreign government pursuant to any existing or future treaty or agreement if the Administrator determines it would be in the national interest to acquire this right.

(4) The reservation in the United States of the rights to the invention in any country in which the contractor does not file an application for patent within such time as the Administration shall determine.

(5) The right in the Administrator to require the granting of a nonexclusive, exclusive, or partially exclusive license to a responsi-

ble applicant or applicants, upon terms reasonable under the circumstances, (A) to the extent that the invention is required for public use by governmental regulations, or (B) as may be necessary to fulfill health, safety, or energy needs, or (C) for such other purposes as may be stipulated in the applicable agreement.

(6) The right in the Administrator to terminate such waiver or license in whole or in part unless the recipient of the waiver or license demonstrates to the satisfaction of the Administrator that he has taken effective steps, or within a reasonable time thereafter is expected to take such steps, necessary to accomplish substantial utilization of the invention.

(7) The right in the Administrator, commencing three years after the grant of a license and four years after a waiver is effective as to an invention, to require the granting of a nonexclusive or partially exclusive license to a responsible applicant or applicants, upon terms reasonable under the circumstances, and in appropriate circumstances to terminate the waiver or license in whole or in part, following a hearing upon notice thereof to the public, upon a petition by an interested person justifying such hearing—

(A) if the Administrator determines, upon review of such material as he deems relevant, and after the recipient of the waiver or license, or other interested person, has had the opportunity to provide such relevant and material information as the Administrator may require, that such waiver or license has tended substantially to lessen competition or to result in undue concentration in any section of the country in any line of commerce to which the technology relates; or

(B) unless the recipient of the waiver or license demonstrates to the satisfaction of the Administrator at such hearing that he has taken effective steps, or within a reasonable time thereafter is expected to take such steps, necessary to accomplish substantial utilization of the invention.

(i) The Administrator shall provide an annual periodic notice to the public in the Federal Register, or other appropriate publication, of the right to have a hearing as provided by subsection (h)(7) of this section, and of the availability of the records of determinations provided in this section.

(j) *Small business status of applicant for waiver or licenses.* The Administrator shall, in granting waivers or licenses, consider the small business status of the applicant.

(k) *Protection of invention, etc., rights by Administrator.* The Administrator is authorized to take all suitable and necessary steps to protect any invention or discovery to which the United States holds title, and to require that contractors or persons who acquire rights to inventions under this section protect such inventions.

(l) *Administration as defense agency of United States for purpose of maintaining secrecy of inventions.* The Administration shall be considered a defense agency of the United States for the purpose of chapter 17 of Title 35.

(m) *Definitions.* As used in this section—

(1) the term "person" means any individual, partnership, corporation, association, institution, or other entity;

(2) the term "contract" means any contract, grant, agreement, understanding, or other arrangement, which includes research, development, or demonstration work, and includes any assignment, substitution of parties, or subcontract executed or entered into thereunder;

(3) the term "made," when used in relation to any invention, means the conception or first actual reduction to practice of such invention;

(4) the term "invention" means inventions or discoveries, whether patented or unpatented; and

(5) the term "contractor" means any person having a contract with or on behalf of the Administration.

(n) *Report concerning applicability of existing patent policies to energy programs; time for submission to President and appropriate congressional committees.* Within twelve months after December 31, 1974, the Administrator with the participation of the Attorney General, the Secretary of Commerce, and other officials as the President may designate, shall submit to the President and the appropriate congressional committees a report concerning the applicability of existing patent policies affecting the programs under this chapter, along with his recommendations for amendments or additions to the statutory patent policy, including his recommendations on mandatory licensing, which he deems advisable for carrying out the purposes of this chapter. (Public Law 93–577, December 31, 1974, 88 Stat. 1887; Public Law 96–517, December 12, 1980, 94 Stat. 3027.)

42 U.S.C. 2457.   Property rights in inventions

(a) Whenever any invention is made in the performance of any work under any contract of the (National Aeronautics and Space) Administration, and the Administrator (of NASA) determines that—

(1) the person who made the invention was employed or assigned to perform research, development, or exploration work and the invention is related to the work he was employed or assigned to perform, or that it was within the scope of his employment duties, whether or not it was made during working hours, or with a contribution by the Government of the use of Government facilities, equipment, materials, allocated funds, information proprietary to the Government, or services of Government employees during working hours; or

(2) the person who made the invention was not employed or assigned to perform research, development, or exploration work, but the invention is nevertheless related to the contract, or to the work or duties he was employed or assigned to perform, and was made during working hours, or with a contribution from the Government of the sort referred to in clause (1),

such invention shall be the exclusive property of the United States, and if such invention is patentable a patent therefor shall be issued to the United States upon application made by the Administrator, unless the Administrator waives all or any part of the rights of the United States to such invention in conformity with the provisions of subsection (f) of this section.

(b) *Contract provisions.* Each contract entered into by the Administrator with any party for the performance of any work shall contain effective provisions under which such party shall furnish promptly to the Administrator a written report containing full and complete technical information concerning any invention, discovery, improvement, or innovation which may be made in the performance of any such work.

(c) *Patent application.* No patent may be issued to any applicant other than the Administrator for any invention which appears to the Commissioner of Patents to have significant utility in the conduct of aeronautical and space activities unless the applicant files with the

Commissioner, with the application or within thirty days after request therefor by the Commissioner, a written statement executed under oath setting forth the full facts concerning the circumstances under which such invention was made and stating the relationship (if any) of such invention to the performance of any work under any contract of the Administration. Copies of each such statement and the application to which it relates shall be transmitted forthwith by the Commissioner to the Administrator.

(d) *Board of Patent Interferences.* Upon any application as to which any such statement has been transmitted to the Administrator, the Commissioner may, if the invention is patentable, issue a patent to the applicant unless the Administrator, within ninety days after receipt of such application and statement, requests that such patent be issued to him on behalf of the United States. If, within such time, the Administrator files such a request with the Commissioner, the Commissioner shall transmit notice thereof to the applicant, and shall issue such patent to the Administrator unless the applicant within thirty days after receipt of such notice requests a hearing before a Board of Patent Interferences on the question whether the Administrator is entitled under this section to receive such patent. The Board may hear and determine, in accordance with rules and procedures established for interference cases, the question so presented, and its determination shall be subject to appeal by the applicant or by the Administrator to the United States Court of Appeals for the Federal Circuit in accordance with procedures governing appeals from decisions of the Board of Patent Interferences in other proceedings.

(e) Whenever any patent has been issued to any applicant in conformity with subsection (d) of this section, and the Administrator thereafter has reason to believe that the statement filed by the applicant in connection therewith contained any false representations of any material fact, the Administrator within five years after the date of issuance of such patent may file with the Commissioner a request for the transfer to the Administrator of title to such patent on the records of the Commissioner. Notice of any such request shall be transmitted by the Commissioner to the owner of record of such patent, and title to such patent shall be so transferred to the Administrator unless within thirty days after receipt of such notice such owner of record requests a hearing before a Board of Patent Interferences on the question whether any such false representation was contained in such statement. Such question shall be heard and determined, and determination thereof shall be subject to review, in the manner prescribed by subsection (d) of this section for questions arising thereunder. No request made by the Administrator under this subsection for the transfer of title to any patent, and no prosecution for the violation of any criminal statute, shall be barred by any failure of the Administrator to make a request under subsection (d) of this section for the issuance of such patent to him, or by any notice previously given by the Administrator stating that he had no objection to the issuance of such patent to the applicant therefor.

(f) *Waiver; Inventions and Contributions Board.* Under such regulations in conformity with this subsection as the Administrator shall prescribe, he may waive all or any part of the rights of the United States under this section with respect to any invention or class of inventions made or which may be made by any person or class of persons in the performance of any work required by any contract of the Administration if the Administrator determines that the interests of the United States will be served thereby. Any such waiver may be made upon such terms and under such conditions as the Administrator shall determine to be required for the protection of the interests of the United States. Each such waiver made with respect to any invention shall be subject to the reservation by the Administrator of an irrevocable, nonexclusive, nontransferable, royalty-free license for the practice of such invention throughout the world by or on behalf of the United States or any foreign government pursuant to any treaty or agreement with the United States. Each proposal for any waiver under this subsection shall be referred to an Inventions and Contributions Board which shall be established by the Administrator within the Administration. Such Board shall accord to each interested party an opportunity for hearing, and shall transmit to the Administrator its findings of fact with respect to such proposal and its recommendations for action to be taken with respect thereto.

(g) (Repealed Public Law 96–517, December 12, 1980, sec. 7(b), 94 Stat. 3027.)

(h) *Protection of title.* The Administrator is authorized to take all suitable and necessary steps to protect any invention or discovery to which he has title, and to require that contractors or persons who retain title to inventions or discoveries under this section protect the inventions or discoveries to which the Administration has or may acquire a license of use.

(i) *Defense agency.* The Administration shall be considered a defense agency of the United States for the purpose of chapter 17 of Title 35.

(j) *Definitions.* As used in this section—

(1) the term "person" means any individual, partnership, corporation, association, institution, or other entity;

(2) the term "contract" means any actual or proposed contract, agreement, understanding, or other arrangement, and includes any assignment, substitution of parties, subcontract executed or entered into thereunder; and

(3) the term "made," when used in relation to any invention, means the conception or first actual reduction to practice of such invention. (Public Law 85–568, July 29, 1958, 72 Stat. 435; Public Law 96–517, December 12, 1980, 94 Stat. 3027; Public Law 97–164, April 2, 1982, 96 Stat. 49.)

42 U.S.C. 2458. Contributions awards

(a) Subject to the provisions of this section, the Administrator is authorized, upon his own initiative or upon application of any person, to make a monetary award, in such amount and upon such terms as he shall determine to be warranted, to any person (as defined by section 2457 of this title) for any scientific or technical contribution to the Administration which is determined by the Administrator to have significant value in the conduct of aeronautical and space activities. Each application made for any such award shall be referred to the Inventions and Contributions Board established under section 2457 of this title. Such Board shall accord to each such applicant an opportunity for hearing upon such application, and shall transmit to the Administrator its recommendation as to the terms of the award, if any, to be made to such applicant for such contribution. In determining the terms and conditions of any award the Administrator shall take into account—

(1) the value of the contribution to the United States;

(2) the aggregate amount of any sums which have been expended by the applicant for the development of such contribution;

(3) the amount of any compensation (other than salary received for services rendered as an officer or employee of the Government) previously received by the applicant for or on account of the use of such contribution by the United States; and

(4) such other factors as the Administrator shall determine to be material.

(b) If more than one applicant under subsection (a) of this section claims an interest in the same contribution, the Administration shall ascertain and determine the respective interests of such applicants, and shall apportion any award to be made with respect to such contribution among such applicants in such proportions as he shall determine to be equitable. No award may be made under subsection (a) of this section with respect to any contribution—

(1) unless the applicant surrenders, by such means as the Administrator shall determine to be effective, all claims which such applicant may have to receive any compensation (other than the award made under this section) for the use of such contribution or any element thereof at any time by or on behalf of the United States, or by or on behalf of any foreign government pursuant to any treaty or agreement with the United States, within the United States, or at any other place;

(2) in any amount exceeding $100,000, unless the Administrator has transmitted to the appropriate committees of the Congress a full and complete report concerning the amount and terms of, and the basis for, such proposed award, and thirty calendar days of regular session of the Congress have expired after receipt of such report by such committees. (Public Law 85–568, July 29, 1958, 72 Stat. 437.)

42 U.S.C. 2473. Functions of the Administration
* * *

(c) In the performance of its functions the (National Aeronautics and Space) Administration is authorized— * * *

(3) to acquire * * * such other real and personal property (including patents), or any interest therein, as the Administration deems necessary within and outside the continental United States; * * * to sell and otherwise dispose of real and personal property (including patents and rights thereunder) in accordance with the provision of the Federal Property and Administrative Service Act of 1949, as amended (40 U.S.C. 471 *et seq.*); * * * (Public Law 85–568, July 29, 1958, 72 Stat. 429.)

*   *   *   *   *   *   *

C. Department of Health and Human Services

30 U.S.C. 937.   Research grants
* * *

(b) The Secretary of Health and Human Services shall initiate research within the National Institute for Occupational Safety and Health, and is authorized to make research grants to public and private agencies and organizations and individuals for the purpose of devising simple and effective tests to measure, detect, and treat respiratory and pulmonary impairments in active and inactive coal miners. Any grant made pursuant to this subsection shall be conditioned upon all information, uses, products, processes, patents, and other developments resulting from such research being available to the general public, except to the extent of such exceptions and limitations as the Secretary of Health and Human Services may deem necessary in the public interest. * * * (Public Law 92–303, May 19, 1972, 86 Stat. 155.)

* * * * * * *

D. Department of the Interior

16 U.S.C. 833a.   Administration of project
* * *

(d) Acquisition of any property or property rights. The Secretary of the Interior shall have power to acquire any property or property rights, including patent rights, which in his opinion are necessary to carry out the purposes of this chapter (ch. 12C—Fort Peck Project) by the exercise of eminent domain and to institute condemnation proceedings therefore in the same manner as is provided by law for the condemnation of real estate. (May 18, 1938, ch. 250, 52 Stat. 404.)

30 U.S.C. 322.   Laboratory research and development, etc.

In order to carry out the purposes of this chapter (ch. 6—Synthetic Liquid Fuel Demonstration Plants), the Secretary of the Interior is authorized—
* * *

(b) to acquire, by purchase, license, lease for a term of years or less, or donation, secret processes, technical data, inventions, patent applications, patents, irrevocable nonexclusive licenses, and other rights and licenses under patents granted by this or any other nation; * * * (Public Law 290, 78th Cong., April 5, 1944, 58 Stat. 190.)

30 U.S.C. 323. Licenses and Patent rights

The Secretary of the Interior is authorized to grant, on such terms as he may consider appropriate but subject to section 488 of Title 40, licenses under patent rights acquired under this chapter (ch. 6—Synthetic Liquid Fuel Demonstration Plants): *Provided,* That such licenses are consistent with the terms of the agreements by which such patent rights are acquired. No patent acquired by the Secretary of the Interior under this chapter shall prevent any citizen of the United States, or corporation created under the laws of the United States or any State thereof, from using any invention, discovery, or process covered by such patent, or restrict such use by any such citizen or corporation, or be the basis of any claim against any such person or corporation on account of such use. (Public Law 290, 78th Cong., April 5, 1944, 58 Stat. 191; amended Public Law 247, 82d Cong., October 31, 1951, 65 Stat. 709.)

30 U.S.C. 951. Studies and research—Appropriate Projects
* * *

(c) * * * No research, demonstrations, or experiments shall be carried out, contracted for, sponsored, cosponsored, or authorized under authority of this chapter (ch. 22—Coal Mine Health and Safety) unless all information, uses, products, patents, and other developments resulting from such research, demonstrations, or experiments will (with such exception and limitation, if any, as the Secretary of the Interior or the Secretary of Health and Human Services in coordination with the Secretary (of the Interior) may find to be necessary in the public interest) be available to the general public. * * * (Public Law 91–173, December 30, 1969, 83 Stat. 799; amended Public Law 95–164, November 9, 1977, 91 Stat. 1320.)

30 U.S.C. 1226. Research—Coordination with existing programs; availability of information to public
* * *

(d) No research, demonstration, or experiment shall be carried out under this chapter (ch. 25—Surface Mining Control and Reclamation) by an institute financed by grants under this chapter, unless all uses, products, processes, patents, and other developments resulting therefrom, with such exception or limitation, if any, as the Secretary (of the Interior) may find necessary in the public interest, be available promptly to the general public. Nothing contained in this section shall deprive the owner of any background patent relating to any such activities of any rights which that owner may have under that patent. * * * (Public Law 95–87, August 3, 1977, 91 Stat. 454.)

30 U.S.C. 1328.   Research, development projects, etc., relating to alternative coal mining technologies—authority of Administrator to conduct, promote, etc.

* * *

(e) Subject to the patent provisions of section 1226(d) of this title, all information and data resulting from any research studies, surveys, experiments, or demonstration projects conducted or financed under this subchapter shall be promptly made available to the public. (Public Law 95–87, August 3, 1977, 91 Stat. 531.)

*   *   *   *   *   *   *

E. Department of Defense

10 U.S.C. 2386.   Copyrights, patents, designs, etc.; acquisition

Funds appropriated for a military department available for making or procuring supplies may be used to acquire any of the following if the acquisition relates to supplies or processes produced or used by or for, or useful to, that department:

(1) Copyrights, patents, and applications for patents.

(2) Licenses under copyrights, patents, and applications for patents.

(3) Designs, processes, and manufacturing data.

(4) Releases, before suit is brought, for past infringement of patents or copyrights.

(August 10, 1956, ch. 1041, 70A Stat. 137; amended Public Law 86–726, September 8, 1960, 74 Stat. 855.)

10 U.S.C. 5151.   Office of Naval Research: duties

(a) The Office of Naval Research shall perform such duties as the Secretary of the Navy prescribes relating to—
* * *

(3) the supervision, administration, and control of activities within or for the Department relating to patents, inventions, trademarks, copyrights, and royalty payments, and matters connected therewith. * * * (August 10, 1956, ch. 1041, 70A Stat. 291.)

10 U.S.C. 7210. Purchase of patents, patent applications, and licenses

(a) The Secretary of the Navy may buy letters patent, applications for letters patent, and licenses under either letters patent or applications for letters patent. The purchases shall be made from appropriations available for the purchase or manufacture of the equipment or material to which the purchased letters patent, applications, or licenses pertain. * * * (August 10, 1956, ch. 1041, 70A Stat. 444.)

22 U.S.C. 526. Protection of patent rights of U.S. citizens

The Secretary of the Army and the Secretary of the Navy, shall in all contracts or agreements for the sale of such matériel fully protect the rights of all citizens of the United States who have patent rights in and to any such matériel which is authorized to be sold and the funds collected for royalties on such patents shall be paid to the owners and holders of such patents. (June 15, 1940, ch. 365, 54 Stat. 397.)

*　*　*　*　*　*　*

F. CONSUMER PRODUCT SAFETY COMMISSION

15 U.S.C. 2054. Product safety information and research
* * *

(d) Whenever the Federal contribution for any information, research, or development activity authorized by this chapter (ch. 47— Consumer Product Safety) is more than minimal, the (Consumer Product Safety) Commission shall include in any contract, grant, or other arrangement for such activity, provisions effective to insure that the rights to all information, uses, processes, patents, and other developments resulting from that activity will be made available to the public without charge on a nonexclusive basis. Nothing in this subsection shall be construed to deprive any person of any right which he may have had, prior to entering into any arrangement referred to in this subsection, to any patent, patent application, or invention. (Public Law 92–573, October 27, 1972, 86 Stat. 1211.)

* * * * * * *

G. Department of Commerce

15 U.S.C. 2218.   **Administrative provisions (National Fire Prevention and Control Administration)**
* * *

(d) *Inventions and discoveries.* All property rights with respect to inventions and discoveries, which are made in the course of or under contract with any government agency pursuant to this chapter (ch. 49—Fire Prevention and Control), shall be subject to the basic policies set forth in the President's Statement of Government Patent Policy issued August 23, 1971, or such revisions of that statement of policy as may subsequently be promulgated and published in the Federal Register. * * * (Public Law 93–498, October 29, 1974, 88 Stat. 1548.)

* * * * * * *

H. Department of State

22 U.S.C. 2572.   **Patents**

All research within the United States contracted for, sponsored, cosponsored, or authorized under authority of this chapter (ch. 35— Arms Control and Disarmament) shall be provided for in such manner that all information as to uses, products, processes, patents, and other developments resulting from such research developed by Government expenditure will (with such exceptions and limitations, if any, as the Director may find to be necessary in the public interest) be available to the general public. This section shall not be so construed as to deprive the owner of any background patent relating thereto of such rights as he may have thereunder. (Public Law 87– 297, September 26, 1961, 75 Stat. 634.)

* * * * * * *

I. Department of Transportation

15 U.S.C. 1395. Research and training, etc.

(a) The Secretary (of Transportation) shall conduct research, testing, development, and training necessary to carry out the purposes of this subchapter (Motor Vehicle Safety Standards).

* * *

(c) Whenever the Federal contribution for any research or development activity authorized by this chapter (ch. 38—Traffic and Motor Vehicle Safety) encouraging motor vehicle safety is more than minimal, the Secretary shall include in any contract, grant, or other arrangement for such research or development activity, provisions effective to insure that all information, uses, processes, patents, and other developments resulting from that activity will be made freely and fully available to the general public. Nothing herein shall be construed to deprive the owner of any background patent of any right which he may have thereunder. (Public Law 89–563, September 9, 1966, 80 Stat. 721.)

* * * * * * *

J. Department of the Treasury

31 U.S.C. 393. Acquisition of production capability for minting clad coins; public contracts and procurement

(a) In order to acquire * * * patents, patent rights, technical knowledge and assistance * * * necessary to produce rapidly an adequate supply of the coins authorized by section 391 of this title (Title 31. Money and Finance), the Secretary (of the Treasury) may enter into contracts upon such terms and conditions as he may deem appropriate and in the public interest. * * * (Public Law 89–81, July 23, 1965, 79 Stat. 255.)

* * * * * * *

K. Environmental Protection Agency

42 U.S.C. 7404(b)(4). Research relating to fuels and vehicles
* * *

(b) In carrying out the provisions of this section, the Administrator (of the Environmental Protection Agency) may—

(4) acquire secret processes, technical data, inventions, patent applications, patents, licenses, * * * by purchase, license, lease, or donation; * * * (As added, Public Law 90–148, November 21, 1967, 81 Stat. 488; amended Public Law 91–604, December 31, 1970, 84 Stat. 1713.)

42 U.S.C. 7608.   Mandatory licensing

Whenever the Attorney General determines, upon application of the Administrator (of the Environmental Protection Agency)—

(1) That—

(A) in the implementation of the requirements of section 7411 (Standards of performance for new stationary sources), 7412 (National emission standards for hazardous air pollutants) or 7521 (Standards governing emission of substances from new motor vehicles or new motor vehicle engines) of this title, a right under any United States letters patent, which is being used or intended for public or commercial use and not otherwise reasonably available, is necessary to enable any person required to comply with such limitation to so comply, and

(B) there are no reasonable alternative methods to accomplish such purpose, and

(2) that the unavailability of such right may result in a substantial lessening of competition or tendency to create a monopoly in any line of commerce in any section of the country,

the Attorney General may so certify to a district court of the United States, which may issue an order requiring the person who owns such patent to license it on such reasonable terms and conditions as the court, after hearing, may determine. Such certification may be made to the district court for the district in which the person owning the patent resides, does business, or is found. (As added Public Law 91–604, December 31, 1970, 84 Stat. 1709.)

42 U.S.C. 6981(c)(3).   Research, demonstrations, training and other activities (Solid Waste Disposal)

* * *

(3) Any invention made or conceived in the course of, or under, any contract under this chapter shall be subject to section 9 of the Federal Nonnuclear Energy Research and Development Act of 1974 (42 U.S.C. 5908) to the same extent and in the same manner as inventions made or conceived in the course of contracts under

such Act, except that in applying such section, the Environmental Protection Agency shall be substituted for the Energy Research and Development Administration and the words "solid waste" shall be substituted for the word "energy" where appropriate. (Public Law 89–272, Title II, sec. 8001, as added Public Law 94–580, October 21, 1976, 90 Stat. 2829.)

* * * * * * *

L. NATIONAL SCIENCE FOUNDATION

42 U.S.C. 1871. Patent rights

(a) Each contract or other arrangement executed pursuant to this chapter (ch. 16—National Science Foundation) which relates to scientific research shall contain provisions governing the disposition of inventions produced thereunder in a manner calculated to protect the public interest and the equities of the individual or organization with which the contract or other arrangement is executed: *Provided,* however, That nothing in this chapter shall be construed to authorize the Foundation to enter into any contractual or other arrangement inconsistent with any provision of law affecting the issuance or use of patents.

(b) No officer or employee of the Foundation shall acquire, retain or transfer any rights, under the patent laws of the United States or otherwise, in any invention which he may make or produce in connection with performing his assigned activities and which is directly related to the subject matter thereof: *Provided,* however, That this subsection shall not be construed to prevent any officer or employee of the Foundation from executing any application for patent on any such invention for the purpose of assigning the same to the Government or its nominee in accordance with such rules and regulations as the Director (of the National Science Foundation) may establish. (Public Law 507, 81st Cong., May 10, 1950, 64 Stat. 154.)

* * * * * * *

M. TENNESSEE VALLEY AUTHORITY

16 U.S.C. 831d. Board Authority
* * *

(i) *Aid of other government services; use of any invention or discovery.*

* * * (A)ny invention or discovery made by virtue of and incidental to such service by an employee of the Government of the United States serving under this section, or by any employee of the Corporation (Tennessee Valley Authority), together with any patents which may be granted thereon, shall be the sole and exclusive property of the Corporation, which is authorized to grant such licenses thereunder as shall be authorized by the board: *Provided further,* That the board may pay to such inventor such sum from the income from sale of licenses as it may deem proper. * * * (May 18, 1933, ch. 32, 48 Stat. 61.)

* * * * * * *

X. TREATMENT OF PATENTS UNDER THE FEDERAL INCOME TAX

26 U.S.C. 186. Recoveries of damages
* * *

(a) *Allowance of deduction.*—If a compensatory amount which is included in gross income is received or accrued during the taxable year for a compensable injury, there shall be allowed as a deduction for the taxable year an amount equal to the lesser of—

(1) the amount of such compensatory amount, or

(2) the amount of the unrecovered losses sustained as a result of such compensable injury.

(b) *Compensable injury.*—For purposes of this section, the term "compensable injury" means—

(1) injuries sustained as a result of an infringement of a patent issued by the United States. * * * (Public Law 91–172, December 30, 1969, 83 Stat. 711.)

26 U.S.C. 861. Income from sources within the United States

(a) *Gross income from sources within United States.*—The following items of gross income shall be treated as income from sources within the United States:
* * *

(4) *Rentals and Royalties.*—Rentals or royalties from property located in the United States or from any interest in such property, including rentals or royalties for the use of or for the privilege of

using in the United States patents, copyrights, secret processes and formulas, good will, trademarks, trade brands, franchises, and other like property. * * * (August 16, 1954, 68A Stat. 275.)

26 U.S.C. 862.   Income from sources without the United States

(a) *Gross income from sources without the United States.*—The following items of gross income shall be treated as income from sources without the United States:
* * *

(4) rentals or royalties from property located without the United States or from any interest in such property, including rentals or royalties for the use of or for the privilege of using without the United States patents, copyrights, secret processes and formulas, good will, trademarks, trade brands, franchises, and other like properties; * * * (August 16, 1954, 68A Stat. 276.)

26 U.S.C. 871.   Tax on nonresident alien individuals

(a) *Income not connected with United States business—30 percent tax.*

(1) *Income other than capital gains.*—There is hereby imposed for each taxable year a tax of 30 percent of the amount received from sources within the United States by a nonresident alien individual as— * * *

(D) gains from the sale or exchange after October 4, 1966, of patents, copyrights, secret processes and formulas, good will, trademarks, trade brands, franchises, and other like property, or of any interest in any such property, to the extent such gains are from payments which are contingent on the productivity, use, or disposition of the property or interest sold or exchanged, or from payments which are treated as being so contingent under subsection (e),

but only to the extent the amount so received is not effectively connected with the conduct of a trade or business within the United States. (As amended, Public Law 89–809, November 13, 1966, 80 Stat. 1547.)

26 U.S.C. 881.   Tax on income of foreign corporations not connected with United States business

(a) *Imposition of tax.*—There is hereby imposed for each taxable year a tax of 30 percent of the amount received from sources within the United States by a foreign corporation as—

* * *

(4) gains from the sale or exchange after October 4, 1966, of patents, copyrights, secret processes and formulas, good will, trademarks, trade brands, franchises, and other like property, or of any interest in any such property, to the extent such gains are from payments which are contingent on the productivity, use, or disposition of the property or interest sold or exchanged or from payments which are treated as being so contingent under section 871(e),

but only to the extent the amount so received is not effectively connected with the conduct of a trade or business within the United States. * * * (As amended, Public Law 89–809, November 13, 1966, 80 Stat. 1555.)

26 U.S.C. 1235.   Sale or exchange of patents

(a) *General.*—A transfer (other than by gift, inheritance, or devise) of property consisting of all substantial rights to a patent, or an undivided interest therein which includes a part of all such rights, by any holder shall be considered the sale or exchange of a capital asset held for more than 1 year, regardless of whether or not payments in consideration of such transfer are—

(1) payable periodically over a period generally coterminous with the transferee's use of the patent, or

(2) contingent on the productivity, use, or disposition of the property transferred.

(b) *"Holder" defined.*—For purposes of this section, the term "holder" means—

(1) any individual whose efforts created such property, or

(2) any other individual who has acquired his interest in such property in exchange for consideration in money or money's worth paid to such creator prior to actual reduction to practice of the invention covered by the patent, if such individual is neither—

(A) the employer of such creator, nor

(B) related to such creator (within the meaning of subsection (d)).

(c) *Effective date.*—This section shall be applicable with regard to any amounts received, or payments made, pursuant to a transfer described in subsection (a) in any taxable year to which this subtitle applies, regardless of the taxable year in which such transfer occurred.

(d) *Related persons.*—Subsection (a) shall not apply to any transfer, directly or indirectly, between persons specified within any one of the paragraphs of section 267(b); except that, in applying section 267(b) and (c) for purposes of this section—

(1) the phrase "25 percent or more" shall be substituted for the phrase "more than 50 percent" each place it appears in section 267(b), and

(2) paragraph (4) of section 267(c) shall be treated as providing that the family of an individual shall include only his spouse, ancestors, and lineal descendants.

(e) *Cross reference.*—

For special rule relating to nonresident aliens, see section 871(a). (August 16, 1954, 68A Stat. 329; amended Public Law 85–866, September 2, 1958, 72 Stat. 1644; Public Law 94–455, October 4, 1976, 90 Stat. 1732.)

26 U.S.C. 1249. Gain from certain sales or exchanges of patents, etc., to foreign corporations

(a) *General rule.*—Gain from the sale or exchange after December 31, 1962, of a patent, an invention, model, or design (whether or not patented), a copyright, secret formula or process, or any other similar property right to any foreign corporation by any United States person (as defined in section 7701(a)(30)) which controls such foreign corporation shall, if such gain would (but for the provisions of this subsection) be ordinary income, be considered as ordinary income.

(b) *Control.*—For purposes of subsection (a), control means with respect to any foreign corporation, the ownership, directly or indirectly, of stock possessing more than 50 percent of the total combined voting power of all classes of stock entitled to vote. For purposes of this subsection, the rules for determining ownership of stock prescribed by section 958 shall apply. (Public Law 87–834, October 16, 1962, 76 Stat. 1945; Public Law 89–809, November 13, 1966, 80 Stat. 1563; amended Public Law 94–455, October 4, 1976, 90 Stat. 1793.)

*　*　*　*　*　*　*

XI. MISCELLANEOUS

A. INTERNATIONAL

22 U.S.C. 269f. International Bureau of Intellectual Property; appropriation

There is authorized to be appropriated to the Department of State
* * *

(b) Such sums as may be required for the payment by the United States of its proportionate share of the expenses of said international bureau as determined under article 16(4) of the Paris Convention for the Protection of Industrial Property, as revised, except that in no event shall the payment for any year exceed 4.5 per centum of all expenses of the bureau apportioned among countries for that year. (Joint Resolution, July 12, 1960, Public Law 86–614, 74 Stat. 381; amended by Joint Resolution, October 20, 1972, Public Law 92–511, 86 Stat. 918.)

19 U.S.C. 2435. Commercial agreements

(a) *Presidential authority.* Subject to the provisions of subsections (b) and (c) of this section, the President may authorize the entry into force of bilateral commercial agreements providing nondiscriminatory treatment to the products of countries heretofore denied such treatment whenever he determines that such agreements with such countries will promote the purposes of this chapter (ch. 12—Trade Act of 1974) and are in the national interest.

(b) *Terms of agreements.* Any such bilateral commercial agreement shall—
* * *

(4) if the other party to the bilateral agreement is not a party to the Paris convention for the Protection of Industrial Property, provide rights for United States nationals with respect to patents and trademarks in such country not less than the rights specified in such convention; * * * (Public Law 93–618, January 3, 1975; 88 Stat. 2061.)

* * * * * * *

XII. COPYRIGHT AND CRIMINAL LAW

A. NATIONAL STOLEN PROPERTY ACT

18 U.S.C. 2314.   Transportation of stolen goods, securities, moneys, fraudulent State tax stamps, or articles used in counterfeiting

Whoever transports in interstate or foreign commerce any goods, wares, merchandise, securities or money, of the value of $5,000 or more, knowing the same to have been stolen, converted or taken by fraud; or

Whoever, having devised or intending to devise any scheme or artifice to defraud, or for obtaining money or property by means of false or fraudulent pretenses, representations, or promises, transports or causes to be transported, or induces any person to travel in, or to be transported in interstate commerce in the execution or concealment of a scheme or artifice to defraud that person of money or property having a value of $5,000 or more; or

Whoever, with unlawful or fraudulent intent, transports in interstate or foreign commerce any falsely made, forged, altered, or counterfeited securities or tax stamps, knowing the same to have been falsely made, forged, altered, or counterfeited; or

Whoever, with unlawful or fraudulent intent, transports in interstate or foreign commerce any traveler's check bearing a forged countersignature; or

Whoever, with unlawful or fraudulent intent, transports in interstate or foreign commerce, any tool, implement, or thing used or fitted to be used in falsely making, forging, altering, or counterfeiting any security or tax stamps, or any part thereof—

Shall be fined not more than $10,000 or imprisoned not more than ten years, or both.

This section shall not apply to any falsely made, forged, altered, counterfeited or spurious representation of an obligation or other security of the United States, or of an obligation, bond, certificate, security, treasury note, bill, promise to pay or bank note issued by any foreign government or by a bank or corporation of any foreign country. (June 25, 1948, ch. 645, 62 Stat. 806; May 24, 1949, ch. 139. sec. 45, 63 Stat. 96; July 9, 1956, ch. 519, 70 Stat. 507; Oct. 4, 1961, Public Law 87–371, sec. 2, 75 Stat. 802; September 28, 1968, Public Law 90–535, 82 Stat. 885.)

18 U.S.C. 2318. Trafficking in counterfeit labels for phonorecords, and copies of motion pictures or other audiovisual works

(a) Whoever, in any of the circumstances described in subsection (c) of this section, knowingly traffics in a counterfeit label affixed or designed to be affixed to a phonorecord, or a copy of a motion picture or other audiovisual work, shall be fined not more than $250,000 or imprisoned for not more than five years, or both.

(b) As used in this section—

(1) the term "counterfeit label" means an identifying label or container that appears to be genuine, but is not;

(2) the term "traffic" means to transport, transfer or otherwise dispose of, to another, as consideration for anything of value or to make or obtain control of with intent to so transport, transfer or dispose of; and

(3) the terms "copy", "phonorecord", "motion picture", and "audiovisual work" have, respectively, the meanings given those terms in section 101 (relating to definitions) of title 17.

(c) The circumstances referred to in subsection (a) of this section are—

(1) the offense is committed within the special maritime and territorial jurisdiction of the United States; or within the special aircraft jurisdiction of the United States (as defined in section 101 of the Federal Aviation Act of 1958);

(2) the mail or a facility of interstate or foreign commerce is used or intended to be used in the commission of the offense; or

(3) the counterfeit label is affixed to or encloses, or is designed to be affixed to or enclose, a copyrighted motion picture or other audiovisual work, or a phonorecord of a copyrighted sound recording.

(d) When any person is convicted of any violation of subsection (a), the court in its judgment of conviction shall in addition to the penalty therein prescribed, order the forfeiture and destruction or other disposition of all counterfeit labels and all articles to which counterfeit labels have been affixed or which were intended to have had such labels affixed.

(e) Except to the extent they are inconsistent with the provisions of this title, all provisions of section 509, title 17, United States

Code, are applicable to violations of subsection (a). (Amended May 24, 1982, Public Law 97–180, sec. 2, 96 Stat. 91.)

18 U.S.C. 2319.   Criminal infringement of a copyright

(a)· Whoever violates section 506(a) (relating to criminal offenses) of title 17 shall be punished as provided in subsection (b) of this section and such penalties shall be in addition to any other provisions of title 17 or any other law.

(b) Any person who commits an offense under subsection (a) of this section—

(1) shall be fined not more than $250,000 or imprisoned for not more than five years, or both, if the offense—

(A) involves the reproduction or distribution, during any one-hundred-and-eighty-day period, of at least one thousand phonorecords or copies infringing the copyright in one or more sound recordings;

(B) involves the reproduction or distribution, during any one-hundred-and-eighty-day period, of at least sixty-five copies infringing the copyright in one or more motion pictures or other audiovisual works; or

(C) is a second or subsequent offense under either of subsection (b)(1) or (b)(2) of this section, where a prior offense involved a sound recording, or a motion picture or other audiovisual work;

(2) shall be fined not more than $250,000 or imprisoned for not more than two years, or both, if the offense—

(A) involves the reproduction or distribution, during any one-hundred-and-eighty-day period, of more than one hundred but less than one thousand phonorecords or copies infringing the copyright in one or more sound recordings; or

(B) involves the reproduction or distribution, during any one-hundred-and-eighty-day period, of more than seven but less than sixty-five copies infringing the copyright in one or more motion pictures or other audiovisual works; and

(3) shall be fined not more than $25,000 or imprisoned for not more than one year, or both, in any other case.

(c) As used in this section—

(1) the terms "sound recording", "motion picture", "audiovisual work", "phonorecord", and "copies" have, respectively, the

meanings set forth in section 101 (relating to definitions) of title 17; and

(2) the terms "reproduction" and "distribution" refer to the exclusive rights of a copyright owner under clauses (1) and (3) respectively of section 106 (relating to exclusive rights in copyrighted works), as limited by sections 107 through 118, of title 17. (Amended May 24, 1982, Public Law 97–180, sec. 3, 96 Stat. 92.)

FINDING LIST FOR NOTES OF OTHER STATUTES*

Section of U.S. Code	Page	Section of U.S. Code	Page
5 U.S.C. 500	223	28 U.S.C. 44	202
5 U.S.C. 501	228	28 U.S.C. 46	204
5 U.S.C. 3104	211	28 U.S.C. 1291	204
5 U.S.C. 3325	212	28 U.S.C. 1292	205
5 U.S.C. 5102	212	28 U.S.C. 1295	207
5 U.S.C. 5316	212	28 U.S.C. 1338	200
5 U.S.C. 6103	220	28 U.S.C. 1391	200
10 U.S.C. 2386	257	28 U.S.C. 1400	201
10 U.S.C. 5151	257	28 U.S.C. 1498	201
10 U.S.C. 7210	258	28 U.S.C. 1694	202
15 U.S.C. 638	228	28 U.S.C. 1733	209
15 U.S.C. 1155	230	28 U.S.C. 1741	210
15 U.S.C. 1395	260	28 U.S.C. 1744	210
15 U.S.C. 1511	211	28 U.S.C. 1745	210
15 U.S.C. 2054	258	28 U.S.C. 1781	210
15 U.S.C. 2218	259	28 U.S.C. 1928	202
16 U.S.C. 831d	262	30 U.S.C. 322	255
16 U.S.C. 833a	255	30 U.S.C. 323	256
18 U.S.C. 201	212	30 U.S.C. 937	255
18 U.S.C. 203	215	30 U.S.C. 951	256
18 U.S.C. 205	216	30 U.S.C. 1226	256
18 U.S.C. 206	218	30 U.S.C. 1328	257
18 U.S.C. 207	223	31 U.S.C. 72	220
18 U.S.C. 208	218	31 U.S.C. 393	260
18 U.S.C. 209	219	31 U.S.C. 725e	220
18 U.S.C. 2314	268	31 U.S.C. 725r	229
18 U.S.C. 2318	269	42 U.S.C. 1871	262
18 U.S.C. 2319	270	42 U.S.C. 2014	231
19 U.S.C. 1337	209	42 U.S.C. 2181	232
19 U.S.C. 1337a	209	42 U.S.C. 2182	233
19 U.S.C. 2435	267	42 U.S.C. 2183	234
21 U.S.C. 372	229	42 U.S.C. 2184	237
22 U.S.C. 526	258	42 U.S.C. 2185	237
22 U.S.C. 269f	267	42 U.S.C. 2186	238
22 U.S.C. 2572	259	42 U.S.C. 2187	238
26 U.S.C. 186	263	42 U.S.C. 2188	239
26 U.S.C. 861	263	42 U.S.C. 2189	240
26 U.S.C. 862	264	42 U.S.C. 2190	240
26 U.S.C. 871	264	42 U.S.C. 2201	240
26 U.S.C. 881	264	42 U.S.C. 2457	250
26 U.S.C. 1235	265	42 U.S.C. 2458	253
26 U.S.C. 1249	266	42 U.S.C. 2473	254

*See page 199 for subject listing.

Section of U.S. Code	Page
42 U.S.C. 5811	241
42 U.S.C. 5814	241
42 U.S.C. 5817	241
42 U.S.C. 5841	242
42 U.S.C. 5845	242
42 U.S.C. 5908	243
42 U.S.C. 6981(c)(3)	261
42 U.S.C. 7151	242

Section of U.S. Code	Page
42 U.S.C. 7261	243
42 U.S.C. 7404(b)(4)	260
42 U.S.C. 7608	261
Sec. 165	203
Sec. 166	203
Sec. 168	203
D.C. Code Sec. 28-2701	222

INDEX

Subject	Title–Sec.	Page

A

Abandoned applications, fee on petition to revive..........................	35–41	15
Abandonment of application by failure to prosecute......................	35–133	27
Abandonment of invention		
Bar to patent..........................	35–102	19
By violation of secrecy order	35–182	37–38
Administrator, executor, or guardian.........	35–117	24
Advertising restrictions...................	5–501	228
Affidavits and depositions in contested cases, rules for taking.................	35–23	12
Agriculture, Secretary of, to furnish information, and detail employees to Commissioner of Patents and Trademarks for plant patent cases	35–164	35
Allowance, notice of.....................	35–151	31–32
Amendment		
Inserting claim of issued patent	35–135	28
Time for	35–132	27
American republics		
Aid to, protection of U.S. patent rights	22–526	262
Annual report of the Commissioner	35–14	11
Anonymous work, defined	17–101	115
Appeals to Board of Appeals	35–134	27
Fee.................................	35–41	15
Hearing of............................	35–7	8–9
Appeals to Court of Customs and Patent Appeals........................	35–141	29
Certificate of decision of Court recorded in the Patent and Trademark Office....	35–144	30
Determination of Appeal; revision of decision.........................	35–144	30
From Board of Appeals..................	35–141	29
From Board of Patent Interferences	35–141	29
Grounds of decision to be furnished court...	35–143	30
Notice of appeal	35–142	29
Proceedings on appeal...................	35–143	29–30
Appeals to United States Court of Appeals regarding trademarks...............	15–1071	91–94
Applicant for international application........	35–373	73
Applicant, notified of interference	35–135	27

Note: Title and section numbers in italics indicate material appearing in the Notes of Other Statutes.

Subject	Title–Sec.	Page
Application for copyright registration	17–409	174–175
Application of equitable principles in inter partes proceedings................	15–1069	91
Application for foreign patent, license required.......................	35–184	39
Application for patent		
Abandonment of, by failure to prosecute....	35–133	27
Assignment of.........................	35–261	56–57
Confidential............................	35–122	26
Continuing	35–120	25–26
Description; specification and claim........	35–112	21–22
Divisional	35–121	26
Drawings.............................	35–113	22
Effect of defective execution.............	35–26	13
Effective as of date of earliest foreign application in certain cases...............	35–119	24
Examination of invention	35–131	27
Fee on filing	35–41	14–17
	35–111	21
For deceased or insane inventors...........	35–117	24
May be made by legal representative of deceased or incapacitated inventor	35–117	24
Must be made and sworn to by inventor, if living, when assigned.............	35–152	32
Must be made within specified time after foreign application for right of priority	35–119	24–25
Oath of applicant, see Oath in patent application Owned by Government	35–267	57
What to contain	35–111	21
When filed by other than inventor	35–118	24
	35–121	26
Application for patent reissue..............	35–251	53–54
Application for trademark.................	15–1051	78–79
Designation of resident for service of process and notice.....................	15–1051	79
Fee on filing	15–1051	79
Refusal of registration..................	15–1052	80–81
Registration..........................	15–1051	78–79
Appointments, how made.................	35–3	6–7
Archives, and reproduction of copyrighted material......................	17–108	122–125
Armed forces		
Patents, designs, etc., acquisition	10–2386	257
Navy; naval research, purchase of patents, etc.	10–5151	257–258
	10–7210	258

Subject	Title–Sec.	Page
Arms control and disarmament research; disposition of patents	22–2572	259
Article patented marked with number of patent	35–287	60–61
Assignee		
May file application in certain cases	35–118	24
May file divisional application	35–121	26
May file reissue application	35–251	53–54
Patent may be issued to	35–152	32
Assignments, patent	35–261	56–57
Establishing prima facie execution of	35–261	56–57
Fees for recording	35–41	15
Must be recorded in Patent and Trademark Office to issue patent to assignee	35–152	32
Patent may issue to assignee	35–152	32
Recording in Patent and Trademark Office . .	35–261	56–57
Assistant Commissioners, how appointed and duties	35–3	6–7
Atomic energy, defined	42–2014	231
Atomic Energy Act of 1954	42–5817	241
	42–5908	243
Atomic Energy Commission	42–5814	241
Atomic Weapons		
Commission patent licenses	42–2186	238
Compensation, awards, and royalties	42–2187	238–239
Confidential information	42–2181	233
Defined	42–2041	231
Federally financed research	42–2189	240
General provisions of commission	42–2201	240
Injunctions	42–2184	237
Inventions conceived during commission contracts	42–2182	233–234
Inventions relating to	42–2181	232
Military utilization	42–2181	232
Monopolistic use of patents	42–2188	239–240
Nonmilitary utilization	42–2183	234–237
Prior art	42–2185	237
Reports to the Commissioner of Patents and Trademarks	42–2181	232–233
Saving clause	42–2190	240
Attorney fees in infringement suit	35–285	60
Attorneys and agents		
Administrative practice	5–500	223
Government officers and employees as	18–203	215–216
May be refused recognition for misconduct . .	35–32	14

Subject	Title–Sec.	Page
Attorneys and agents—Contd.		
Petition to District Court, D.C.	35–32	14
Rules for recognition made by		
Commissioner	35–31	13–14
Suspension or exclusion from practice	35–32	14
Unauthorized practitioners	35–33	15
Audiovisual works, defined.	17–101	115

B

Subject	Title–Sec.	Page
Bars to grant of a patent	35–102	19
	35–103	20
Benefit of earlier filing date in foreign		
country	35–119	24–25
Benefit of earlier filing date in United States . .	35–120	25–26
Best edition, defined.	17–101	115
Best mode required.	35–112	21
Bill in equity (*See* Civil Action)		
Board of Appeals, how constituted	35–7	8–9
(*See also* Appeals to Board of Appeals)		
Board of Patent Interferences	*42–2457*	251–252
Bribery of public official.	*18–201*	212–215

C

Subject	Title–Sec.	Page
Cable system		
Defined	17–111	137
Secondary transmissions	17–111	130–138
Certificate of correction		
Applicant's mistake.	35–255	55
Office mistake.	35–254	55
Certificates of trademark registration	15–1057	82–84
Certification mark.	15–1054	81–82
Defined	15–1127	109–110
Certified copies		
Department records and papers	*28–1733*	219–220
Of any records, books, papers, or drawings		
belonging to the Patent and Trade-		
mark Office may be obtained.	*28–1744*	220
Of drawings and specifications of patents		
issued	35–10	10
Of foreign patents.	*28–1745*	220
Of Patent and Trademark Office records, to		
be used in evidence.	*28–1744*	220
Of records, furnished to Court of Customs		
and Patent Appeals in appeals	35–143	30

278

Subject	Title–Sec.	Page

Chapter 22

Intent of 15–1127 110–111

Circuit judges

Appointment, tenure, residence and salary .. 28–44 202–203

Assignment of........................ 28–46 204

Citizenship required in oath............... 35–115 23

Civil action

Election of in case of interference.......... 35–141 29

In case of interference.................. 35–146 30–31

Jurisdiction, plurality of parties, foreign

party 35–146 31

To obtain patent...................... 35–145 30

Claim of patent

Independent or dependent 35–41 15

                                         35–112 21–22

Independent or dependent, validity 35–282 59

Invalid, effect of...................... 35–253 54–55

Invalid, suits on patent with 35–288 61

Notice of rejection 35–132 27

Too extensive or narrow, remedy 35–251 53–54

What to cover........................ 35–112 21–22

Classification of patents 35–9 9–10

Clerk of United States Court may summon

witness in interference cases 35–24 12

Must notify Commissioner of patent suits ... 35–290 61–62

Coin-operated phonorecord player, defined 17–116 149

Collective mark.......................... 15–1054 81–82

Defined 15–1127 110

Collective work, defined.................... 17–101 115

Colorable imitation, defined................ 15–1127 110

Commerce, Department of

Patent and Trademark Office in........... 35–1 6

Patents 15–2218 259

Commerce, Secretary of

Appointments by 35–3 7

Commissioner under direction of 35–6 8

May vest functions 35–3 7

To approve rules...................... 35–6 8

                                         35–31 13–14

Commercial name, defined................. 15–1127 109

Commissioner

Annual report to Congress 35–14 11

Duties of............................ 35–6 8

How appointed 35–3 7

May disbar attorneys................... 35–32 14

May establish charges 35–41 14

Subject	Title–Sec.	Page

Commissioner—Contd.

May make rules for taking affidavits and
depositions 35–23   12
Member of Board of Appeals 35–7   9
Position at level V 5–5316   212
Shall cause examination to be made........ 35–131   27
To establish regulations 35–6   8
To furnish court with grounds of decision,
on appeal...................... 35–143   30
To have charge of property.............. 35–6   8
To prescribe rules and regulations
governing recognition of attorneys
and agents..................... 35–31   13–14
To sign patents or have name printed
thereon and attested 35–153   32
To superintend grant of patents.......... 35–6   8
Vacancy in office...................... 35–3   7
Compilation, defined 17–101   115
Compilations and derivative works.......... 17–103   120
Composition of matter
Patentable.......................... 35–101   19
Specimens of ingredients may be required... 35–114   22–23
Compulsory license for making and distributing
phonorecords................... 17–115   143–145
Computer program
Defined............................ 17–101   119
Exclusive rights and 17–117   149–150
Confidential status of application 35–122   26
  35–205   47
Conflict of interest 18–203   215–216
  18–205   216–217
  18–206   218
  18–207   223–228
  18–208   218–219
Congressmen
May not be attorney or agent............. 18–203   215–216
Constitutional provisions .... —   vi
Consumer Product Safety Commission........ 15–2054   258–259
Continuing application................... 35–120   25–26
Contributory infringement 35–271   57–58
Copies of records, fees 35–41   17
Copyright
Compilations and derivative works........ 17–103   120
Criminal law and 18–2314   268
  18–2318   269–270
  18–2319   270–271

Subject	Title–Sec.	Page

Copyright—Contd.

Deposit of copies or phonorecords for Library of Congress	17–407	169–171
Duration	17–302	160–161
	17–303	161
	17–304	161–165
	17–305	165
Exclusive rights	17–106	121–122
Importation prohibitions	17–603	186
Infringement	17–501	177
	17–502	177–178
	17–503	178
	17–504	178–179
	17–505	179
	17–506	179–180
	17–507	180
	17–508	180–181
	17–509	181
	17–510	182
	18–2319	270–271
Infringing importation of copies on phonorecords	17–602	185–186
Injunctions	17–502	177–178
Limitations on exclusive rights	17–107	122
	17–108	122–125
	17–109	125
	17–110	126–128
	17–111	128–139
	17–112	139–141
	17–117	149–150
Manufacture, importation and public distribution of certain copies	17–601	182–185
National origin and	17–104	120–121
Notice	17–401	166
	17–402	166–167
	17–403	167
	17–404	167
	17–405	167–168
	17–406	168–169
Ownership	17–201	153–154
	17–202	154
Preemption with respect to other laws	17–301	159–161
Registration	17–408	171–174
	17–409	174
	17–410	175
	17–411	175–176
	17–412	176

Copyright—Contd.
Renewal............................ . 17–304   162–163
                                     17–408   173
Subject matter, general................. 17–102   119–120
Termination of transfers and licenses granted
    by author 17–203   154
Transfer of ownership.................. 17–201   154
United States government works 17–105   121
Copyright Office
Copies of records...................... 17–706   189
Copyright registration................. 17–408   171–172
Delay in forms and fees due to postal system
    delays 17–709   191
Effective date of actions by.............. 17–703   188
Fees................................ 17–708   190–191
Forms and publications................. 17–707   189–190
General responsibilities................. 17–701   187
Records: Preparation, maintenance, public
    inspection, and searching 17–705   189
Regulations.......................... 17–702   187
Reproductions for use by blind and handi-
    capped......................... 17–710   192
Retention and disposition of articles
    deposited...................... 17–704   188–189
Copyright owner, defined................ 17–101   116
Copyright Royalty Tribunal
Administrative support................. 17–806   197
Deduction of costs of proceedings 17–807   198
Effective date of final determination 17–809   198
Establishment and purpose.............. 17–801   192–195
Institution and conclusion of proceedings ... 17–804   196–197
Judicial review 17–810   198
Membership 17–802   195
Procedures.......................... 17–803   195–197
Reports 17–808   198
Staff................................ 17–805   197
Correction of letters patent............... 35–254   55
                                     35–255   55
Cost of suits (*See* Infringement, patent)
Counterfeit mark...................... 15–1127   110
Court of Appeals
Appointment of chief judge.............. 166   203
Appointment of judges by the President.... 168   203–204
Judges, service of 165   203
Jurisdiction of....................... *28–1295*   207–208

Subject	Title–Sec.	Page
Court of Claims, may grant compensation for use of invention by United States . . .	28–1498	201
Court of Customs and Patent Appeals		
Appeal to (See Appeals to Court of Customs and Patent Appeals)		
Courts of appeals		
Circuit judges, appointment, tenure, residence and salary	28–44	202–203
Interlocutory decisions of	28–1292	205–206
Jurisdiction of	15–1121	103–104
	28–1291	204–205

D

Subject	Title–Sec.	Page
Damages for infringement (See Infringement, patent)		
Day for taking any action or paying any fee falling on Saturday, Sunday, or holiday	35–21	11
Death of author and duration of copyright	17–302	160–161
Death or incapacity of inventor	35–117	24
Decisions in patent cases, printing of	35–11	10
Declaration in lieu of oath	35–25	12–13
Dedication of term	35–253	55
Defective execution of documents, effect of	35–26	13–14
Defense, Department of		
Acquisition of copyrights, patents, designs, etc.	10–2386	257
Office of Naval Research: duties	10–5151	257–258
Patent rights protection of U.S. citizens	22–526	258
Purchase of patents, patent applications, and licenses	10–7210	258
Defenses in action for infringement	35–282	59
Deposit of copies or phonorecords for Library of Congress	17–407	169–171
Depositions, Commissioner may establish rules for	35–23	12
Derivative work, defined	17–101	116
Description of invention	35–112	21
Design patents		
Double recovery, not allowed	35–289	61
Fees	35–41	15
For what granted	35–171	35–36
Liability for infringement of	35–289	61
Penalty for unauthorized use of patented design	35–289	61

Subject	Title–Sec.	Page
Design patents—Contd.		
Prior foreign application.................	35–172	36
Right of priority.......................	35–172	36
Subject to same provisions as other patents..	35–171	35–36
Term of...............................	35–173	36
Unauthorized use of	35–289	61
Designated office........................	35–363	69
	35–366	70
	35–367	70–71
	35–371	71–72
	35–372	72–74
Disbarment of attorneys and agents..........	35–32	13
Disclaimer		
Fee...................................	35–41	15
How filed and by whom	35–253	54–55
Must be filed before commencement of suit		
to recover costs..................	35–288	61
	28–1928	202
Nature of............................	35–253	54–55
Distant signal equivalent, defined	17–111	138
District Court for District of Columbia		
Jurisdiction..........................	35–146	31
Review of disbarment of attorneys and		
agents	35–32	14
District Courts		
Jurisdiction of patent, copyright and trade-		
mark cases.....................	28–1338	200
Venue generally.......................	28–1391	200
Venue in patent cases	28–1400	201
Division of application	35–121	26
Division of patent on reissue	35–251	53–54
Drawing		
Attached to patent	35–154	32–33
Keeping of	35–1	6
Printing of	35–11	10
When necessary.......................	35–113	22
Drugs		
Secretary of Health, Education, and Welfare		
authorized to furnish information		
upon request of Commissioner of		
Patents and Trademarks	21–372	229
Duration of copyright		
Subsisting copyrights	17–304	161–165
Terminal date	17–305	165
Works on or after January 1, 1978	17–302	160–161

Subject	Title–Sec.	Page

Duration of copyright—Contd.

Works created but not published or copyrighted before January 1, 1978 17–303   161

Duties of Commissioner 35–6   8

E

Effect of transfer of particular copy or
phonorecord..................... 17–109   125

Employees of Patent and Trademark Office.... 35–3   6–7

How appointed...................... 35–3   6–7

Restrictions on as to interest in patents..... 35–4   7

Scientific positions 5–3104   211

                                    5–3325   212

Energy, Department of (previously Energy
Research and Development Administration)

Establishment....................... 42–5811   241

                                    42–7151   243

Patent, copyright, and inventions 42–5908   243

                                    42–7261   243–249

Power of the Secretary 42–5817   241–242

                                    42–7151   243

Environmental Protection Agency patents 42–6981c3   261–262

                                    42–7404b4   260–262

                                    42–7608   262

Ephemeral recordings 17–112   139–141

Establishment of date of invention by reference
to knowledge or use in foreign
country 35–104   20

Establishment, Patent and Trademark Office... 35–1   6

Ethics

Government employees................. 18–203   215–216

                                    18–205   216–217

                                    18–206   217

                                    18–207   223–228

Evidence

Copies of department records as........... 28–1733   209–210

Copies of foreign patent specifications and
drawings 28–1745   210

Copies of Patent and Trademark Office
records as 28–1744   210

Government records and papers 28–1733   209–210

Examination

Applicants shall be notified of rejection on .. 35–132   27

Subject	Title–Sec.	Page

Examination—Contd.

To be made of application and alleged

invention	35–131	27
Classification definitions	5–5102	212
Duties of	35–7	8–9
How appointed	35–3	6–7
Qualifications	35–7	8–9

Exchange of Patent and Trademark Office

| publications for other publications | 35–11 | 10 |

Exchange of printed copies of patents with

| foreign countries | 35–12 | 10 |

Exclusive rights in copyrighted works

Effect of transfer of particular copy or

| phonorecord | 17–109 | 125 |

Exemptions of certain performances and

displays	17–110	126–128
Fair use limitations	17–107	122
General information	17–106	121–122
Limitations	17–107	122
	17–108	122–125
	17–109	125
	17–110	126–128
	17–111	126–139
	17–112	139–141
Nondramatic musical works	17–115	143–145
Pictorial, graphic, and sculptural works	17–113	141–142
Reproduction by libraries and archives	17–108	122–125
Secondary transmissions	17–111	128–139
Sound recordings	17–114	142–143
Executors, administrators or guardians	35–117	24

F

Fair use of copyrighted material	17–107	122
False designations of origin	15–1125	105–106
False descriptions of goods	15–1125	105–106

Falsely marking or labeling articles as

| patented | 35–292 | 62 |
| Federal agency, defined | 35–200 | 41 |

Federal Assistance, inventions made with

Confidentiality	35–205	47
Definitions	35–201	41–42
Disposition of rights	35–202	42–46

Domestic and foreign protection of federally

| owned inventions | 35–207 | 48 |

Subject	Title–Sec.	Page
Federal Assistance—Contd.		
March-in rights.........................	35–203	46–47
Policy and objective of.................	35–200	41
Precedence of chapter	35–210	51–53
Preference for United States industry.......	35–204	47
Regulations governing federal licensing.....	35–208	48
Relationship to antitrust laws.............	35–211	53
Restrictions on licensing of federally owned		
inventions	35–209	48–51
Uniform clauses and regulations...........	35–206	47–48
Federal Nonnuclear Energy Research and		
Development Act of 1974	42–6981c3	262–263
Federal Property and Administrative Service		
Act of 1949	42–2473	254
Fee, copyright..........................	17–708	190–191
Fees, patent		
Amount of...........................	35–41	15–16
Deposited in Treasury..................	31–725r	229
Designation..........................	35–361	68
For records, publications and services not		
specified in statute	35–41	17
International	35–361	68
	35–376	74
How paid and refunded	35–42	17–18
To witness in interference cases	35–24	12
Fees, trademark.........................	15–1113	98
Filing application by other than inventor	35–118	24
Foreign applications		
License to file required..................	35–184	39
Penalty for filing without license..........	35–185	39–40
Foreign countries, exchange of printed copies		
of patents with	35–12	10
Foreign country, knowledge or use in, not		
used to establish date of invention...	35–104	20
Foreign documents; authentication..........	28–1741	210
Foreign patent documents; copies...........	28–1745	210
Foreign patents		
Certified copies of, as evidence............	28–1745	210
Copies of, exchanged for United States		
patents........................	35–12	10
Prior, effect on United States application		
for patent	35–102	19
Foreign priority.........................	35–119	24–25
	35–365	69–70
Funding agreement, defined...............	35–200	41

Subject	Title–Sec.	Page

G

General Accounting Office to examine
accounts of Patent and Trademark
Office salaries and expenses . . . . | *31–72* | 120

Government employee
Ethics . . . . | *18–203* | 215–216
| | *18–205* | 216–217
| | *18–206* | 217
| | *18–207* | 223–228
| | *18–208* | 218–219

Suit against United States for infringement. . | *28–1498* | 201
Government interests in patents. . . . . | *35–266* | 57
| | *35–267* | 57

H

Health and Human Services, Department of;
patents. . . . . | *30–937* | 255
| | *30–951* | 256
Holiday, time for action expiring on . . . . | *35–21* | 11
Holidays, District of Columbia . . . . | D.C. Code |
| | *28–2701* | 222
Holidays, Federal . . . . | *5–6103* | 220–222

I

Importation prohibitions of works under copy-
right . . . . | *17–603* | 186
Importations of goods bearing infringing
marks or names forbidden . . . . | *15–1124* | 104–105
Importation of product made by patented
process. . . . . | *19–1337* | 209
| | *19–1337a* | 209
Improvements, patents may be granted for . . . . | *35–101* | 19
Incontestability of right to use mark under
certain conditions . . . . | *15–1065* | 89–90
Indexes of patents and patentees, printing of . . | *35–11* | 10
Indian Arts and Crafts Board . . . . | *15–1113* | 98
Infringement, copyright
Alteration of programing by cable systems . . | *17–510* | 182
Costs and attorney's fees. . . . . | *17–505* | 179
Criminal infringement . . . . | *17–506* | 179–180
Damage and profits. . . . . | *17–504* | 178–179
General information . . . . | *17–501* | 177

Subject	Title–Sec.	Page
Infringement, copyright—Contd.		
Impounding and disposition of infringing articles.....................	17–503	178
Injunctions	17–502	177–178
Limitation on actions	17–507	180
Notification of filing and determination of actions......................	17–508	180–181
Registration as prerequisite to suit.........	17–411	175–176
Seizure and forfeiture	17–509	181
Infringement, patent		
Action for	35–281	59
Attorney fees........................	35–285	60
By United States, compensation for........	28–1498	201
By United States, time limitation in suit for	35–286	60
Clerk of court to notify Patent and Trademark Office of suit...............	35–290	61–62
Contributory	35–271	57–58
Costs not recoverable in certain suits.......	28–1928	202
Damages for	35–284	60
Defenses in suit for....................	35–282	59
Defined............................	35–271	57–58
Injunction	35–283	59–60
Notice of, necessary to recovery of damages..	35–287	60–61
Pleading defense and special matters to be proved in suit..................	35–282	59
Process, service of in action for	28–1694	202
Suit for, jurisdiction..................	28–1338	200
	28–1391	
Suit for, when a claim is invalid	35–288	61
Temporary presence in United States.......	35–272	58
Time limitation	35–286	60
Infringement, trademark..................	15–1114	98–99
	15–1115	99–101
Destruction of infringing articles..........	15–1118	103
Recovery of profits and damages in suit	15–1111	97
Infringing importation of copies or phonorecords........................	17–602	185–186
Injunctions, enforcement	15–1116	101–102
Injunctions may be granted by court having jurisdiction	35–283	59–60
Insane persons, patent applications of	35–117	24
Interference, patent		
Agreements, between parties, relating to termination, to be filed in Patent and Trademark Office.............	35–135	28

Subject	Title–Sec.	Page
Interference, patent—Contd.		
Appeal to court........................	35–141	29
Determination of priority...............	35–102	19–20
	35–135	27–28
Parties to be notified of................	35–135	27–28
Review of decision by civil action........	35–145	30
Rules for taking testimony..............	35–23	12
Interference, trademark		
Declaration by Commissioner............	15–1066	90
Involvement of Trademark Trial and Appeal		
Board........................	15–1067	90–91
Interfering patents		
How set aside.......................	35–291	62
Jurisdiction, plurality of parties, foreign		
party.........................	35–146	30–31
	35–291	62
Relief against	35–291	62
Interior, Department of; patents	30–322	255–256
	30–323	256
	30–951	256
	30–1226	256–257
	30–1328	257
	16–833a	255
International application..................	35–351	67
	35–363	69
	35–364	69
	35–366	70
	35–367	70–71
	35–375	74
International bureau	35–351	67–68
	35–361	68
	35–362	69
	35–371	71–72
Register of marks communicated by	15–1126	106
International Bureau For Protection of Intel-		
lectual Property; appropriation......	22–269f	267
International commercial agreements	19–2435	267
International conventions, trademarks	15–1126	106–108
International Searching Authority	35–351	67
	35–362	69
	35–364	69
	35–368	71
International studies and programs funds......	35–6	8
Intervening rights on reissue	35–252	54
Invention date as affected by activity abroad...	35–104	20
Invention, defined......................	35–100	18–19

Subject	Title–Sec.	Page
Invention made abroad	35–104	20
Inventions and Contributions Board	42–2457	163
Inventions patentable	35–101	19
Inventions previously patented abroad	35–102	19
Inventions, right to, from sponsored R&D	42–5908	243–249
Inventor		
Death or incapacity	35–117	24
May obtain patent	35–101	19
Oath for joint	35–116	23
To make application	35–111	21
Inventor's certificate as reference	35–102	19
Inventor's certificate priority right	35–119	24
Issue of patent	35–151	31–32
Issue fee		
Delayed payment	35–41	16
	35–151	32
If not paid within three months, patent withheld	35–151	32
Nonpayment	35–41	16
	35–151	32
Payment of	35–151	31–32

J

Joint inventors	35–116	23–24
Joint owners	35–262	57
Joint work, defined	17–101	116
Juristic person, defined	15–1127	109
Jurisdiction over patent actions		
Court of Appeals, interlocutory decisions	28–1292	205–206
District Court for District of Columbia	35–32	14
United States district courts	28–1338	200
Jurisdiction over trademark actions	15–1121	103–104

K

Knowledge or use in foreign country no bar to patent	35–102	19

L

Legal representative of dead or incapacitated inventor	35–117	24
Letters rogatory issued by a foreign or international tribunal, transmittal by Department of State	28–1781	210–211

291

Subject	Title–Sec.	Page
Libraries, and reproduction of copyrighted material	17–108	122–125
Libraries, public, copies of patents for	35–13	10–11
	35–41	17
Library	35–8	9
Library of Congress		
Deposit of copies or phonorecords for copyright purposes	17–407	169–171
	17–408	172
Limitation on damages	35–286	60
Limitations on exclusive rights in copyrighted works	17–107	122
	17–108	122–125
	17–109	125
	17–110	126–128
	17–111	128–139
	17–112	139–141
	17–117	149–150
Literary works, defined	17–101	117
Local service area of a primary transmitter, defined	17–111	138

M

Subject	Title–Sec.	Page
Machines patentable	35–101	19
Manufacture, importation, and public distribution of certain copies of works under copyright	17–601	182–185
Manufactures patentable	35–101	19
Manufacturing requirements and importation for works under copyright	17–601	182–185
	17–602	185–186
	17–603	186
Mark, use of	15–1127	110
Marking articles falsely as patented	35–292	62
Marking articles patented	35–287	60–61
Members of Congress		
May not be attorney or agent	18–203	215–216
Names prohibited in advertising	5–501	228
Misjoinder of inventor	35–116	23
	35–202	44
	35–256	56
Mistake in patent registration	35–254	55
	35–255	55
Mistake in trademark registration	15–1057	84
Model, shall be furnished if required	35–114	22–23

Subject	Title–Sec.	Page

Money
Paid by mistake, or in excess, refunded   35–42   18
Received for fees, etc., to be paid into the
    Treasury.   35–42   17–18
Motion pictures, defined.   17–101   117
Multiple dependent claim.   35–112   21–22
    Fee.   35–41   15

N

National Aeronautics and Space Act, patents . .   42–2457   250–253
                                                         42–2458   253–254
National Aeronautics and Space Administration
Acquisition of patents.   42–2473   254
National Science Foundation patents   42–1871   262
National stage of international application.   35–371   71–72
                                                         35–372   72–73
                                                         35–373   73
National Stolen Property Act   18–2314   268
New matter inadmissible in reissue   15–251   53–54
New matter, may not be introduced by
    amendment   35–132   27
Noncommercial broadcasting
Use of certain works in connection with   17–118   150–153
Nondramatic musical works, exclusive rights to.   17–115   143–145
                                                         17–116   145–149
Nonjoinder of inventor   35–256   56
Nonobviousness.   35–103   19
Nonprofit organization, defined   35–200   42
Nonresident patentee   35–293   62–63
Notice as regards patents
As to proof in infringement suits.   35–282   59
Of allowance of patent   35–151   31–32
Of appeal to the Court of Customs and
    Patent Appeals   35–142   29
                                                         35–143   29–30
Of interference   35–135   27–28
Of patent suit, decision to be given Patent
    and Trademark Office by clerk of
    court   35–290   61–62
Of rejection of an application.   35–132   27
To the public by Federal agency   35–209   49–50
To the public that invention is patented   35–287   60–61
Notice of copyright
Contributions to collective works   17–404   167
Error in name of date.   17–406   168–169

Subject	Title–Sec.	Page
Notice of copyright—Contd.		
False representation	17–506	180
Fraudulent notice	17–506	180
Omission of notice	17–405	167–168
Phonorecords of sound recordings	17–402	166–167
Publications incorporating United States government works	17–403	167
Visually perceptible copies	17–401	166
Novelty	35–102	19–20
Nuclear Regulatory Commission	42–5841	242
Nuclear Regulatory Research, Office of	42–5845	242

O

Subject	Title–Sec.	Page
Oath in patent application	35–115	23
	35–152	32
Before whom taken in foreign countries	35–115	23
Before whom taken in the United States	35–115	23
Declaration in lieu of	35–25	12–13
Joint inventors	35–116	23–24
Must be made by inventor, if living	35–115	23
	35–152	33
Requirements of	35–115	23
To be made by legal representative if inventor is dead or incapacitated	35–117	24
Oath in trademark application	15–1061	86
Obviousness	35–103	20
Officer of Patent and Trademark Office may attest patents	35–153	32
Officers and employees		
Government, acting as attorneys or agents	18–203	215–216
Of Patent and Trademark Office	35–3	6–7
Of Patent and Trademark Office, restrictions on as to interest in patents	35–4	7
Official Gazette		
Exchange for publications	35–11	10
Printing and distribution of	35–11	10
Publication of trademark in	15–1062	86–87
	15–1092	95
Opposition to trademark registration	15–1067	90–91
	15–1068	91
Ownership of copyright	17–201	153–154
Distinct from ownership of material object	17–202	154
Execution of transfers	17–204	157
Ownership of trademark	15–1057	83

Subject	Title–Sec.	Page

P

Paris Convention........................	35–119	25
Patent attorneys and agents (*See* Attorneys and agents)		
Patent Compensation Board	42–2187	238–239
Patent Cooperation Treaty		
Definitions	35–351	67–68
Patent fees...............................	35–41	14–17
Disposition of, return of excess	35–42	17–18
Patent laws, printing of..................	35–11	10
Patent and Trademark Office		
In Department of Commerce	*35–1*	6
	15–1511	211
	5–3104	211–212
Library...............................	35–8	9
Printing...............................	35–11	10
Receipts to be deposited into Treasury as miscellaneous receipts.............	*31–725e*	220
Rules, authority for	35–6	8
	15–1123	104
Seal of................................	35–2	6
	15–1057	81, 83
Trademark records.....................	35–1057	82–84
Patent pending, false marking as...........	35–292	62
Patentability, conditions for...............	35–102	19
	35–103	20
Patented article		
Marked as such.......................	35–287	60–61
Used by Government, compensation for	*28–1498*	201
Patentee		
Defined	35–101	19
Notified of interference.................	35–135	27–28
Patents		
Application for	35–111	21
Assignment of........................	35–261	56–57
Atomic energy and fissionable material	*42–2014*	231
Based on international application	35–375	74
Certified copies of......................	35–10	10
Classification of.......................	35–9	9–10
Contents and duration of	35–154	32–33
Copies supplied to public libraries	35–13	10–11
	35–41	17
Copying claim of	35–135	27–28
Design (*See* Design Patents)		
Effect of adverse interference decision	35–135	27–28

295

Subject	Title–Sec.	Page
Patents—Contd.		
Exchange of printed copies with foreign		
countries	35–12	10
Fee on issuing	35–41	14–16
Filing application in foreign country	35–184	39
For what granted	35–101	19
Foreign knowledge or use no bar to		
grant of	35–102	19
On government sponsored work	42–5908	243–249
How issued, attested, and recorded	35–153	32
May be issued to assignee	35–152	32
May be withheld in certain cases	35–181	36–37
Obtainable by civil action	35–145	30
Personal property	35–261	56–57
Plant, see Plant patents		
Presumption of validity	35–282	59
Price of copies	35–41	17
Printing of	35–11	10
Reissuing of, when defective	35–251	53–54
Rights of inventions made with federal		
assistance	35–200	40–52
	to 211	
Restrictions on officers and employees of		
Patent and Trademark Office as to		
interest in	35–4	7
Surrender of, to take effect on reissue	35–251	53–54
Term	35–154	32–33
	35–155	33
	35–155A	33–34
Time of issue, payment of issue fee	35–151	31–32
To be authenticated by seal of Patent and		
Trademark Office	35–2	6
When to issue	35–151	31–32
Withheld for nonpayment of issue fee	35–151	31–32
Payment to international intergovernmental		
organizations	35–6	8
Payment of trademark filing fee	15–1051	78–79
Performing rights society	17–116	149
Phonorecords, defined	17–101	117
Photolithography: Headings of drawings		
printed	35–11	10
Pictorial, graphic, and sculptural works,		
exclusive rights to	17–113	141–142
Piracy and counterfeiting amendments of		
1982	18–2318	269–270
	18–2319	270–271

Subject	Title–Sec.	Page
Plant patents		
Claim	35–162	35
Description	35–162	35
Nature of right	35–163	35
Plants patentable	35–161	35
Secretary of Agriculture to furnish information and detail employees	35–164	35
Pleading and proof in action for infringement	35–282	59
Practical application, defined	35–200	42
Presumption of validity of patents	35–282	59
Primary transmission	17–111	137
Principal register, defined	15–1127	108–109
Printed publication bar to a patent	35–102	19
Printing		
Decisions in patent cases	35–11	10
Of papers filed	35–22	11
Patent and Trademark Office	35–11	10
Printing headings of drawings by Patent and Trademark Office	35–11	10
Prior Art		
Appeal	35–306	66
Certificate of patentability, unpatentability, and claim cancellation	35–307	66–67
Citation of	35–301	64
Conduct of reexamination proceedings	35–305	66
Determination of issue by Commissioner	35–303	65
Reexamination order by Commissioner	35–304	65–66
Request for reexamination	35–302	64–65
Prior patenting or publication bar to patent	35–102	19
Priority, foreign	35–119	24–25
	35–365	69–70
Priority of invention	35–102	19–20
Priority of invention, determined by board of patent interferences	35–135	27–28
Priority, right of, under treaty or law	35–119	24–25
For design applications	35–172	36
Proceedings for concurrent trademark use Registration or cancellation	15–1067	90–91
	15–1068	91
Process patentable	35–101	19
Process, service of in patent infringement action	28–1694	202
Produce, defined	42–2014	231
Product safety information and research	15–2054	258, 259
Property of Patent and Trademark Office	35–1	6
	35–6	8

Subject	Title–Sec.	Page
Protection of foreign nationals against unfair competition	15–1126	108
Pseudonymous work, defined	17–101	117
Public performances of a work		
By means of coin-operated phonorecord players	17–116	145–149
Defined	17–101	118
Public use or sale	35–102	19
Of invention bar to a patent	35–102	19
Publication, defined	17–101	117–118
Publication of international application effect	35–374	73–74
Publication of marks	15–1062	86–87
Publications of copyright office	17–707	189–190
Publications regarding patents and trademarks	35–11	10
Published works, and national origin	17–104	120–121

R

Subject	Title–Sec.	Page
Receiving office	35–351	67–68
	35–361	68
	35–364	69
	35–367	70–71
	35–368	71
Recording copyright transfer, other document	17–205	157–158
Recording of assignments	35–261	56–57
Records of Patent and Trademark Office		
Copies of, as evidence	28–1744	210
Keeping of	35–1	6
Reexamination to be made after first rejection, if desired	35–132	27
References, to be cited on examination	35–132	27
Refundment of money paid by mistake or in excess	35–42	18
Refunds		
Patent and Trademark Office fees deposited in Treasury to be available for	31–725r	140
Refusal of trademark registration	15–1052	80–81
Registered mark, defined	15–1127	110
Registration of copyright		
Application	17–409	174
Claim and issuance certificate	17–410	175
General information	17–408	171
Prerequisite to certain remedies for infringement	17–412	176
Prerequisite to infringement suit	17–411	175–176

Subject	Title–Sec.	Page
Registration of trademark.................	15–1051	78–80
Assignment of mark...................	15–1060	85–86
Cancellation.........................	15–1064	88–89
	15–1093	95
Certificates	15–1057	82–84
Certification and collective marks.........	15–1054	81–82
Classification of goods and services	15–1112	97–98
Duration	15–1058	84–85
Examination	15–1062	86–87
Exclusive rights.......................	15–1115	99–100
Fees.................................	15–1113	98
Foreign applicant	15–1126	108
Mistakes in registration	15–1057	82–84
Opposition to	15–1063	87–88
Power of court	15–1119	103
Prior registration in country of origin	15–1126	106
Refusal of	15–1063	86–87
Registrable trademarks	15–1052	80–81
Renewal..............................	15–1059	85
Right of priority.......................	15–1126	107
Service marks	15–1053	81
Use by related companies................	15–1055	82
Reissue of patents		
Application fee	35–41	15
Application may be made by assignee in certain cases........................	35–251	53–54
By reason of defective claims	35–251	53–54
Effect of..............................	35–252	54
For unexpired term of original patent	35–251	53–54
Intervening rights......................	35–252	54
Of defective patents	35–251	53–54
To contain no new matter	35–251	53–54
Rejection, applicant shall be notified of reasons for patent	35–132	27
Related company, defined.................	15–1127	109
Report to Congress, annual	35–14	11
Reproduction by libraries and archives of copyrighted material	17–108	122–125
Research		
Arms control..........................	22–2572	259
Small Business Administration.............	15–638	228
Restoration of patent	35–155A	33–34
Restrictions on officers and employees of Patent and Trademark Office as to interest in patents	35–4	7
Right of foreign priority.................	35–365	69–70

Subject	Title–Sec.	Page
Right to compensation because of secrecy order	35–183	38–39
Royalties, copyright, payable under compulsory license	17–115	144–145
	17–116	146–147
Rules for taking testimony, Commissioner to establish	35–23	12
Rules of practice		
Authority for	35–6	8
Printing of	35–11	10

S

Subject	Title–Sec.	Page
Salary of Government officials and employees payable only by United States	18–209	219
Saturday, time for action expiring on	35–21	11
Seal of Patent and Trademark Office	35–2	6
Secondary transmissions of performances or displays	17–111	128–139
Secrecy of applications	35–122	26
Secrecy of certain inventions	35–181 to 188	36–40
Secrecy of international applications	35–368	71
Security classification	15–1155	230
Service mark	15–1053	81
Defined	15–1127	109
Service, upon defendant in patent suit	28–1694	202
Signature of inventor necessary to application	35–111	21
Small Business Administration Research; patent services	15–638	228
Small business firm, defined	35–200	42
Solid waste disposal	42–6981(c)3	260–262
Sound recordings, exclusive rights to	17–114	142–143
Source material, defined	42–2014	231
Space Act (See National Aeronautics and Space Act)		
Specification(s)		
Contents of	35–112	21–22
If defective, reissue to correct	35–251	53–54
Keeping of	35–1	6
Printing of	35–11	10
	35–41	17
Shall be part of patent	35–154	32
Uncertified copies, price of	35–41	17

Subject	Title-Sec.	Page
Special nuclear material	*42-2014*	232
Specially qualified research and development	*5-3104*	211-212
personnel......................	3325	212
Specimens, may be required...............	35-114	22-23
State, Department of; patents..............	22-2572	259
Subpoenas to witnesses....................	35-24	12
Suit against the United States	35-286	60
	28-1498	201
Suit for infringement (*See* Infringement, patent)		
Suit in equity (*See* Civil Action)		
Sunday, time for action expiring on	35-21	11
Supplemental register	15-1091	94-95
Applicable provisions	15-1094	96
Application and proceedings for		
registration	15-1091	94-95
Defined	15-1127	109
Mark used in foreign commerce...........	15-1091	94-95
Marks registrable on...................	15-1091	94-95
Nature of mark.......................	15-1091	94-95
Publication of.......................	15-1092	95-96
Registration on principal register not pre-		
cluded........................	15-1095	96
Registration not used to stop importations ..	15-1096	96

T

Taxation		
Gain from certain sales of patents to foreign		
corporation	*26-1249*	266
Income from patents outside the United		
States........................	*26-862*	264
Income from sources within the United		
States........................	*26-861*	263-264
Recoveries of damages..................	*26-186*	263
Sale or exchange of patents; rules for deter-		
mining capital gains and losses	*26-1235*	265-266
Tax on income of foreign corporations......	*26-881*	264-265
Tax on nonresident alien individuals	*26-871*	264
Tennessee Valley Authority		
Ownership of inventions of employees......	*16-831d*	262-263
Term of patent		
Design.............................	35-173	36
Extension...........................	35-155	33
Disclaimer of........................	35-253	54-55
Period	35-154	32
Restoration	35-155A	33-34

Subject	Title–Sec.	Page
Termination of copyright		
Transfers and licenses covering extended renewal	17–304	162–165
Transfers and licenses granted by the author	17–203	154–157
Testimony, rules for taking	35–23	12
Time		
Expiring on Saturday, Sunday or holiday....	35–21	11
For payment of issue fee	35–151	32
For taking action in Government cases	35–267	57
Within which action must be taken	35–133	27
Title of invention	35–154	32–33
Trademark		
Application for	15–1051	78–79
Certificates of registration	15–1057	82–84
Change of ownership	15–1057	82–84
Concurrent registration	15–1052	80–81
Defined	15–1127	109
Designation of resident for service of process and notice	15–1051	78–79
Disclaimer of unregistrable matter	15–1056	82
Payment of filing fee	15–1051	78–79
Registrable on principal register	15–1052	80–81
Registration of	15–1051	78–79
Registration notice	15–1111	97
Use by related companies	15–1055	82
Trademark Trial and Appeal Board	15–1067	90
Appeals to	15–1070	91
Dissatisfaction with decision of	15–1071	91–94
Trade name, defined	15–1127	109
Trafficking in counterfeit labels for phono-records, and copies of motion pictures or other audiovisual works	18–2318	269–270
Transfer of copyright ownership	17–201	154
	17–205	157–158
Transmission program, defined	17–101	118
Transportation, Department of; patents	15–1395	260
Transportation of stolen goods, securities moneys, fraudulent state tax stamps, or articles used in counterfeiting	18–2314	268
Treasury, Department of; patents	31–393	260

U

Unauthorized disclosure	35–182	37–38

Subject	Title–Sec.	Pag
Unauthorized person may not lawfully assist persons in transaction of business before the Office..................	35–33	14
United States as designated office	35–363	69
United States, defined	35–100	19
Unpatented article, penalty for deceptive marking.........................	35–292	62
Use in foreign countries, no bar to grant of patent	35–102	19

V

Violation of right of trademark registrant	15–1116	101–102
Injunctions	15–1116	101
Recovery; profits, damages and costs; attorney fees	15–1117	102–103

W

Withdrawal of international application........	35–366	70
Withholding of patent	35–181	36–37
Witness		
Failing to attend or refusing to testify......	35–24	12
Fees of, interference cases	35–24	12
In interference summoned by clerk of United States court...............	35–24	12
When in contempt, punishment	35–24	12
Work made for hire		
Defined	17–101	119
Duration of copyright...................	17–302	160